NATIONAL PORTRAIT GALLERY

THE COLLECTION

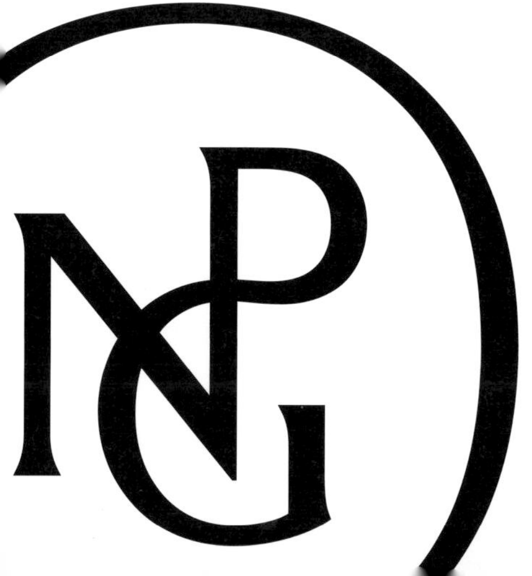

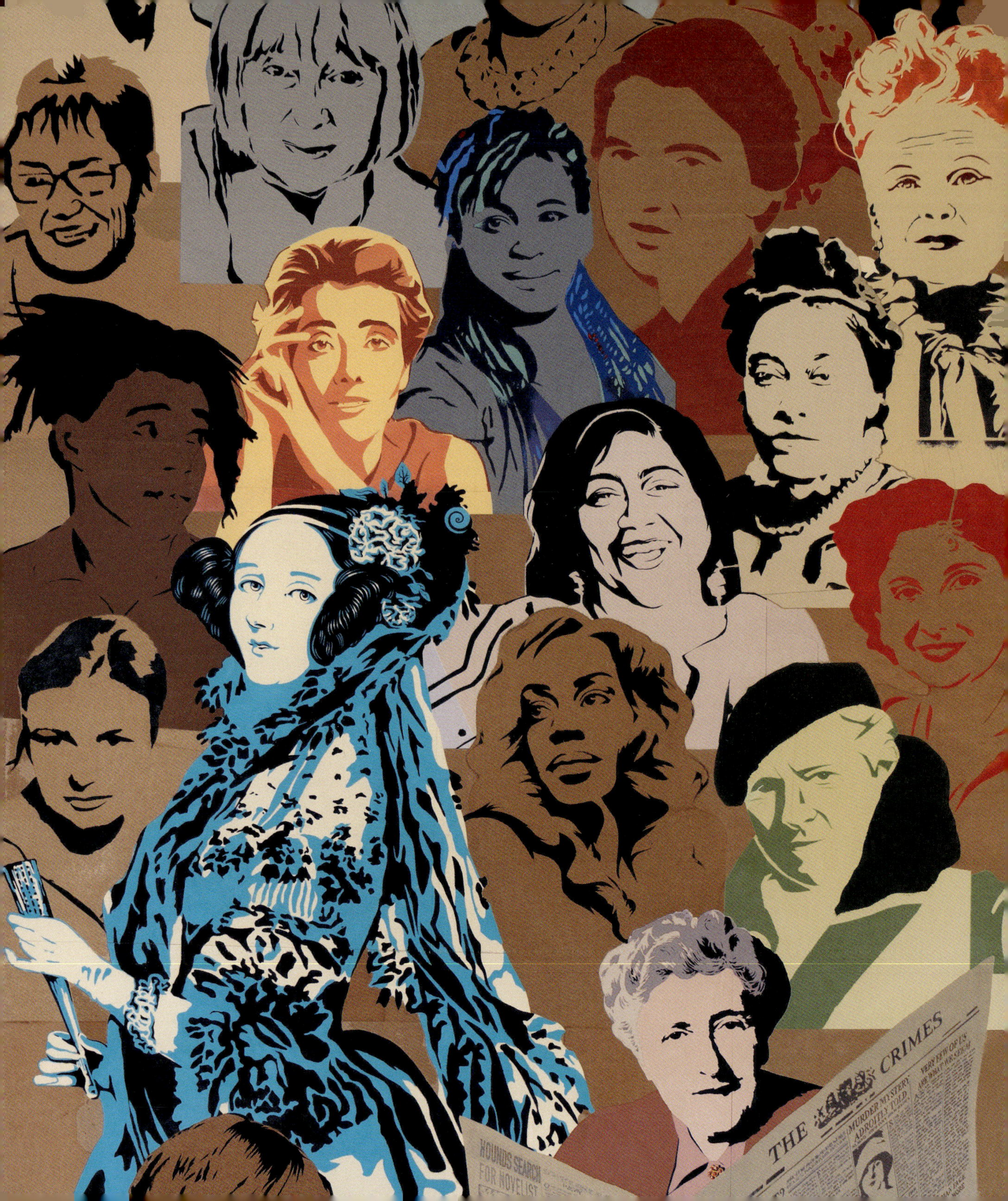
THE TIMES CRIMES
MURDER MYSTERY
ADROITLY TOLD
VERY FEW OF US
ARE WHAT WE SEEM
HOUNDS SEARCH
FOR NOVELIST

Contents

A Living Portrait of Britain

'Often I have found a Portrait superior in real instruction to half a dozen written Biographies ... or rather ... I have found that the Portrait was as a small lighted candle, by which the Biographies could for the first time be read, and some human interpretation be made of them.'
Thomas Carlyle, letter to David Laing, 2 May 1854

Nicholas Cullinan

The National Portrait Gallery tells the story of Britain through portraiture and champions that art form internationally. From global icons, to unsung heroes, we are about the personalities that have shaped, and continue to shape, our nation, using art to bring history to life and explore living today. Our history has always been one of innovation: we were the first portrait gallery in the world when we were founded. This letter of 1854 by the Victorian essayist and historian, Thomas Carlyle, stated that portraiture had the unique ability to illuminate history and biography, and was cited by Lord Stanhope in his speech to the House of Lords in February 1856, in which he argued successfully for a 'gallery of the portraits of the most eminent persons in British history'. The National Portrait Gallery was established later that year. Carlyle thus became the intellectual cornerstone of the Gallery (indeed a bust dedicated to him sits in a roundel on our façade) and his observation that looking at a portrait transcends time and provides a unique encounter between the viewer and the sitter, as mediated by the artist, remains true today.

As the global centre of portraiture our role remains the same as when we began — telling the story of the nation through the people who shape it — although we have broadened our understanding of achievement to reflect the diversity and dynamism of contemporary culture and conversations. Housing the greatest collection of portraits in the world, on our walls are people from all four corners of this country, who have shaped our society over the past 500 years. Now more than ever, we have a unique role to inspire and enrich society through enabling deeper connections with the nation's stories — to be the living portrait of Britain.

Portraits spark curiosity about the life and character of the person depicted and raise questions about the time and society in which they are made. This dual interest in biography and art, as well as in the potential of portraiture to reanimate the past, lies at the heart of the Gallery. Our Collection represents a constantly evolving picture of the nation, of how we view ourselves and who we choose to remember. The Gallery's ethos — uninterrupted from our founding in 1856, to our reopening in 2023, after the biggest transformation in our history — is to enlighten audiences about history and to create a forum in which 'face-to-face' encounters with Britain's most influential people can take place.

The founding portrait to enter the Collection in 1856 was emblematic in this respect: it was not of a monarch or a politician but of the playwright and poet William Shakespeare, whose achievements were the result of his own extraordinary talent and effort. Crucially, it is the only portrait of Shakespeare with a good claim to having been painted from life, around 1610, and may be by an artist called John Taylor.

David Hockney (*Portraits*)
(b.1937)
Tacita Dean, 2016
16mm colour film and
optical sound
NPG 7062

Dean's portrait of Britain's most famous contemporary artist, Hockney, was acquired following its inclusion in the Gallery's first exhibition devoted to film, *Tacita Dean: PORTRAIT* (2018). It was jointly acquired with the Royal Academy of Arts in 2019.

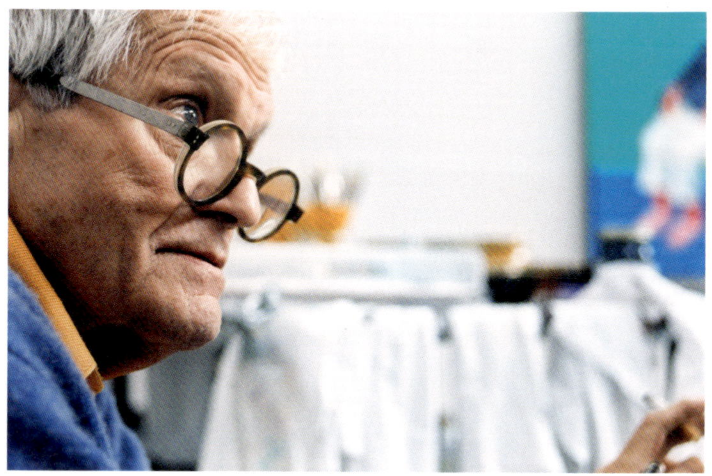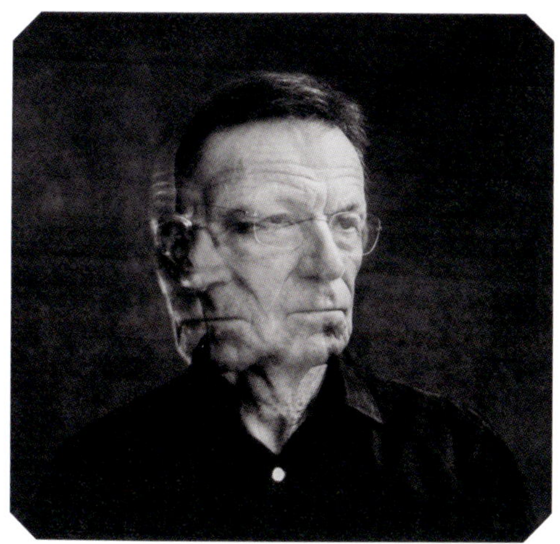

This emphasis given to authenticity finds its roots in Carlyle's influential letter to David Laing of 2 May 1854, which stated that for him 'it has been and is one of the most primary wants to procure a Likeness of the personage inquired after; a good *portrait* if such exists; failing that … *any* representation made by a faithful human creature of that Face and Figure which *he* saw with his eyes'. It was only through a portrait that an historian would know 'what manner of man' an historical figure was, argued Carlyle.

The importance of a portrait having been 'painted from the life' was paramount to the Collection from its inception. There are certain exceptions, such as Marlene Dumas's commemorative painting of the singer and songwriter Amy Winehouse, made following her untimely death at the age of 27 in 2011, and deliberately painted after media images of her, to mark the way her life and death were played out in public.

The portrait of Shakespeare also asserts one of our central principles: that the Gallery should be predominantly a museum of British history, as opposed to being devoted to portraiture as an art form. Within a week of their first meeting on 9 February 1857, the Trustees decided that, in acquiring works, the Gallery should 'look to the celebrity of the person represented rather than to the merit of the artist'. The Trustees also decided from the outset that impact was just as important as achievement, meaning that those who were widely perceived to have had 'great faults and errors' should be included. Although Lord Palmerston, another of the Gallery's founding figures, hoped the Collection would serve, overall, as an 'incentive to mental exertion, to noble actions, to good conduct on the part of the living'.

Today, we continue to encourage our audiences to find inspiration in the artworks and human stories within the Collection, but the Gallery has never been an uncritical 'temple of worthies', or a mere pantheon of 'the great and the good'. Acquisitions have always been guided by the principle of political and religious neutrality and an objective evaluation of a sitter's importance in expanding our understanding of British history, culture and identity. Impartiality remains a central concern when acquiring historical portraits or assessing who among us today might be remembered in the future. However, we equally recognise that the selection of portraits on display in the Gallery, and presented through initiatives such as this

Sir Nicholas Serota
(b.1946)
Sir Steve McQueen, 2022
Fine art giclée print,
155 × 155mm
NPG 7139

A leading art world figure, Serota is Chair of Arts Council England and was previously Director of Tate. This double exposure photograph by the Turner Prize-winning artist and Oscar-winning director McQueen continues the Gallery's tradition of commissioning outstanding portraits.

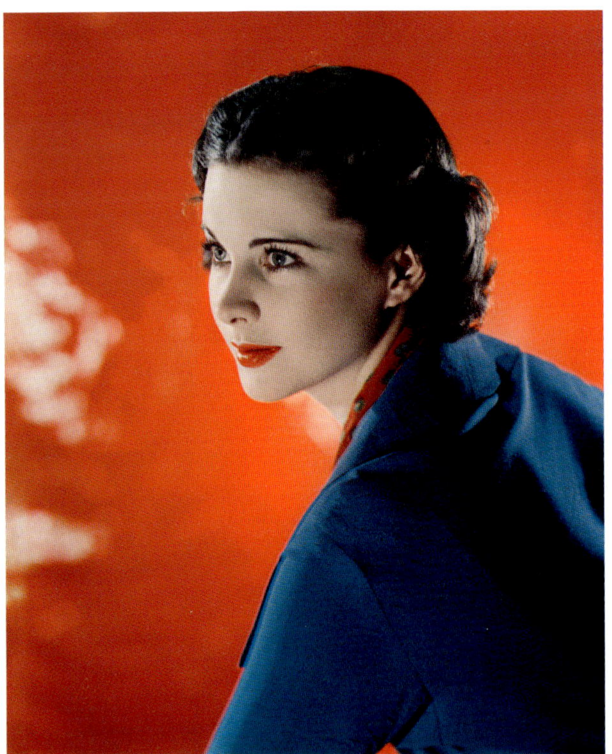 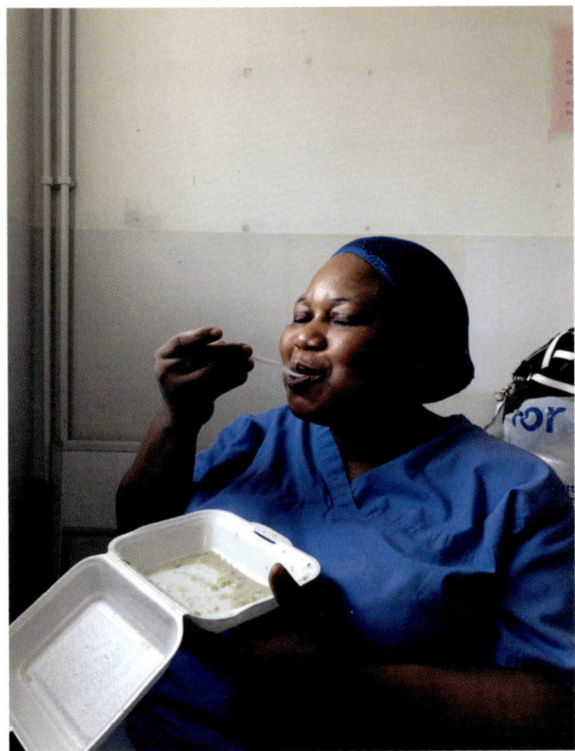

Vivien Leigh
(1913–67)
Yevonde, 1936
Tri-colour separation negative
NPG x222907

Yevonde was a pioneer of
colour photography at a time
when it was not considered a
serious medium for art. This
vividly coloured portrait of
actor Leigh is from the Yevonde
Archive of 2,500 negatives
acquired in 2021.

Gimba – The Ward Host
Hassan Akkad, 2020
Digital image file
NPG x201402

Akkad's portrait shows NHS
worker Gimba Bariketu on her
lunch break at Whipps Cross
Hospital during the COVID-19
pandemic. It is one of 100
photographs that have entered
the Collection from the online
and community exhibition *Hold
Still* (2020).

book, reveals as much about the culture of the present day as the past. Indeed, in addition to the many acquisitions that form the Collection, since 1980 the Gallery has engaged in the conversation about national self-reflection through its pioneering programme of commissions, which has resulted in portraits as diverse and outstanding as Glastonbury Festival founder Michael Eavis by Peter Blake, curator Nicholas Serota by Steve McQueen, author Zadie Smith by Toyin Ojih Odutola and women's activist Malala Yousafzai by Shirin Neshat — all featured in this book.

For the first 40 years of its existence, the Gallery was peripatetic: initially, for 13 years, the Collection was housed in three rooms and a staircase in an elegant Georgian town house (now demolished) at 29 Great George Street, Westminster. Its custodian, the Gallery's first Director Sir George Scharf, lived on the second floor. Despite the cramped conditions, in 1859 the Gallery allowed ticketed entry to the public two days a week and received 5,305 visitors in its first year of opening. By the end of 1869, the Collection comprised 288 portraits and its relocation to larger quarters in South Kensington saw visitor numbers leap from 24,416 that year to well over 100,000 just six years later. In 1885, it was temporarily moved to the Bethnal Green Museum, east London, while a more fitting and permanent home was finally built at St Martin's Place, near Trafalgar Square, by the architect Ewan Christian. Indeed, this publication marks the first time our building has been entirely refreshed and transformed in order to celebrate its original beauty since its opening in 1896, and this has been led by Jamie Fobert Architects in partnership with heritage consultants, Purcell. The entire Collection has been rehung, with a new entrance, forecourt and learning centre created as part of our biggest ever development. At the heart of this project has been a comprehensive redisplay of the Collection — from the Tudors to today. Beyond the Gallery walls, innovative partnerships, outreach and digital programmes engage with broad and varied audiences across the UK and internationally, as part of our extensive programme of activities in order to reach new audiences and be a truly national gallery for everyone.

Indeed, our project *Hold Still*, launched during the COVID-19 pandemic and spearheaded by our Patron, HRH The Princess of Wales, was groundbreaking in representing people from all walks of life in our Collection and in reaching new audiences. Participants were encouraged to submit portraits that conveyed the experiences and emotions of the nation during the pandemic. An overwhelming 31,500 entries came from all corners of the UK, with entrants ranging from 4 to 75 years old. In addition to being included in a digital exhibition, the final 100 images featured in a nationwide poster campaign and outdoor exhibition seen by 5 million people. Thanks to the project's expansive appeal, the *Hold Still* book reached number one in *The Sunday Times* Best Sellers List — unprecedented for a gallery or museum publication. The images from *Hold Still* are now an important part of our Collection and will serve as a unique record of this extraordinary moment in our history.

The Gallery, which has the most extensive portrait collection in the world, consists of three distinct elements: the Primary Collection which comprises 4,000 paintings, sculptures and miniatures, as well as 7,000 works on paper; the Photographs Collection of about 220,000 original photographic images; and the Reference Collection of about 80,000 images, mostly prints, but also some drawings. Each of these areas is featured in this book, highlighting the extraordinary range of artists and different

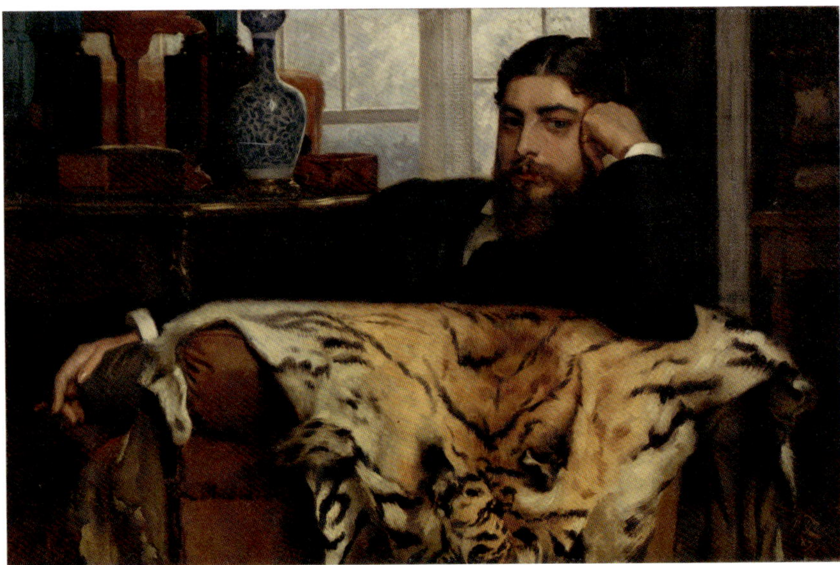

Algernon Moses Marsden
(1847–1920)
Jacques Joseph Tissot, 1877
Oil on canvas, 480 × 725mm
NPG 7135

Tissot was an outstanding painter of cosmopolitan society. His portrait of the art dealer Marsden shows a man at ease with his luxurious surroundings. In 2022, the painting became the first work to be acquired jointly with the National Gallery.

types of portraiture within the Collection. Images in this introduction are drawn from recent acquisitions that illustrate our current and future priorities for the Collection. The book's portraits are then presented in broadly chronological groupings alongside introductions to the periods in which they were made over the past 500 years, from a time of absolute monarchy under the Tudors — during which time painted portraiture in this country flourished, creating some of our most famous works — to our multifaceted, media-saturated world of the digital era in the present day. The publication's starting date of around 1500 reflects the fact that the practice of portrait making in Britain only fully began in the sixteenth century. From the Tudor period to today, the chapters reveal much about the sorts of portrait medium that were available, and the types of people to whom portraiture was accessible, during each era. However, rather than presenting an exhaustive overview of British history, this book is intended to give a fascinating insight into the evolving and dynamic nature of British society and cultural identity.

Through our Collection displays, exhibitions, research, learning, publishing and digital programmes, we aim to bring history to life, stimulate debate, address questions of identity, and promote engagement with portraiture in all media — whether onsite or online — to a diverse global public. As the only national museum exclusively focused on British identity, the Gallery is uniquely placed to encourage reflection on the nature of our society and to celebrate individual achievement. We recognise those who have in some way shaped British history and culture, and, in so doing, show the potential in everyone to make a difference.

I hope that the selection of portraits in this book sparks your curiosity to learn more about British history and society, the art of portraiture, or the remarkable life stories of the sitters. If you have picked this book up at the Gallery, I hope that you have an enjoyable, absorbing and thought-provoking visit. If you have not yet engaged with the Collection in person, we very much look forward to welcoming you!

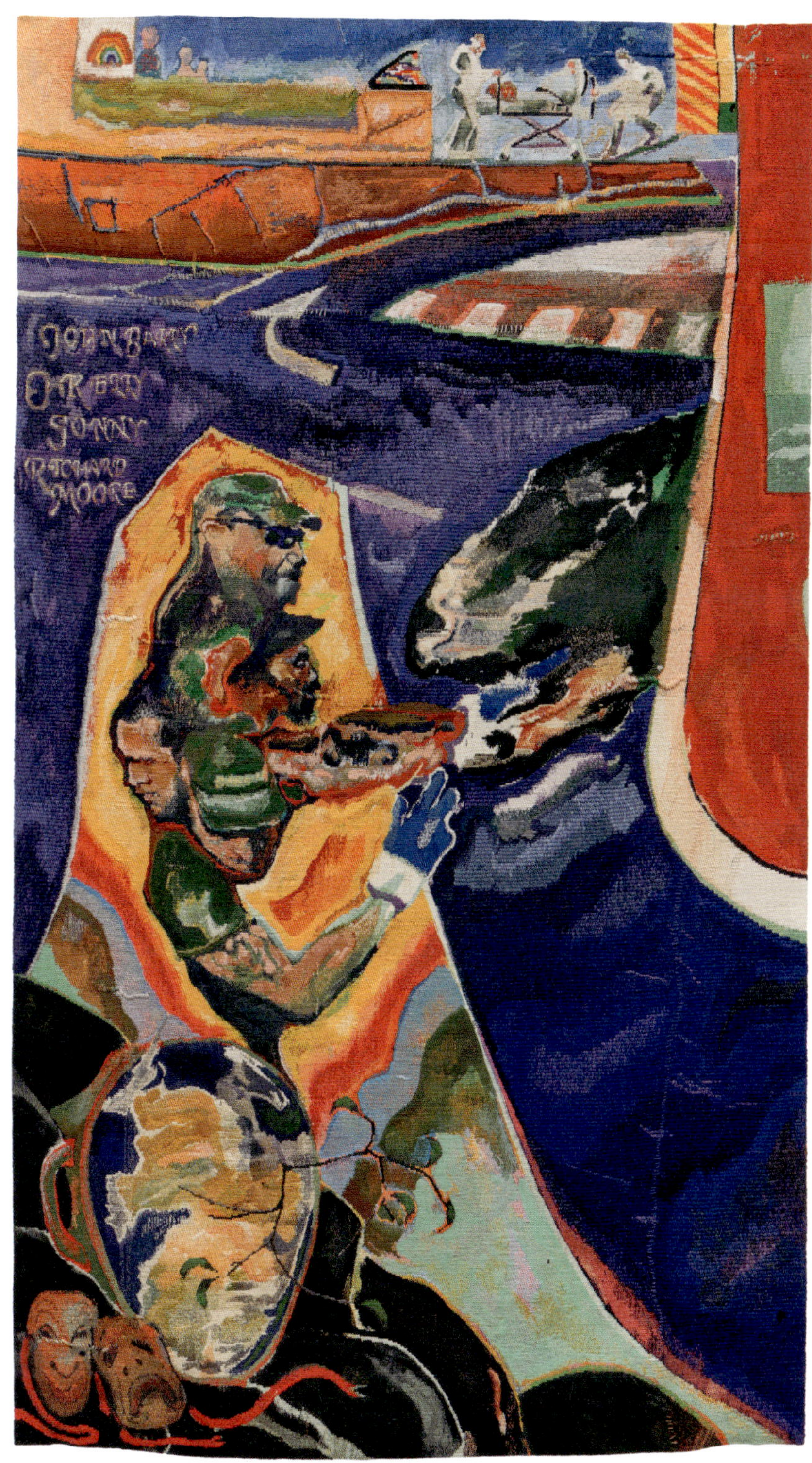

**John Barry, O Kelly,
Sonny and Richard Moore**
Michael Armitage, 2022
Tapestry, 3002 × 1755mm
NPG 7144

This tapestry is after Armitage's painting showing the four refuse collectors named in the title working through the 2020 lockdowns. The patient being stretchered into an ambulance and the rainbow are further references to the 'everyday heroes' of the pandemic.

The Sixteenth Century

During the sixteenth century, the Tudors ruled over a period of seismic change in England, Wales and Ireland. The Church of England was created, along with the Kingdom of Ireland, the Royal Navy, international trading companies and the first English colonies in the Americas.

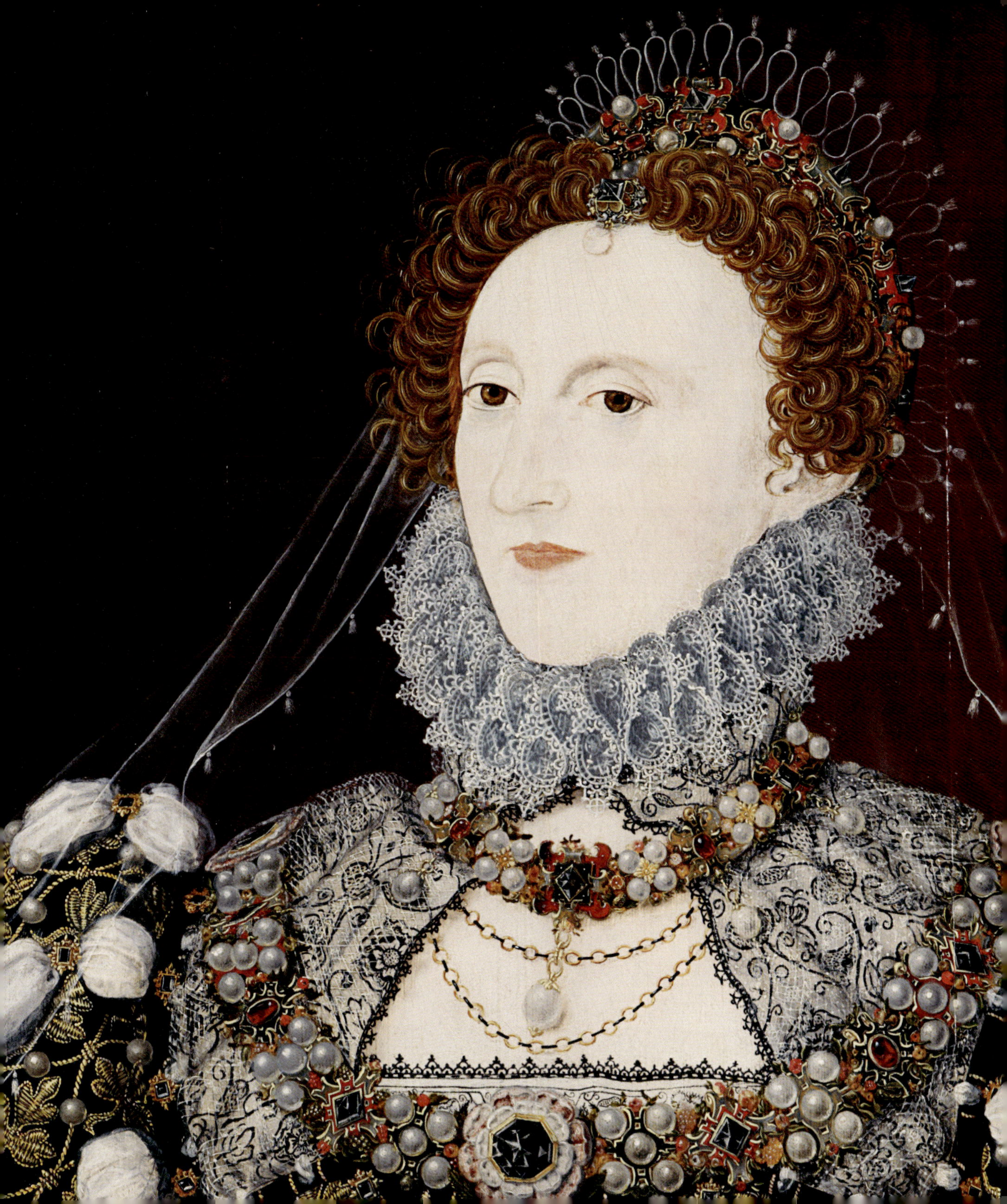

Realm and Reformation

The Tudor monarchs ruled England, Wales and Ireland between 1485 and 1603. Scotland was a separate country ruled by the Stuarts. The first Tudor king, Henry VII, seized the throne from Richard III at the Battle of Bosworth in 1485. Henry Tudor's victory ended a period of civil conflict that has come to be known as the Wars of the Roses (1455–87). Henry VII united the rival branches of the Plantagenet family, the Houses of York and Lancaster, by marrying Elizabeth of York.

Henry VII was succeeded by his son Henry VIII, who in turn was succeeded by his three children, Edward VI, Mary I — England's first queen regnant — and Elizabeth I. Over the course of the sixteenth century, the Tudors centralised power in England, annexed Wales and created the Kingdom of Ireland. Also under their rule, the last English territories in France were lost.

During this period, the religious revolution known as the Reformation had a fundamental impact on society and national identity across Western Europe. Henry VIII's break from the Catholic Church in Rome, claiming the title of Supreme Head of the Church of England, granted the monarch greater personal power than at any previous point in history. Mary, who ruled from 1553 to 1558, attempted to return the nation to Catholicism but, by the end of Elizabeth's reign in 1603, England was an overwhelmingly Protestant country. The Bible was printed in English for the first time and the new printing presses supported a flourishing literary culture.

Many of the changes and innovations of the period had a lasting impact on the country and beyond. Rivalry with Catholic European countries and the threat of invasion by Spain led to the development of the Royal Navy. England's expanding maritime ambitions led to global exploration, the establishment of the first overseas colonies, the formation of international trading companies, and the beginning of the transportation of enslaved people from Africa to the Americas.

The Tudors sought to build their reputation on the international stage by projecting a sophisticated court culture. The court was a site of cultural exchange, with scholars, soldiers, musicians, merchants and diplomats visiting from all over Europe and further afield. Power was exercised through royal patronage and favour, with courtiers vying for appointments and rewards dispensed by the monarch. During the reign of Elizabeth I, male courtiers competed with each other through the performance of their intimacy with the queen. This included the staging of pageants, feasts and tournaments and displays of personal wealth through jewellery, clothes and works of art.

Art became a more potent form of cultural consumption and self-presentation. Standalone painted portraiture became increasingly popular, and was commissioned not only by the royal family and members of the court, but also by the upper and middle classes. The change was influenced by Renaissance humanist ideas from continental Europe, where there was a renewed emphasis on individual identity. The outstanding artists of the period include Hans Holbein the Younger, Anthonis Mor and Nicholas Hilliard.

This is the earliest painted portrait in the Collection. The inscription records that it was made on 29 October 1505. It was sent to Margaret of Austria as part of an unsuccessful marriage negotiation following the death of Henry's wife, Elizabeth of York.

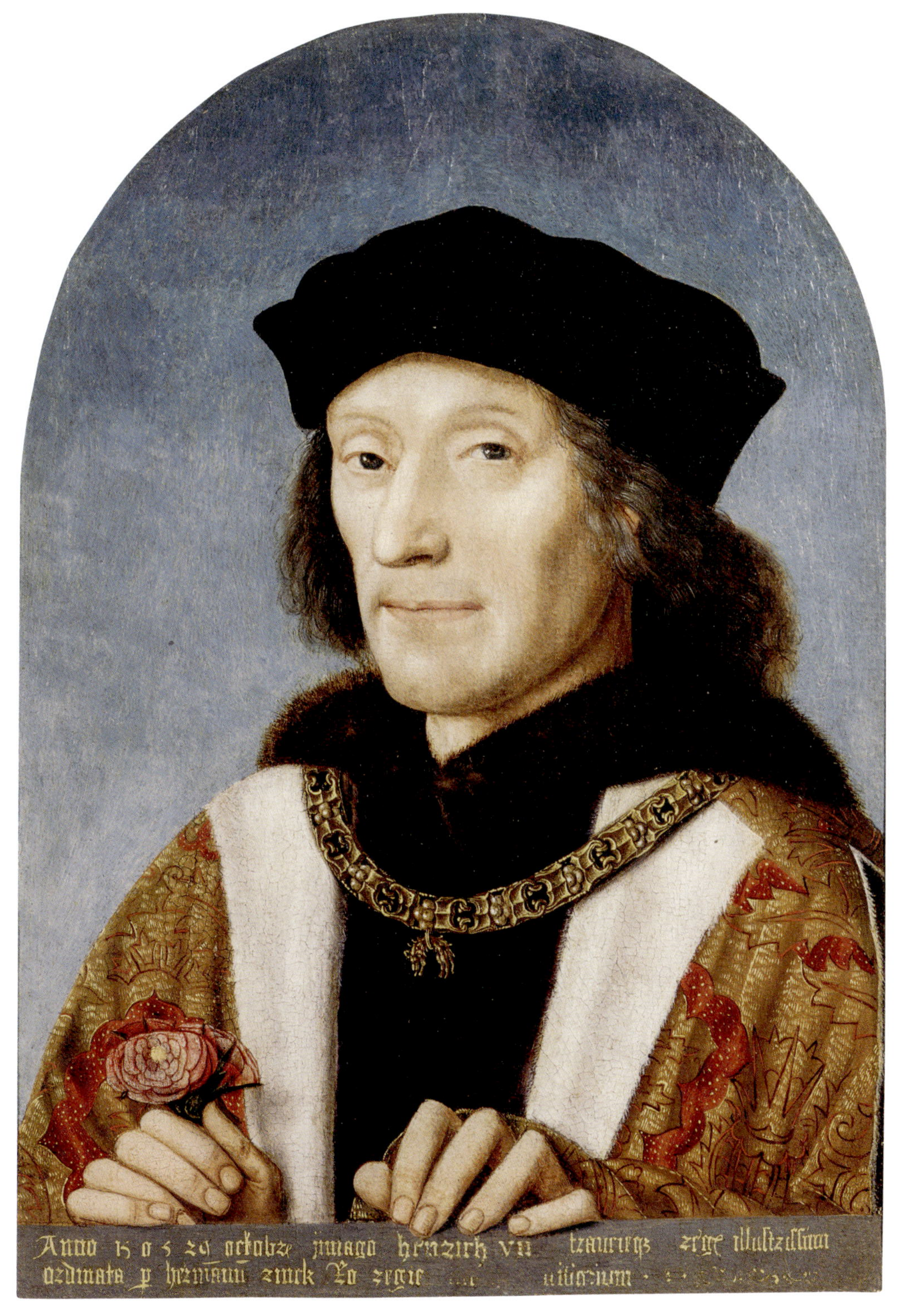

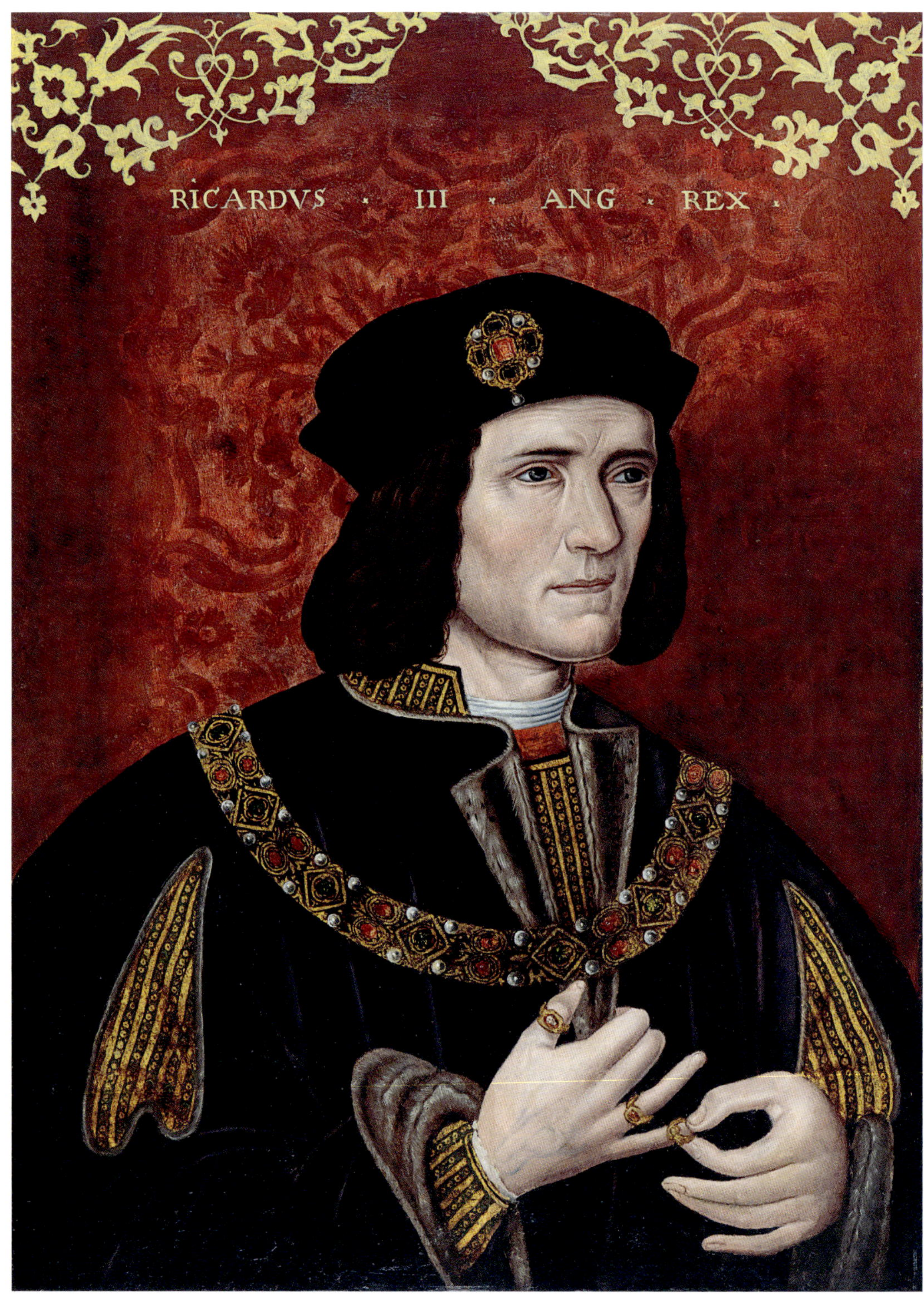

RICARDVS · III · ANG · REX ·

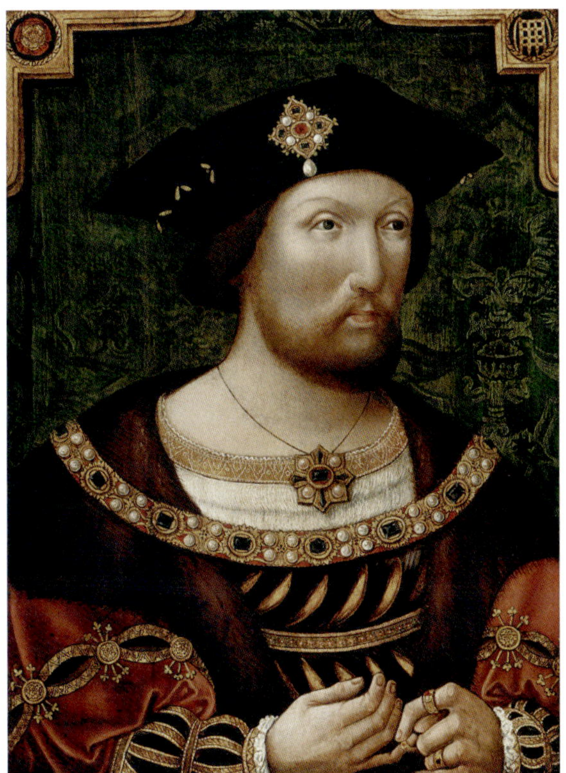 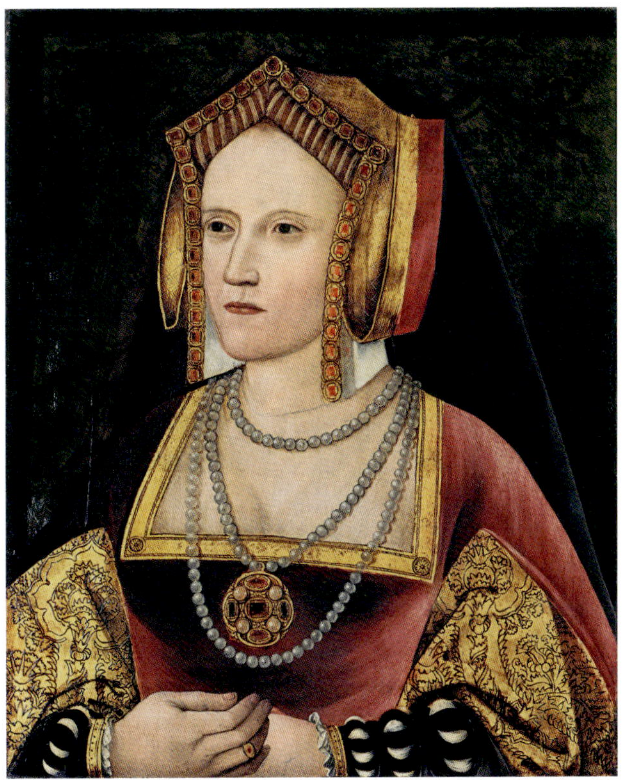

King Richard III
(1452–85)
Unknown artist,
late sixteenth century
Oil on panel, 638 × 470mm
NPG 148

The last Yorkist king of England, Richard III was killed at the Battle of Bosworth and buried in a friary in Leicester. Tudor writers, including William Shakespeare, went on to shape his reputation as an archetypal villain.

King Henry VIII
(1491–1547)
Unknown artist, *c*.1520
Oil on panel, 508 × 381mm
NPG 4690

Henry VIII was crowned shortly before his 18th birthday, succeeding his father, Henry VII, to the throne. He is well known for his six marriages, and for ordering the dissolution of religious houses, which took place in 1536–40.

Katherine of Aragon
(1485–1536)
Unknown artist, *c*.1520
Oil on panel, 520 × 420mm
NPG L246

Katherine of Aragon married Henry VIII in 1509. They struggled to have children and only their daughter Mary survived infancy. The annulment of their marriage after 23 years was at the heart of Henry VIII's break with the Catholic Church.

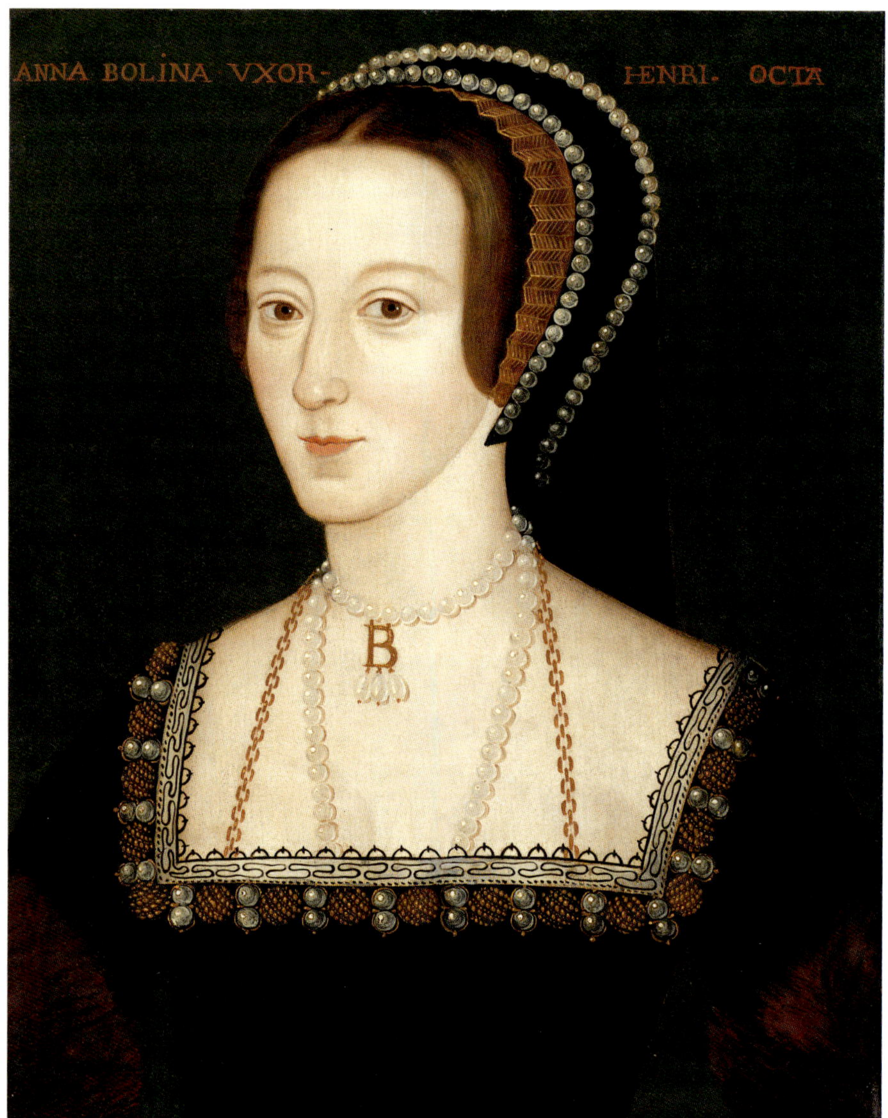

Anne Boleyn
(*c.*1500–36)
Unknown artist,
late sixteenth century
Oil on panel, 543 × 416mm
NPG 668

Boleyn was courted by Henry VIII for years but refused to become his mistress. She finally married Henry in secret in 1533, before his first marriage had been annulled, giving birth to a daughter, Elizabeth, that same year. She was later accused of committing adultery and executed in 1536.

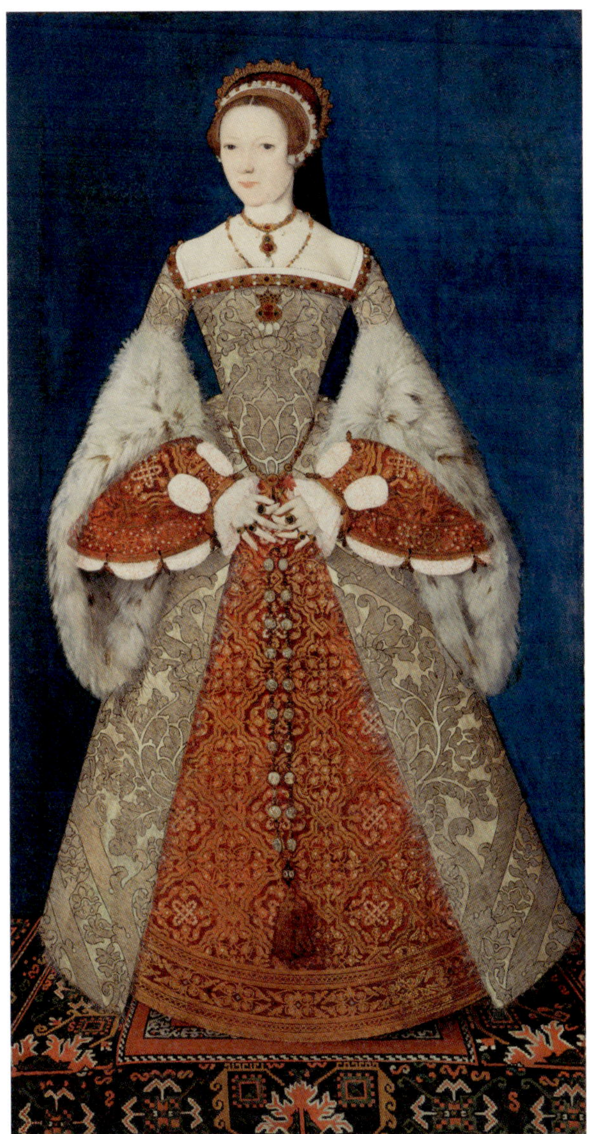

Katherine Parr
(1512–48)
Unknown artist, *c.*1545
Oil on panel, 1803 × 940mm
NPG 4451

Parr married Henry VIII in 1543
and used her position as queen
consort to promote religious reform,
becoming the first English woman to
publish books in her own name.

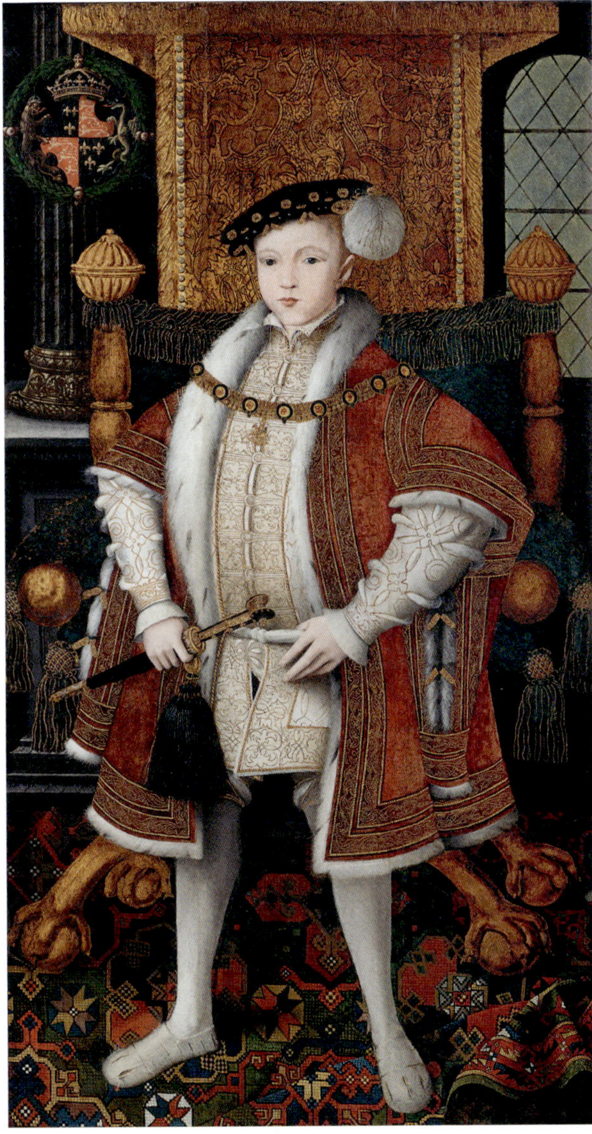

King Edward VI
(1537–53)
Unknown artist, *c.*1547
Oil on panel, 1556 × 813mm
NPG 5511

Edward VI became king aged 9, and
died aged only 15. He ruled with a
group of councillors, and together
they moved quickly to establish
Protestantism in the country.

Sir Henry Lee
(1533–1611)
Anthonis Mor, 1568
Oil on panel, 641 × 533mm
NPG 2095

Lee was educated by his uncle, the poet Sir Thomas Wyatt, and entered royal service at the age of 14. He served five monarchs over the course of his long career and, as his epitaph records, 'kept himself right and steady in many dangerous shocks and utter turns of state'. He achieved his greatest renown at the court of Elizabeth I, serving as the queen's Champion. In this role he devised the Accession Day tilts, held annually on 17 November in her honour. These elaborate celebrations, which combined theatrical elements with jousting, became the most important Elizabethan court festival and created an environment in which courtiers could compete for the queen's favour.

This portrait was painted in Antwerp in 1568 while Lee was travelling in Europe. The Netherlandish painter Mor (*c.*1516–*c.*1576) was court artist to Philip II of Spain and one of the most highly esteemed portraitists in Europe. Mor's exceptionally subtle handling of paint creates a powerful sense of presence. Lee's gesture, with his thumb through a ring suspended from a cord around his neck, may signify a bond of love or friendship. This theme is echoed by the lovers' knots embroidered on his sleeves. The armillary spheres on his sleeves symbolise wisdom and may also refer to his closeness to the queen. Elizabeth I similarly wears an armillary sphere as an earring in the 'Ditchley' portrait, also in the Gallery's Collection, which was commissioned by Lee as part of entertainments staged for the queen at his house in Oxfordshire in 1592.

'I was at Court this morning, where nothing is so much thought upon as dancing and playing. Some are there, hoping for preferment, as my Lord North and Sir Henry Lee. They play at cards with the Queen, and it is likely to be all the honour that will fall unto them this year.'

Rowland Whyte, 27 December 1595

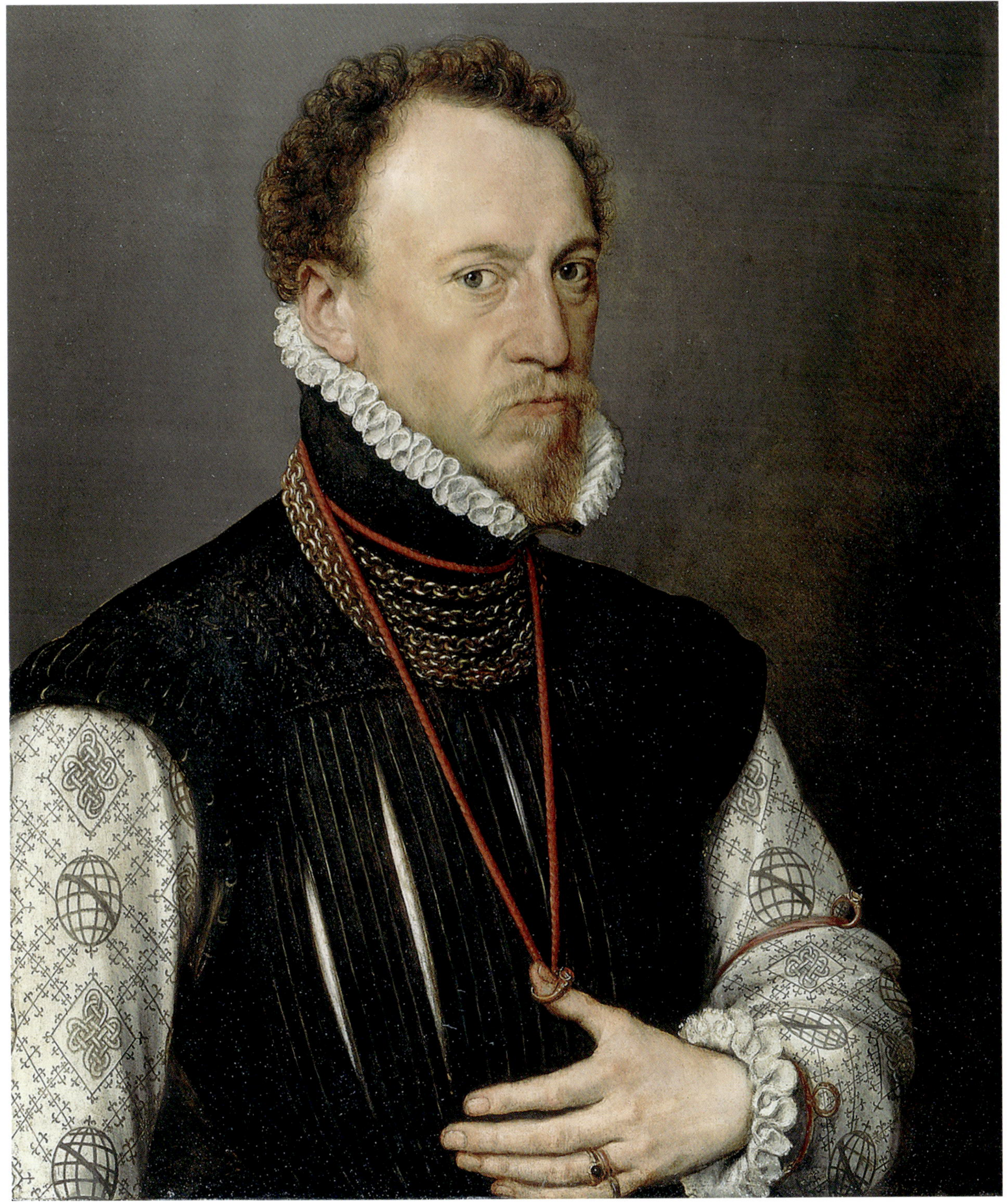

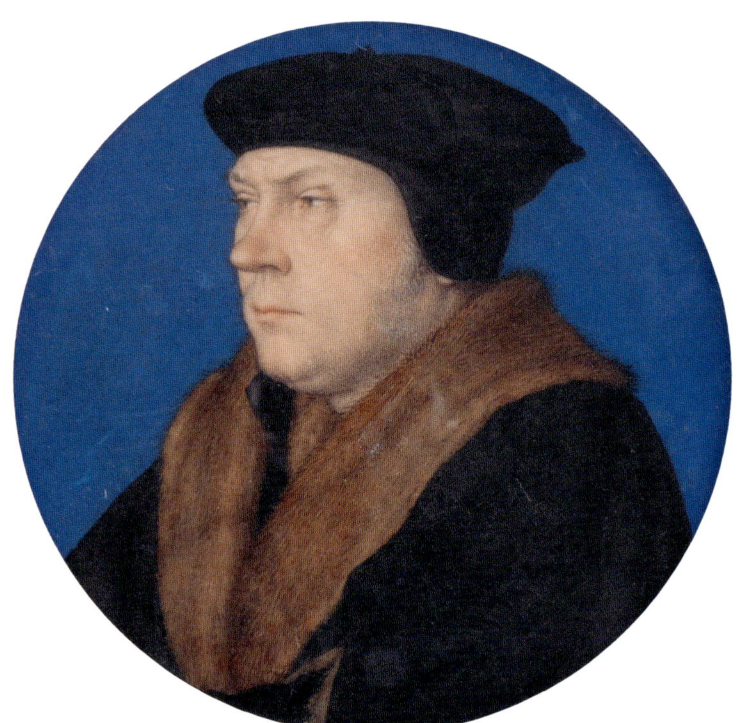

Henry VIII's principal secretary
and chief minister, Cromwell
enforced the king's supremacy
and drove religious reform in
England through the dissolution
of the monasteries and the
dissemination of the Bible in
English. In 1540, he lost the
king's favour and was beheaded
at the Tower of London.

A handsome and ambitious
soldier who made his name
during the English campaigns
in Ireland, Ralegh used his skills
as a poet to gain the favour of
Elizabeth I, whom he praised as
Cynthia, the moon goddess.

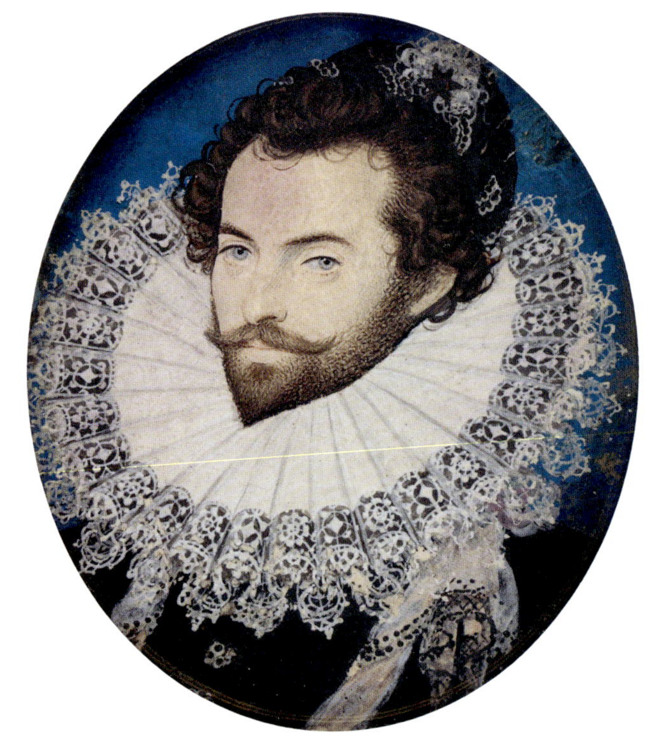

Mary, Queen of Scots
(1542–87)
After Nicholas Hilliard,
inscribed 1578
Oil on panel, 791 × 902mm
NPG 429

Mary became Queen of Scotland
as an infant, but was forced to
abdicate and flee to England
after her second husband
was murdered. As the great-
granddaughter of Henry VII,
Mary had a claim to the English
throne and became the focal
point for Catholic attempts to
remove the Protestant Elizabeth I.
After years of imprisonment, she
was executed in 1587.

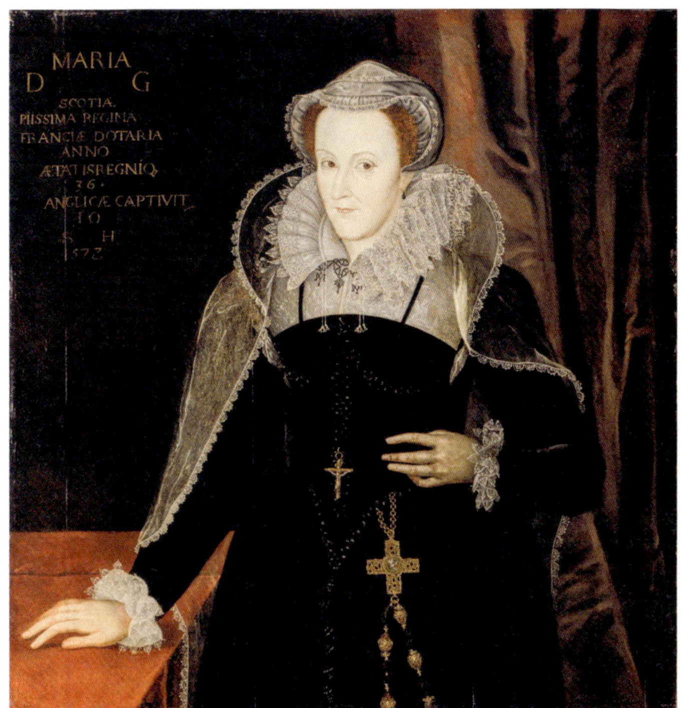

Queen Mary I
(1516–58)
Hans Eworth, 1554
Oil on panel, 216 × 169mm
NPG 4861

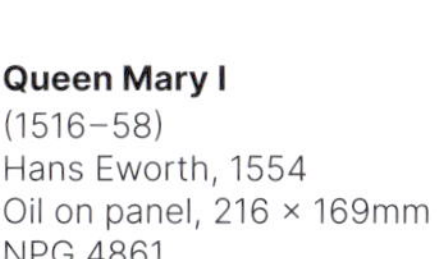

The only surviving child of
Henry VIII and Katherine
of Aragon, Mary became
England's first queen regnant
aged 37, after the death of her
half-brother, Edward VI. Her
marriage to Philip II of Spain
and persecution of Protestants
contributed to her unpopularity.

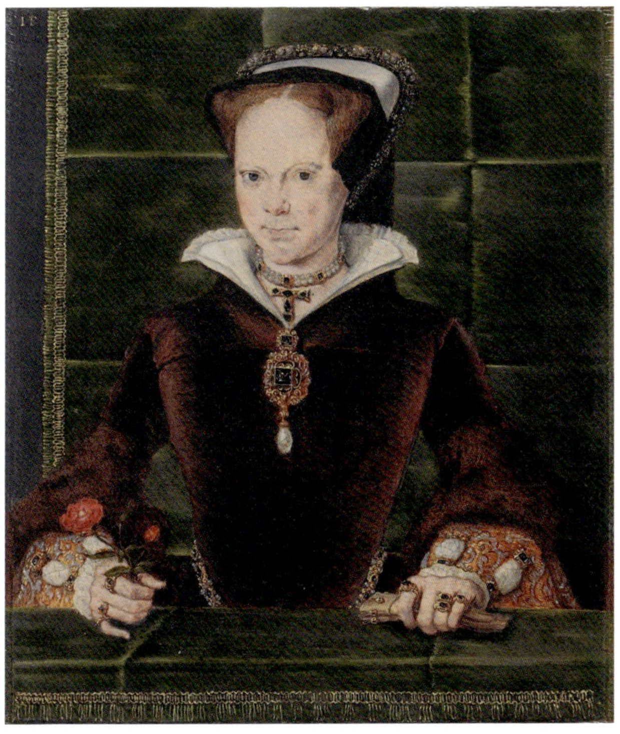

Queen Elizabeth I
(1533–1603)
Nicholas Hilliard, *c.*1575
Oil on panel, 787 × 610mm
NPG 190

The only surviving child of Henry VIII and his second wife, Anne Boleyn, Elizabeth was 25 years old when she inherited the throne from her half-sister, Mary. Her long reign was characterised by the re-establishment of the Protestant Church of England, conflict with Catholic Spain, the growth of foreign trade and exploration, and a flourishing literary culture. She refused widespread pressure to marry and so ensured that she retained her personal authority as queen until her death in 1603.

The most celebrated English artist of the Tudor period, Hilliard (*c.*1547–1619) was one of the few artists to be granted direct access to Elizabeth I. He once painted her portrait from life during a sitting outside in a garden. Hilliard is primarily known as a supremely talented miniaturist but this is one of two large-scale oil portraits of the queen that were painted in the studio at the same time on panel supports cut from the same piece of wood. In this version she wears a phoenix jewel, and in the other a pelican jewel. Elizabeth was highly skilled at using clothing and jewellery to symbolically represent her power and authority. Here she wears a heavily jewelled collar with a red and white Tudor rose in the centre. Taken with the phoenix jewel below, an emblem of rebirth and chastity, the symbols in the portrait promote Elizabeth's role in regenerating and sustaining the dynasty.

'She is a young woman, whose mind is considered no less excellent than her person ... she has fine eyes and above all a beautiful hand of which she makes a display; and her intellect and understanding are wonderful.'

Giovanni Michiel, Venetian Ambassador, 1557

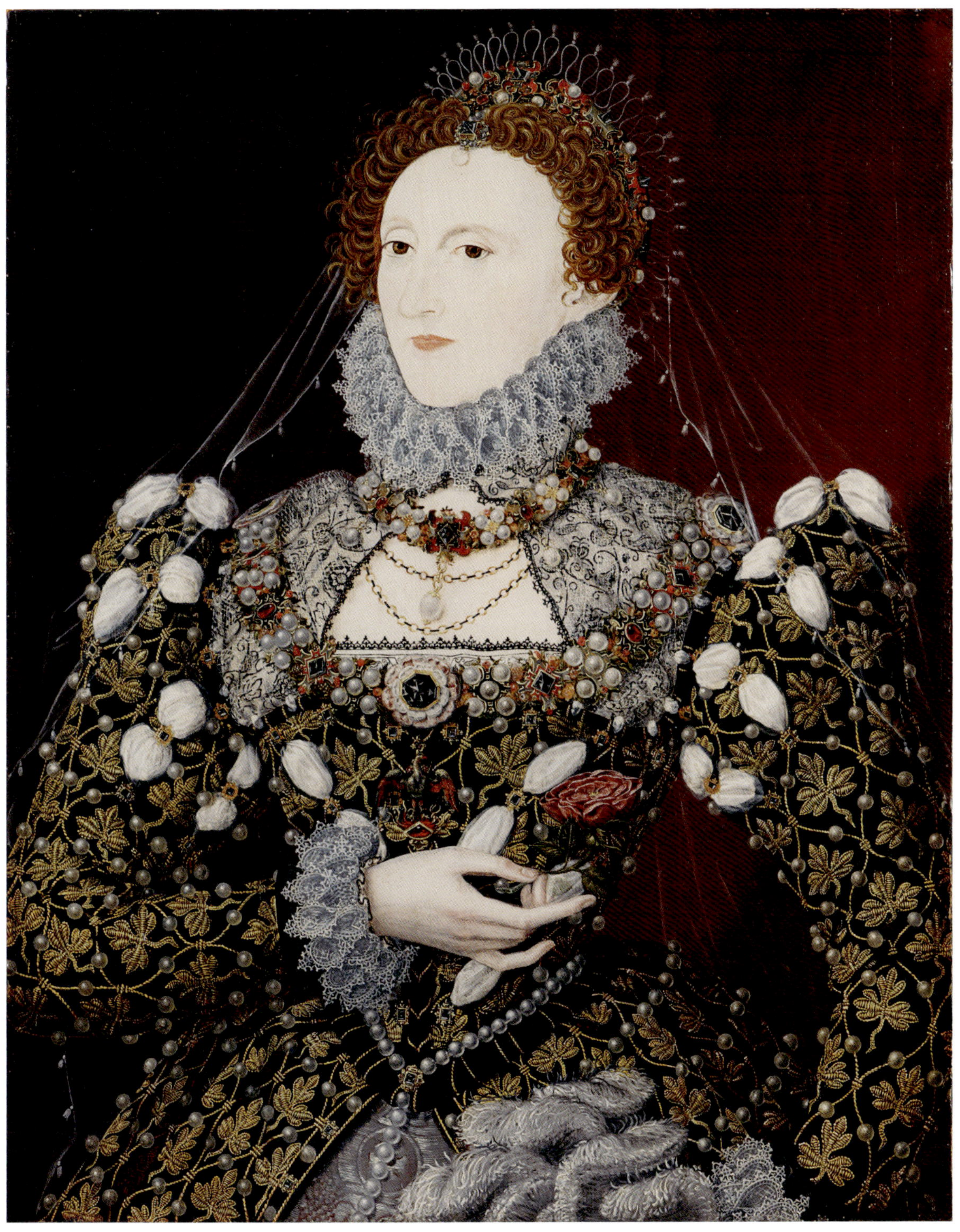

The Seventeenth Century

The seventeenth century was a period of political and religious upheaval featuring civil wars and revolution. Out of the conflict emerged the foundation of today's parliamentary democracy, as well as familiar institutions such as the British army and the Bank of England.

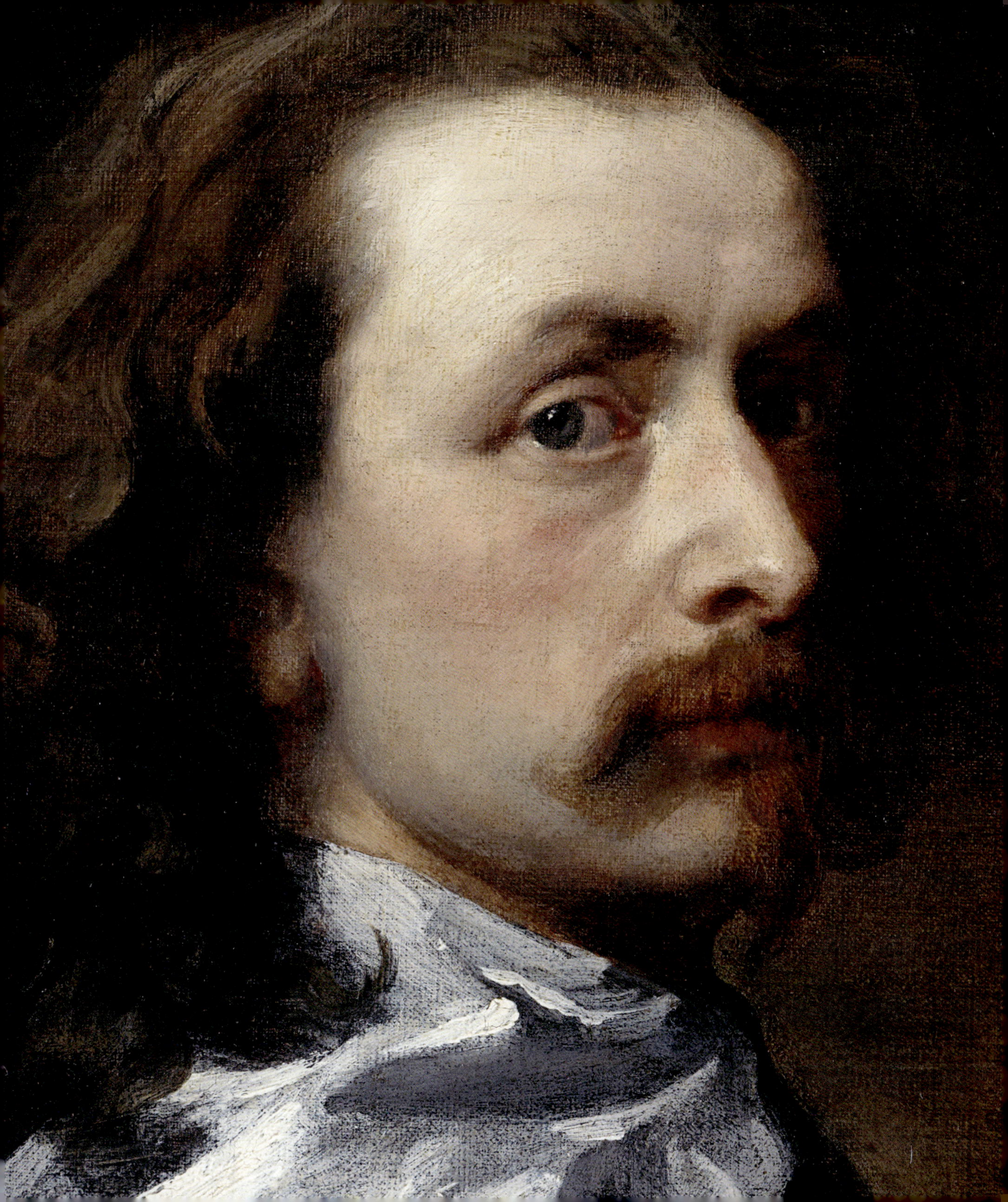

Court and Revolution

Following the death of Elizabeth I in 1603, the English throne passed to her cousin James VI of Scotland, the son of Mary, Queen of Scots. For the first time, England, Wales, Scotland and Ireland were ruled by the same monarch. King James brought the Stuart dynasty to England and the family would remain central to the national story until 1714. As James I of England, he made peace with Spain and sought to maintain the balance of power in Europe.

During this period, literature and theatre flourished. King James and his queen consort, Anne of Denmark, rivalled the cultural patronage of other European monarchies. William Shakespeare wrote some of the most important plays and poems in the English language and the King James Bible was published. The visual arts continued to thrive under the patronage of Charles I, who succeeded to the throne in 1625. Portraiture was radically transformed by the Flemish artist Sir Anthony van Dyck, who is perhaps the most influential portraitist to have worked in Britain.

Like all monarchs before him, Charles I believed in his right to rule with absolute authority: the Divine Right of Kings. But this belief was beginning to be challenged among the wider population. His imposition of unpopular taxes, restrictions on the freedom of worship, and autocratic rule eventually led to civil war. From 1639 to 1651, a series of conflicts known as the Wars of the Three Kingdoms raged across England, Scotland and Ireland. The victor was the army of the English Parliament. Charles I was tried for treason and executed in 1649.

There followed 11 years of republican rule under the leadership of Oliver Cromwell, the Parliamentary commander. An uprising led by Charles II was crushed in 1651, with the young king narrowly escaping the same fate as his father, and Cromwell ruled as Lord Protector of the newly formed Commonwealth of England, Scotland and Ireland from 1653. The republic was thrown into chaos by his death and, in 1660, the Stuart dynasty was restored with the return of Charles II. The following years saw great cultural developments, such as the first women on the public stage, and scientific progress including Sir Isaac Newton's groundbreaking discoveries.

During this period, the Royal Africa Company became the first and largest British company to trade and transport enslaved Africans to the Americas. Britain's first permanent colony in North America had been established in 1607 and, by the end of the century, many plantations there relied on the labour of enslaved people.

While the decadence of Charles II's court provoked disapproval from the public, under his Catholic brother, James II, widespread concerns about the political and religious direction of the country grew into revolt. For the second time, a Stuart king was dethroned but the 1688 revolution had a more enduring legacy than the civil wars. James II fled abroad after William of Orange, husband of James's daughter, Mary, sailed with an army to England from the Netherlands. The political, religious and social changes brought about during the seventeenth century remain with us today. Above all, Britain's constitutional monarchy, in which executive power would increasingly be held by parliament, paved the way for the modern British state.

The playwright and poet Shakespeare is regarded as one of the greatest and most influential writers of all time. This was the first portrait acquired by the Gallery and is probably the only portrait of Shakespeare painted from life.

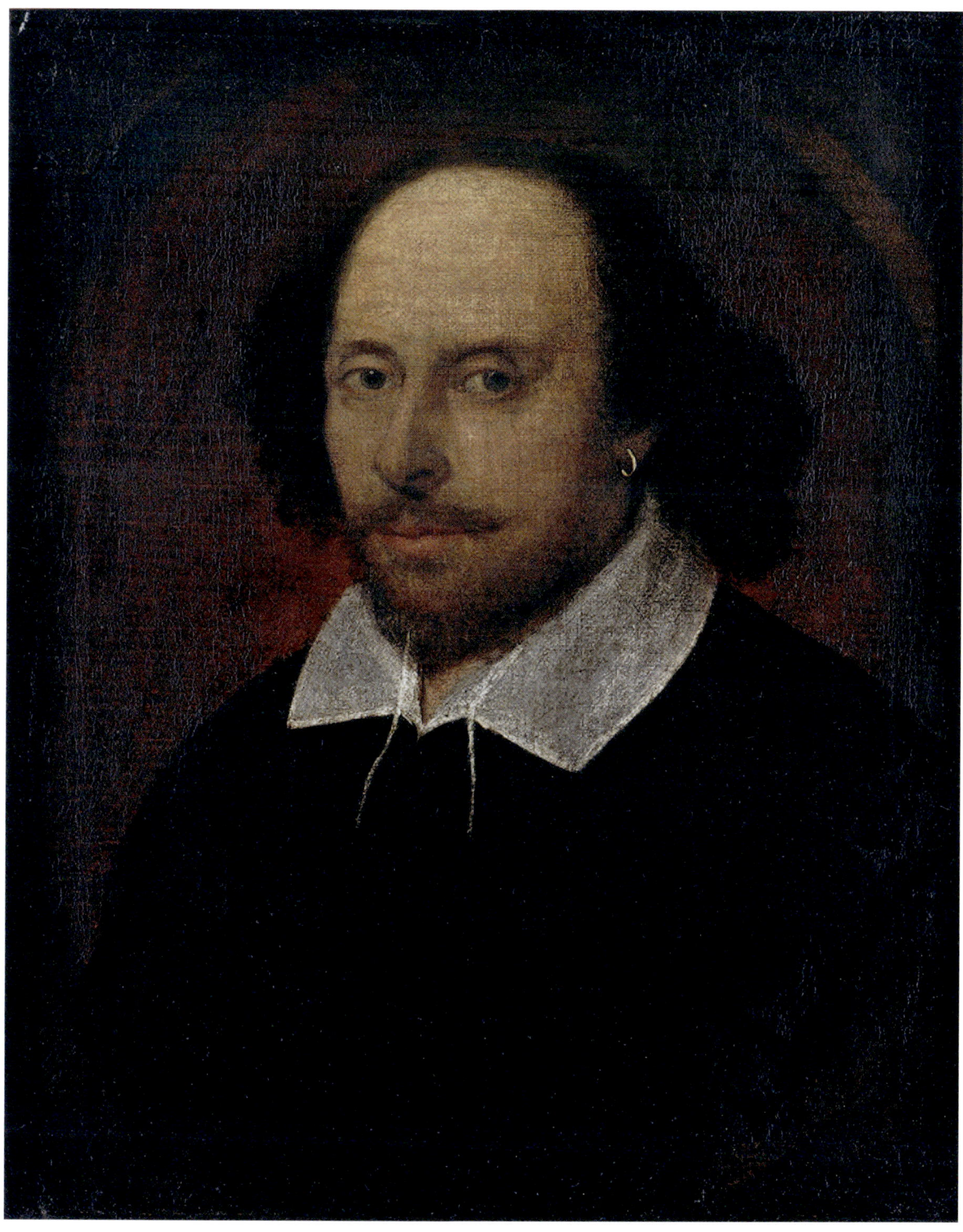

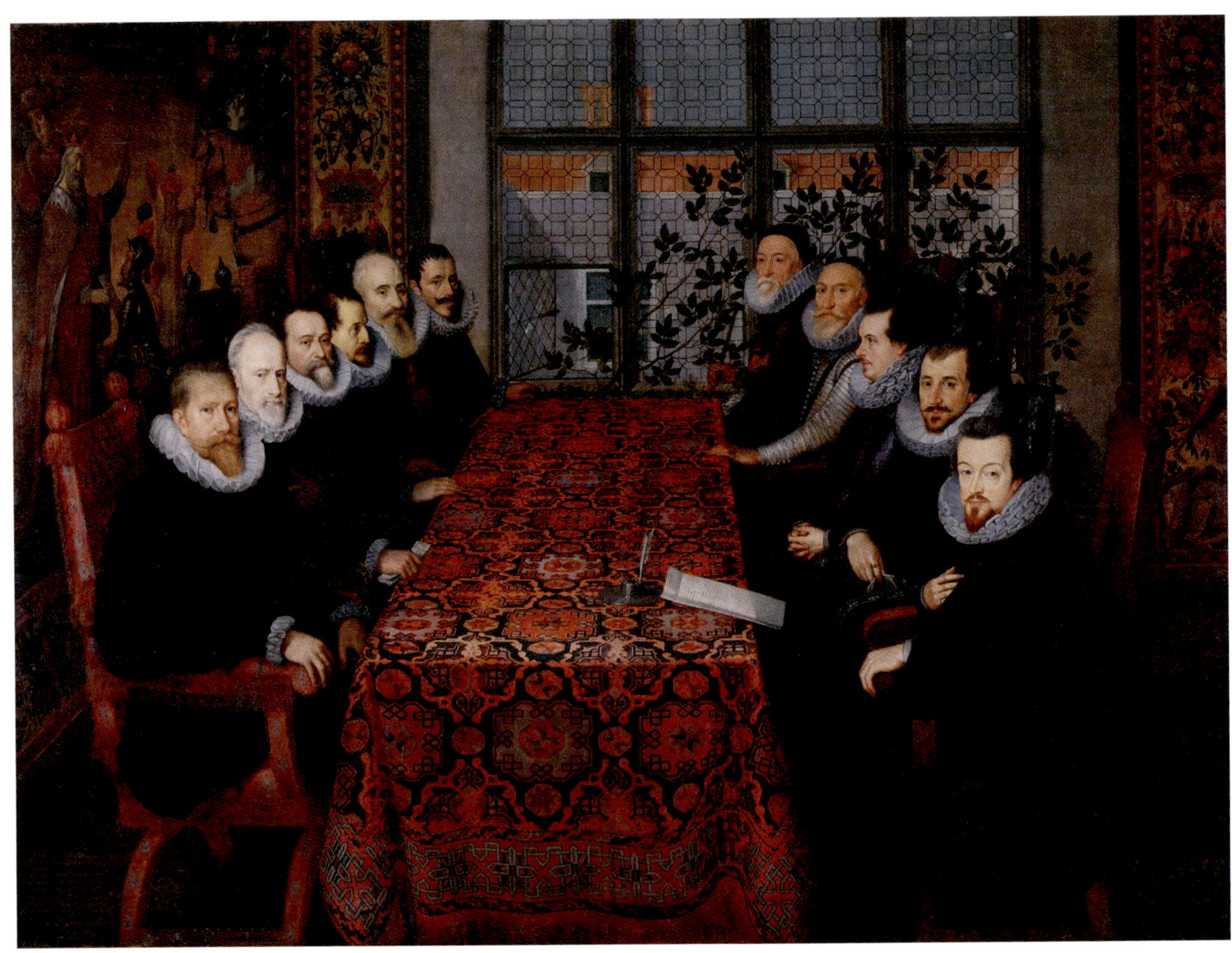

The Somerset House Conference, 1604
Unknown artist, 1604
Oil on canvas, 2057 × 2680mm
NPG 665

Peace in Europe was a key aim of James VI and I. In 1604, following the negotiations depicted in this painting, a treaty was signed between England and Spain, ending 19 years of war.

Anne of Denmark
(1574–1619)
Isaac Oliver, *c.*1612
Watercolour on vellum,
51 × 41mm
NPG 4010

Anne was a Danish princess who
married James VI of Scotland
in 1589. James ascended to
the English throne in 1603 and,
with their increased wealth,
Anne became an important
patron of innovative artists,
soon employing Oliver to make
miniature paintings.

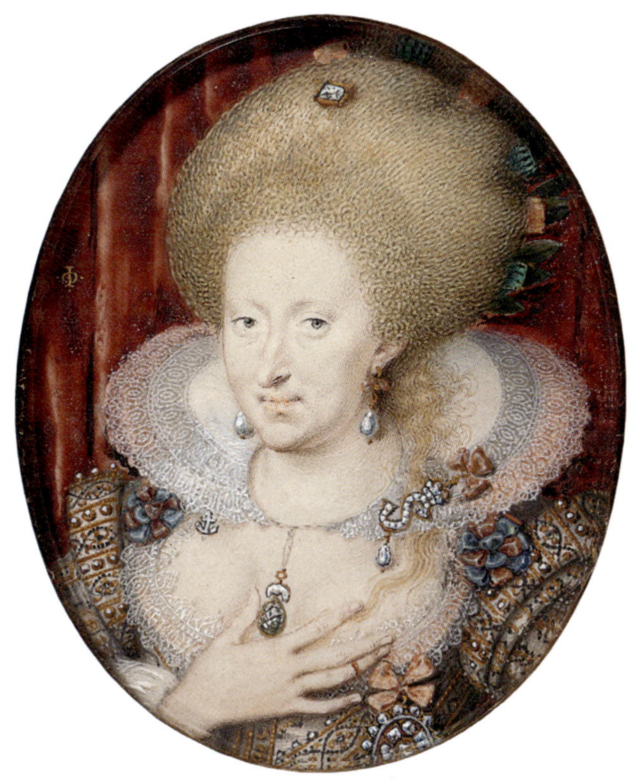

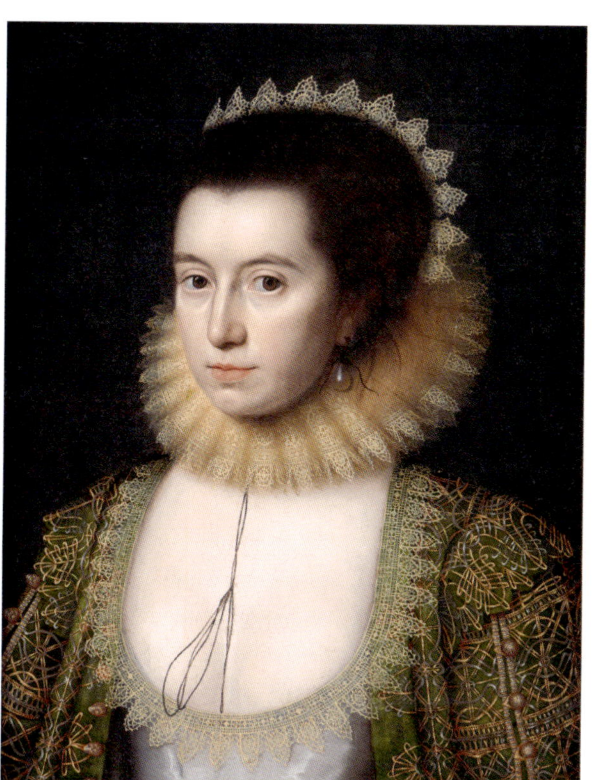

**Lady Anne Clifford,
Countess of Pembroke**
(1590–1676)
William Larkin, *c.*1618
Oil on panel, 575 × 435mm
NPG 6976

Clifford spent most of her adult
life fighting a legal battle to
inherit her father's extensive
estates. Although her family
attempted to silence her, as did
the Archbishop of Canterbury
and even the king, she was not
deterred, eventually inheriting
in middle age.

Sir Anthony van Dyck
(1599–1641)
Self-portrait, c.1640
Oil on canvas, 560 × 460mm
NPG 6987

Van Dyck was by far the most influential painter to have
worked in Britain during the seventeenth century, and
arguably the most influential portrait painter ever to work
in this country. Flemish by birth, he found patronage in
a number of European cities, but his longest stay was in
England, which he made his home from the beginning of his
second visit in 1632 until his death in 1641.

Van Dyck decisively turned British portraiture away from
the stiff, intricately detailed, formal approach of Tudor and
Jacobean painting. His distinctive, fluid, shimmering style
would go on to dominate portraiture in Britain until the early
years of the twentieth century. He was knighted by Charles I
on his arrival in England and appointed the king's Principal
Painter. His high status and renown means that he can be
regarded as the first artist in Britain to become a celebrity.

This is one of three known self-portraits painted by Van
Dyck during his time in Britain. He shows himself fashionably
dressed and apparently in the act of painting, the line of his
arm suggesting his hand raised in the process of applying
paint to a canvas. The marked contrast between the broad,
rapid handling of paint in the garments and the high level
of finish in the face could indicate that the costume is
unfinished, or it may be that this self-portrait is simply more
experimental than his grand, commissioned portraits.

'When Van Dyck came hither
he brought Face-Painting to
us; ever since which time ...
England has excell'd all the
World in that great Branch of
the Art.'

Jonathan Richardson, 1715

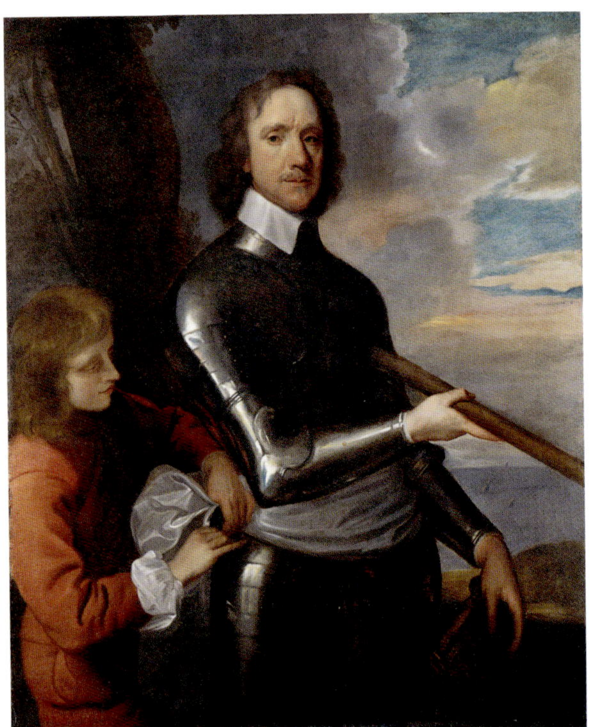

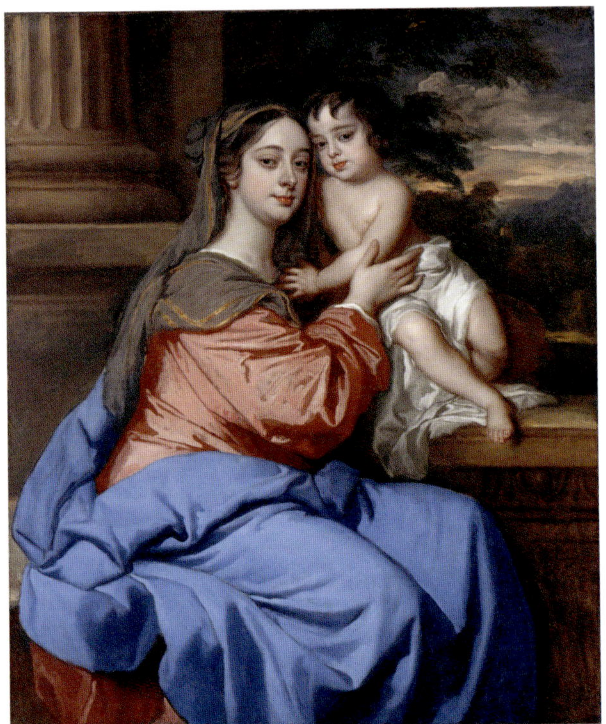

Oliver Cromwell
(1599–1658)
Robert Walker, c.1649
Oil on canvas, 1257 × 1016mm
NPG 536

Cromwell was the only
non-royal head of state in
British history. Having led
the Parliamentarian army to
victory against Charles I in the
English civil wars, defeated
the Scots and Charles II in
1651, and conquered Ireland,
he ruled the British Isles as
Lord Protector from 1653 until
his death in 1658.

**Barbara Villiers, Duchess
of Cleveland, with her son,
Charles FitzRoy**
(1640–1709; 1662–1730)
Sir Peter Lely, c.1664
Oil on canvas, 1247 × 1021mm
NPG 6725

Villiers was Charles II's mistress
when he was restored to the
throne in 1660. She had at
least five children with him and
wielded political influence by
facilitating access to him. This
portrait presents her as the
Virgin Mary with her son by the
king as the Christ Child.

King Charles I
(1600–49)
Daniel Mytens, 1631
Oil on canvas, 2159 × 1346mm
NPG 1246

Charles I, a passionate and
knowledgeable art patron
and collector, is portrayed
here by the fashionable Dutch
artist Mytens. Leader of the
Royalist army in the civil wars,
Charles I was defeated by the
Parliamentarians. He was tried
for treason and executed on
30 January 1649, outside the
Banqueting House, Whitehall.

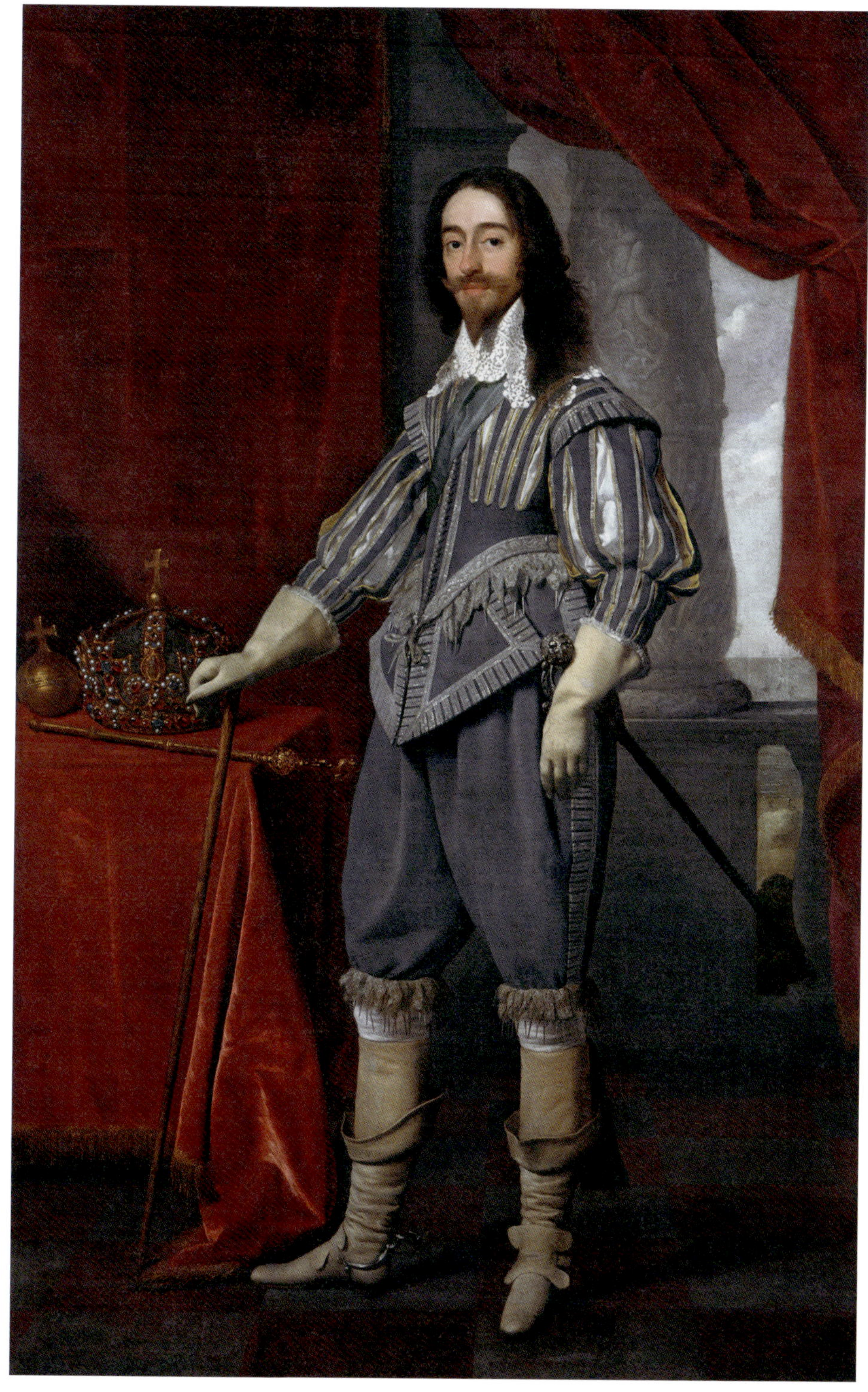

Nell Gwyn
(*c.*1651–87)
Simon Verelst, *c.*1680
Oil on canvas, 737 × 632mm
NPG 2496

Perhaps the most famous name of the Restoration court, Gwyn was also one of the first women to act on the public stage. Most likely born in London, she grew up in its slums in the shadow of civil war. After living hand to mouth as an orange seller in Covent Garden, she established herself as a comic actor in London's Drury Lane during the 1660s.

Gwyn caught the attention of the diarist Samuel Pepys, who described her as 'pretty witty Nell'. More importantly, she was introduced to Charles II and became his mistress. Her irreverent wit and humour were as important as her looks in ensuring her favour with the king. They had two sons, Charles, later Duke of St Albans, and James. The king bought her a house in Pall Mall, paid her a pension and is said to have remembered her on his deathbed with the words, 'Let not poor Nelly starve.'

Verelst (1644–*c.*1710) was a Dutch artist who arrived in England as a specialist flower painter but also depicted many members of the royal court. His theatrical style was particularly well suited to Gwyn, who he painted on a number of occasions and in different poses. This revealing portrait reflects how female actors at the time were seen as operating outside the conventions of respectable society.

'But so great performance of a comical part was never, I believe, in the world before as Nell ... It makes me, I confess, admire her.'

Samuel Pepys, 2 March 1667

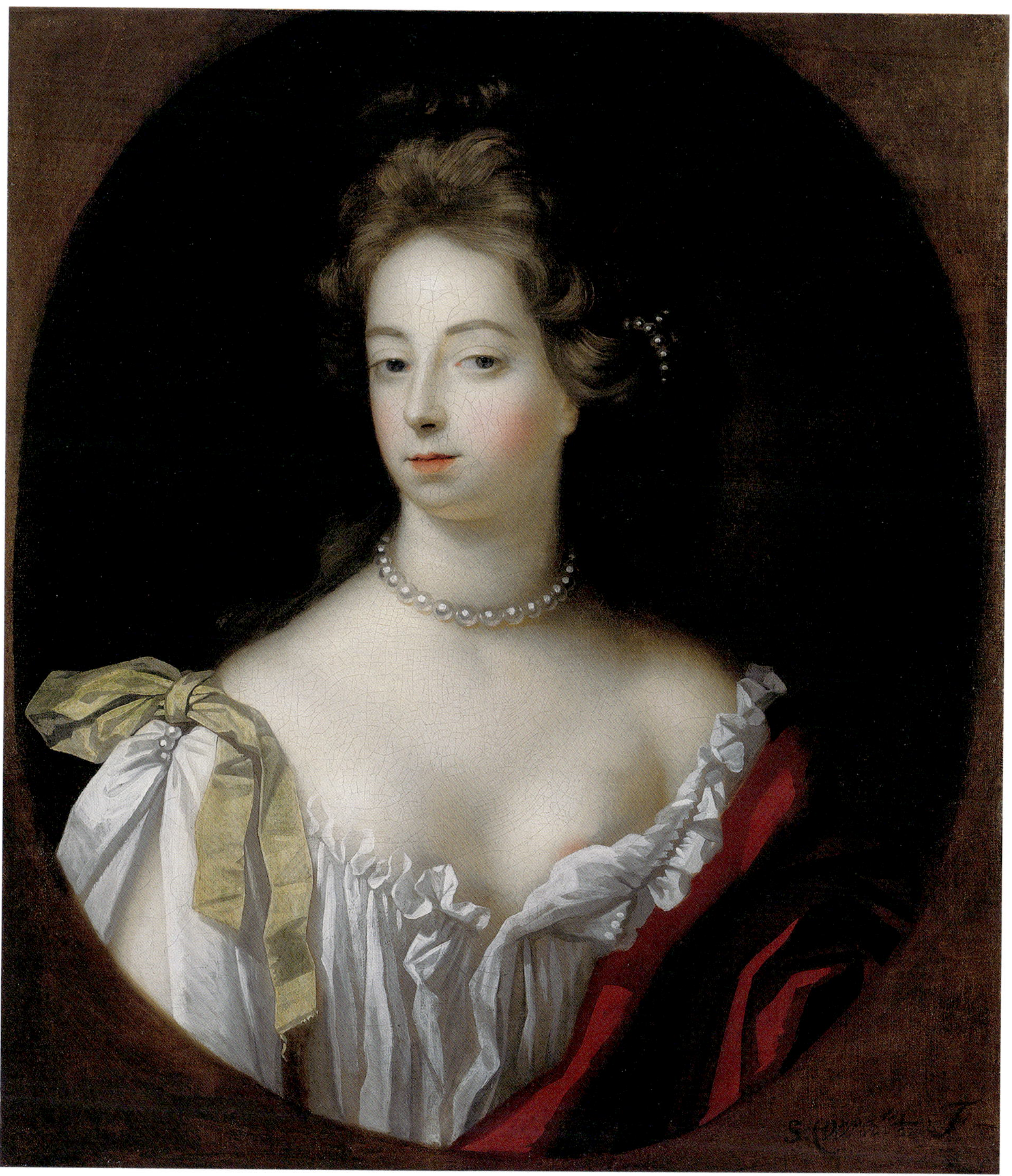

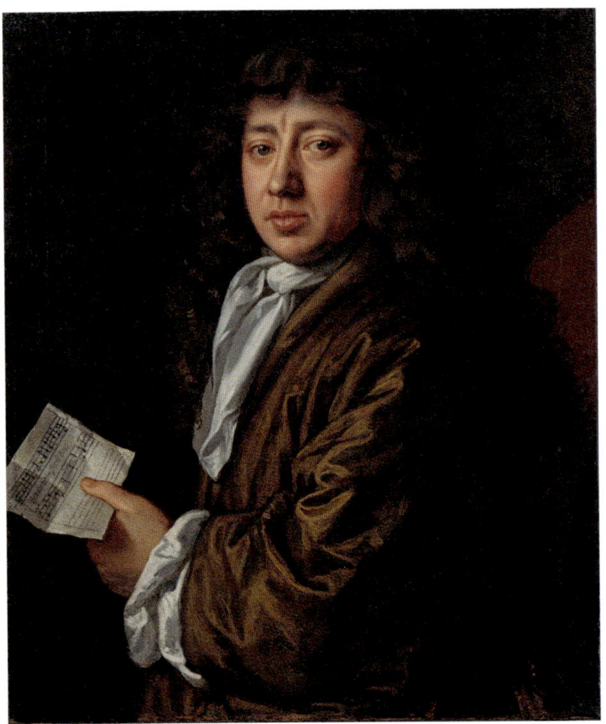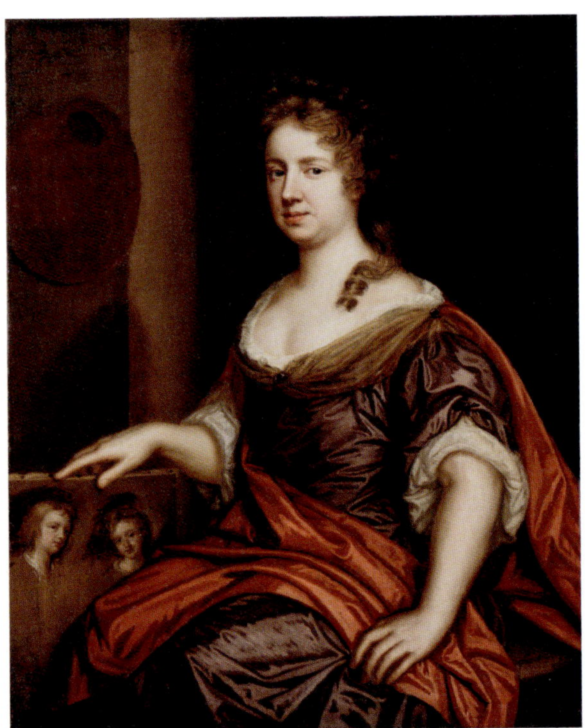

Samuel Pepys
(1633–1703)
John Hayls, 1666
Oil on canvas, 756 × 629mm
NPG 211

Pepys is most famous for his remarkable *Diary*, kept from 1600 until 1669, which serves as a unique record of life in Restoration London. It provides valuable and lively descriptions of national events such as the Great Plague (1665) and the Great Fire of London (1666).

Mary Beale
(1633–99)
Self-portrait, *c*.1666
Oil on canvas, 1092 × 876mm
NPG 1687

Beale is the earliest professional woman artist in the Gallery's Collection. With her artist's palette, and a canvas with portraits of her two sons, Beale shows herself balancing her roles as professional painter, mother and fashionable woman of the period.

Sir Isaac Newton
(1642–1727)
Sir Godfrey Kneller, 1702
Oil on canvas, 756 × 622mm
NPG 2881

Newton was one of the most influential scientists in world history. His achievements include the theory of universal gravitation, published in *Principia* (1687), which supposedly first came to him when he saw an apple fall from a tree.

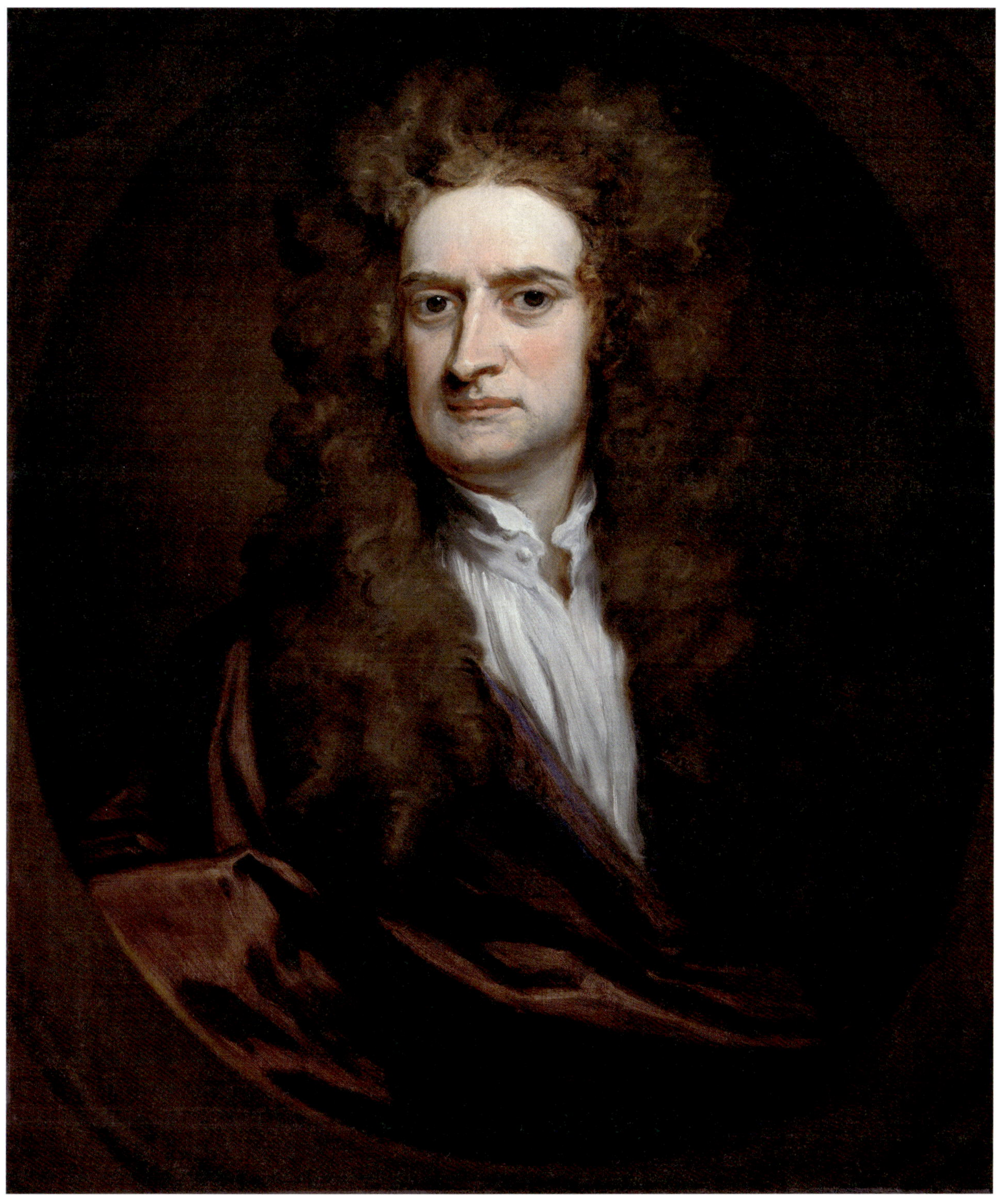

The Eighteenth Century

During the eighteenth century, Britain became a world power, an industrial pioneer and a dynamic commercial society. Through wars and conquest, its colonial rule was extended over millions of people around the globe. Britain also suffered its first colonial defeat when America won its independence.

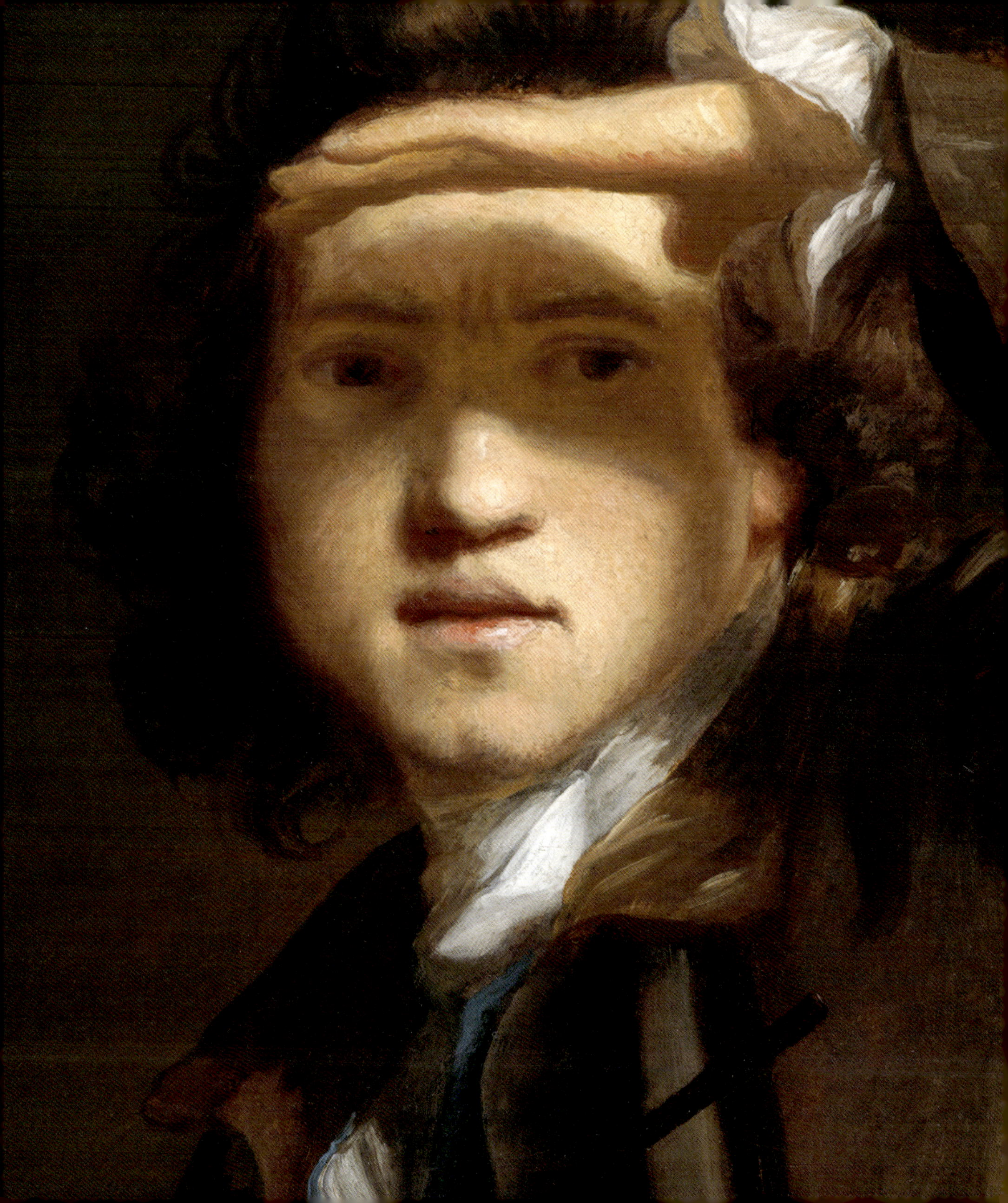

Exploration and Commerce

Britain was at war for most of the eighteenth century. France was the principal opponent, with British forces fighting the armies of Louis XIV at the beginning of the century, Louis XV in the middle decades and the French Revolutionary forces of Napoleon at the century's end.

The period was also framed by two acts of union. The first, between England and Scotland in 1707, formed the United Kingdom of Great Britain; the second, with Ireland in 1800, created the United Kingdom of Great Britain and Ireland. Queen Anne was the first queen of the new nation of Great Britain but her death in 1714 ended the rule of the Stuart dynasty. She was succeeded by her nearest Protestant relative, George I, ruler of the German state of Hanover. Rebellions by Jacobite supporters of the Catholic Stuart claimants to the throne followed in 1715 and 1745.

Following a financial crash in 1720, Britain entered a long period of economic growth and relative political stability. Prosperity increased social mobility and expanded the middle classes as Britain developed into a consumer society. New levels of wealth generated by agricultural and industrial modernisation supported artists, musicians, actors and writers. A rise in the demand for luxury goods and cultural commodities saw the beginning of mass media and the development of modern literary genres such as the novel and biography. The end of press censorship in 1695 facilitated an unprecedented growth in periodicals, which increased the public appetite for cultural criticism, news and gossip.

The taste for art and entertainment expanded rapidly from the 1750s. Artists of the previous generation, like William Hogarth, were frustrated by the limited support and opportunities that they were afforded. Now, art exhibitions became a highlight of the social calendar. The leading British artist of the day, Sir Joshua Reynolds, was the driving force behind the establishment of the Royal Academy of Arts and became its founding president in 1768. The Academy summer exhibitions gave artists an unparalleled opportunity to showcase their skill, enhance their prestige and attract clients. These shows were dominated by portraits by artists such as Thomas Gainsborough, Angelica Kauffmann and Sir Thomas Lawrence.

Significant British wealth was also derived from the exploitation of enslaved people in its colonies. Britain's global ambitions extended to North America, the Caribbean, Australasia and Asia. On the Indian subcontinent, a commercial business, the East India Company, laid the foundations of an empire. British efforts to control India and other territories increased after suffering a major colonial defeat with the loss of America in the War of Independence (1775–83).

From the 1760s, there was growing resistance to the long-standing hierarchies of class, gender and race. Agitation for voting reform and the abolition of slavery followed, with radical politicians and activists, which included people of African heritage, pushing for change. The campaign against slavery resulted in the abolition of the slave trade in 1807 and colonial slavery in 1833, but racial inequality remained deep-rooted in society.

Sir Christopher Wren
(1632–1723)
Sir Godfrey Kneller, 1711
Oil on canvas, 1245 × 1003mm
NPG 113

Described by a contemporary as 'once a prodigy of a boy; now, a miracle of a man', Wren was a scientist and architect, instrumental in founding the Royal Society in 1660, and one of the most famous men of his day. This portrait celebrates the completion of St Paul's Cathedral in 1711.

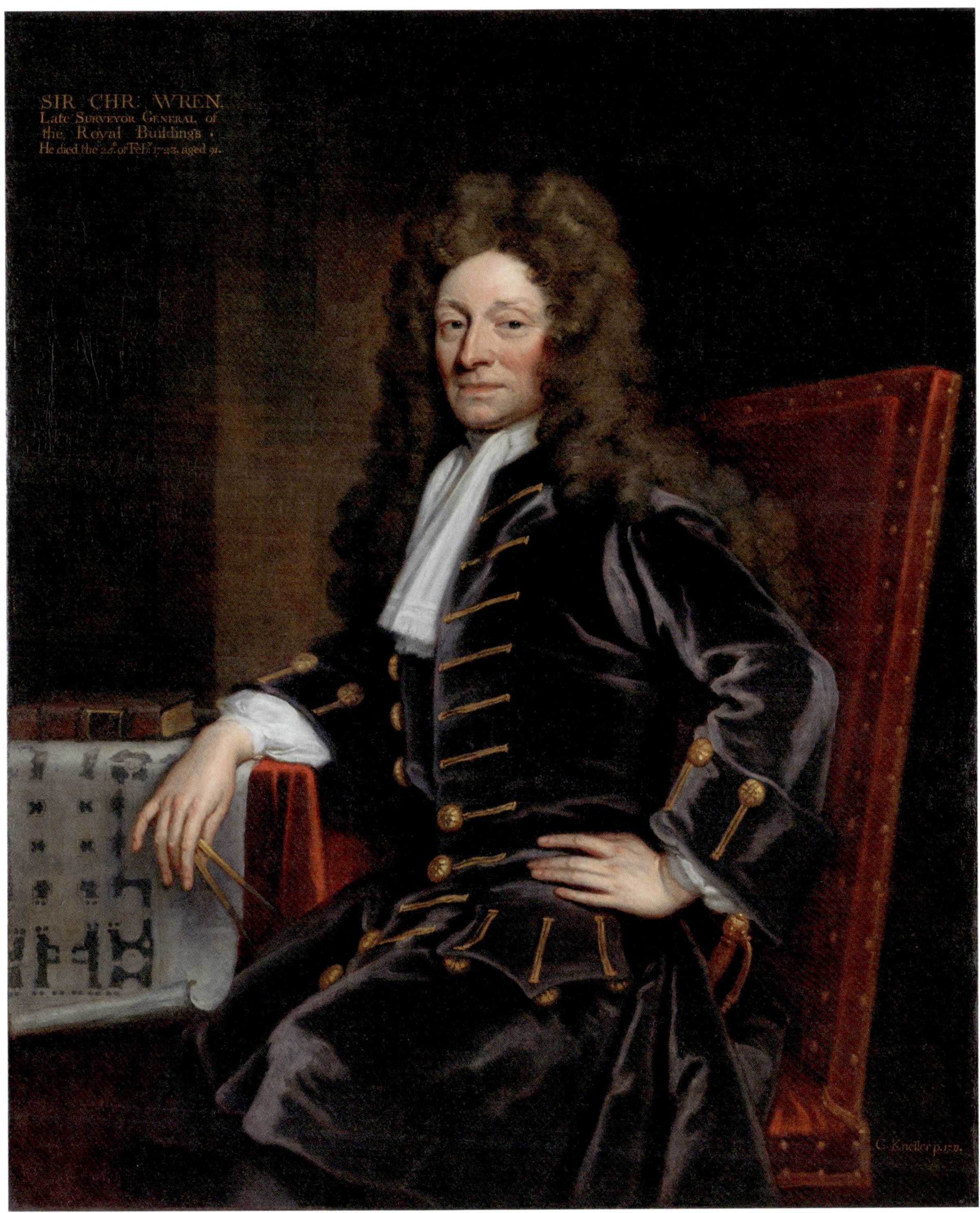

SIR CHR: WREN,
Late Surveyor General of
the Royal Buildings.
He died the 25 of Feb. 1723. aged 91.
G. Kneller p. 1711.

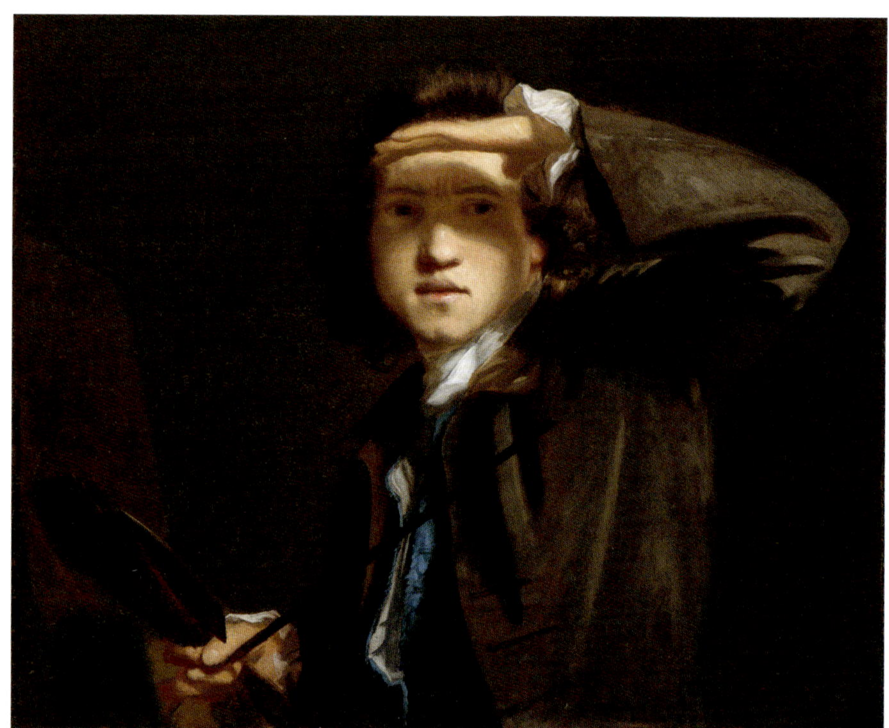

Sir Joshua Reynolds
(1723–92)
Self-portrait, *c.*1747–9
Oil on canvas, 635 × 743mm
NPG 41

Reynolds moved to London from Devon in 1753 and quickly became the leading portrait painter in Britain. As first president of the Royal Academy of Arts, he gave lectures that have had a lasting impact on the theory and practice of art.

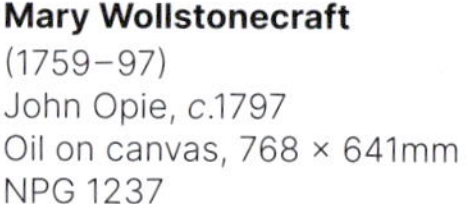

Mary Wollstonecraft
(1759–97)
John Opie, *c.*1797
Oil on canvas, 768 × 641mm
NPG 1237

Wollstonecraft was a founder of British feminism, calling for the equal rights of all people. She argued powerfully for the education, liberation and independence of women in *A Vindication of the Rights of Woman* (1792), which has become a hugely influential feminist text.

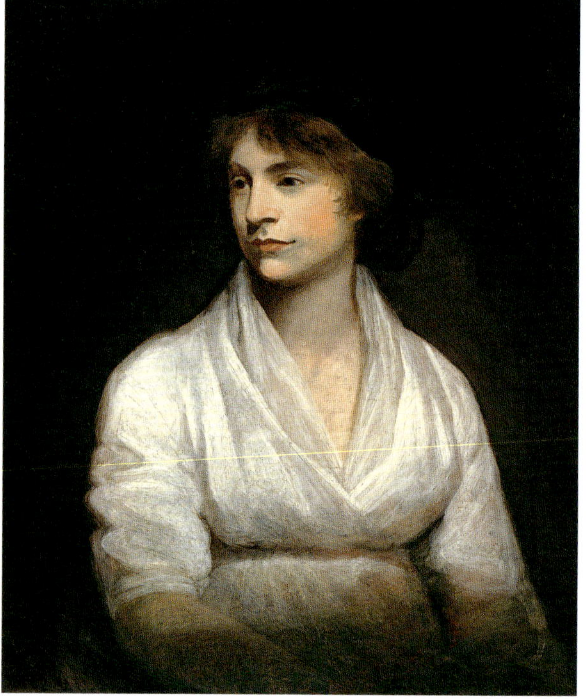

Ayuba Suleiman Diallo
(1701–73)
William Hoare, 1733
Oil on canvas, 762 × 635mm
NPG L245

This is the earliest known British oil portrait of a formerly enslaved African person. Diallo expresses his African Muslim identity by wearing religious dress with his Qur'an, written from memory, around his neck. Through the publication of his memoirs in 1734, Diallo was an important influence on the movement to abolish slavery.

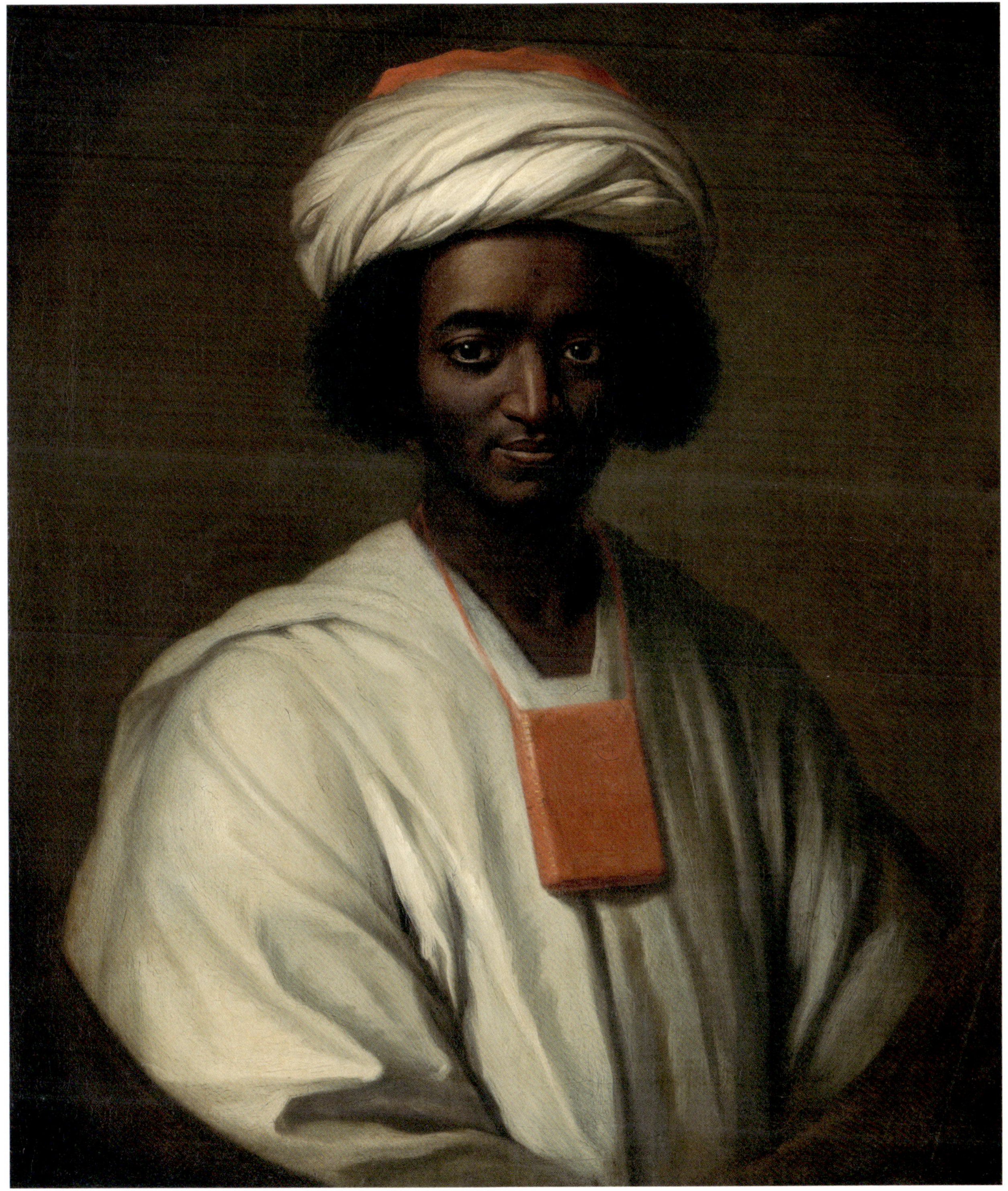

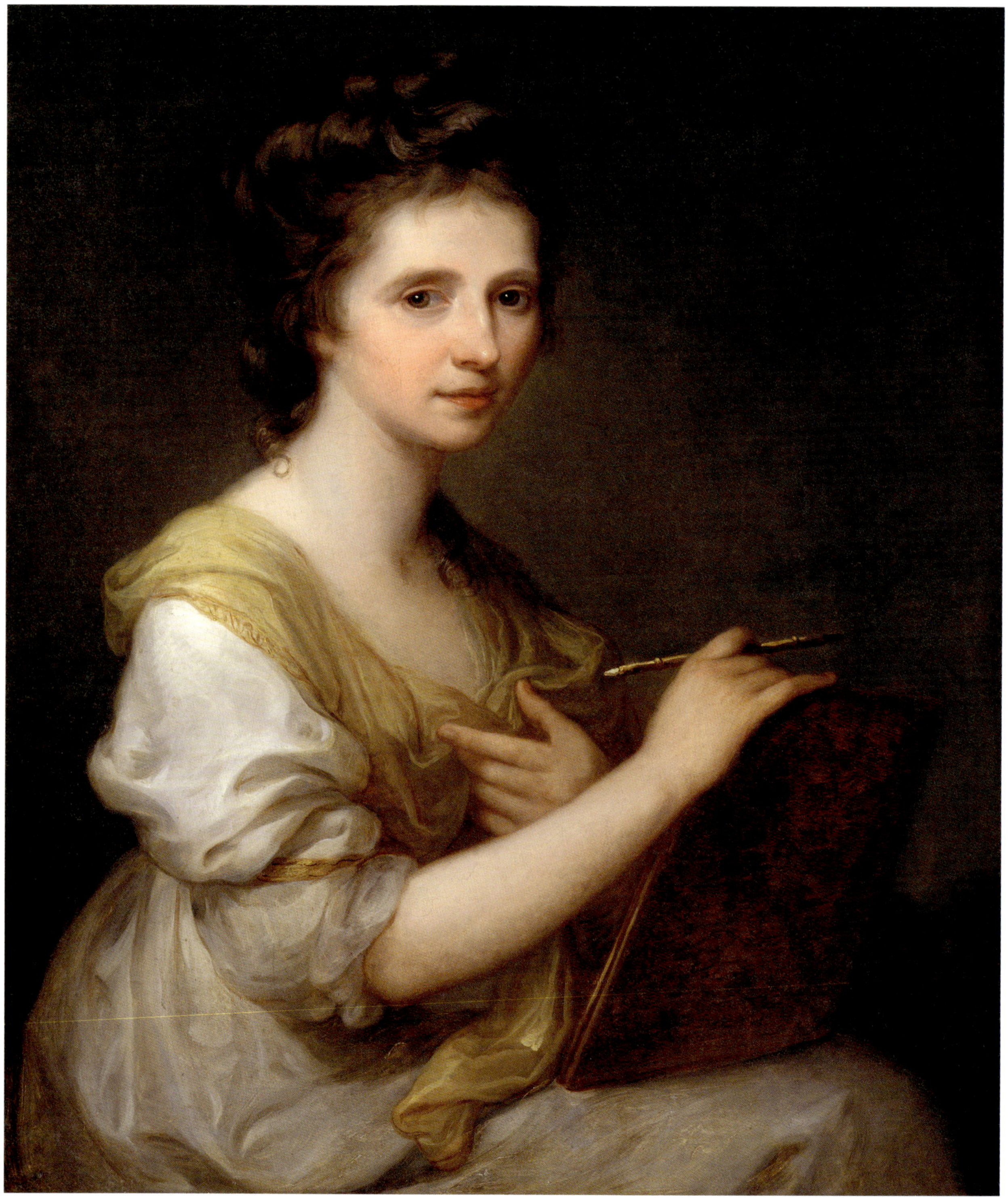

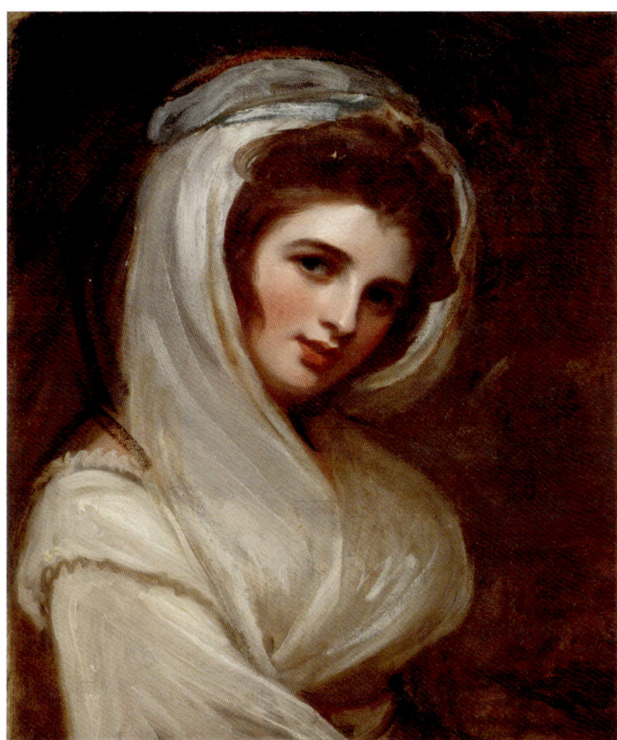

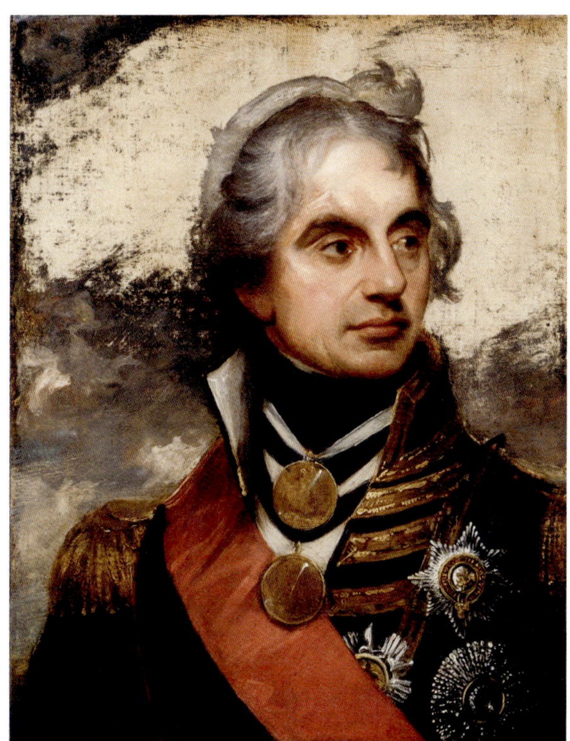

Angelica Kauffmann
(1741–1807)
Self-portrait, *c.*1770–5
Oil on canvas, 737 × 610mm
NPG 430

Swiss-born Kauffmann was
part of London's vibrant artist
community and one of only two
female founders of the Royal
Academy in 1768. Excluded from
life-drawing classes because of
her gender, she developed her
own brand of painting, focusing
on female subjects from history
and mythology.

Emma Hamilton
(1765–1815)
George Romney, *c.*1785
Oil on canvas, 623 × 521mm
NPG 4448

Hamilton achieved celebrity
through her charisma, beauty
and skill as a model and
performer. Her fame, and that
of the artist Romney, was
enhanced by his numerous
paintings of her. Society was
scandalised by her relationship
with Nelson, who she met when
both were married.

**Horatio Nelson, Viscount
Nelson**
(1758–1805)
Sir William Beechey, 1800
Oil on canvas, 623 × 483mm
NPG 5798

Admiral Lord Nelson's victories
during the Napoleonic Wars
gripped the popular imagination,
making him one of Britain's
greatest war heroes. When he
was killed by a sniper during
the Battle of Trafalgar in 1805,
there was a vast outpouring of
public grief.

Chevalier d'Eon
(1728–1810)
Thomas Stewart, after
Jean-Laurent Mosnier, 1792
Oil on canvas, 765 × 640mm
NPG 6937

Born Charles Geneviève Louis Auguste André Timothée d'Eon de Beaumont in Tonnerre, France, d'Eon was a soldier, diplomat and spy who first came to London in 1762 during negotiations of the Treaty of Paris, which ended the Seven Years' War (1756–63). D'Eon's work on the treaty was rewarded with the Order of St Louis, after which the Chevalier remained living in London, as a man, until 1777.

D'Eon later claimed to have been born female but raised as a boy, and had attended events as a woman on various occasions. During negotiations to return secret papers that were damaging to Louis XVI, the French king agreed to pay d'Eon a pension on the condition that the Chevalier henceforth dressed permanently in women's clothes. Returning to London in 1785, d'Eon mixed in fashionable society and had a successful career as a celebrity female fencer. D'Eon's expression of an alternative gender identity is remarkable for the time.

D'Eon's public profile created a demand for images of the fencer, including numerous popular prints. This is a contemporary copy of a portrait by the French society painter Mosnier (1743–1808), which was exhibited at the Royal Academy in 1791. Visible in the painting is the black dress d'Eon was famed for wearing during fencing demonstrations and the Order of St Louis medal. The hat cockade signals d'Eon's brief support for the new French revolutionary government, which ended with the execution of the royal family in 1793.

'It must indeed be acknowledged, that she is the most extraordinary person of the age ... we have seen no one who has united so many military, political, and literary talents.'

The Annual Register for 1781

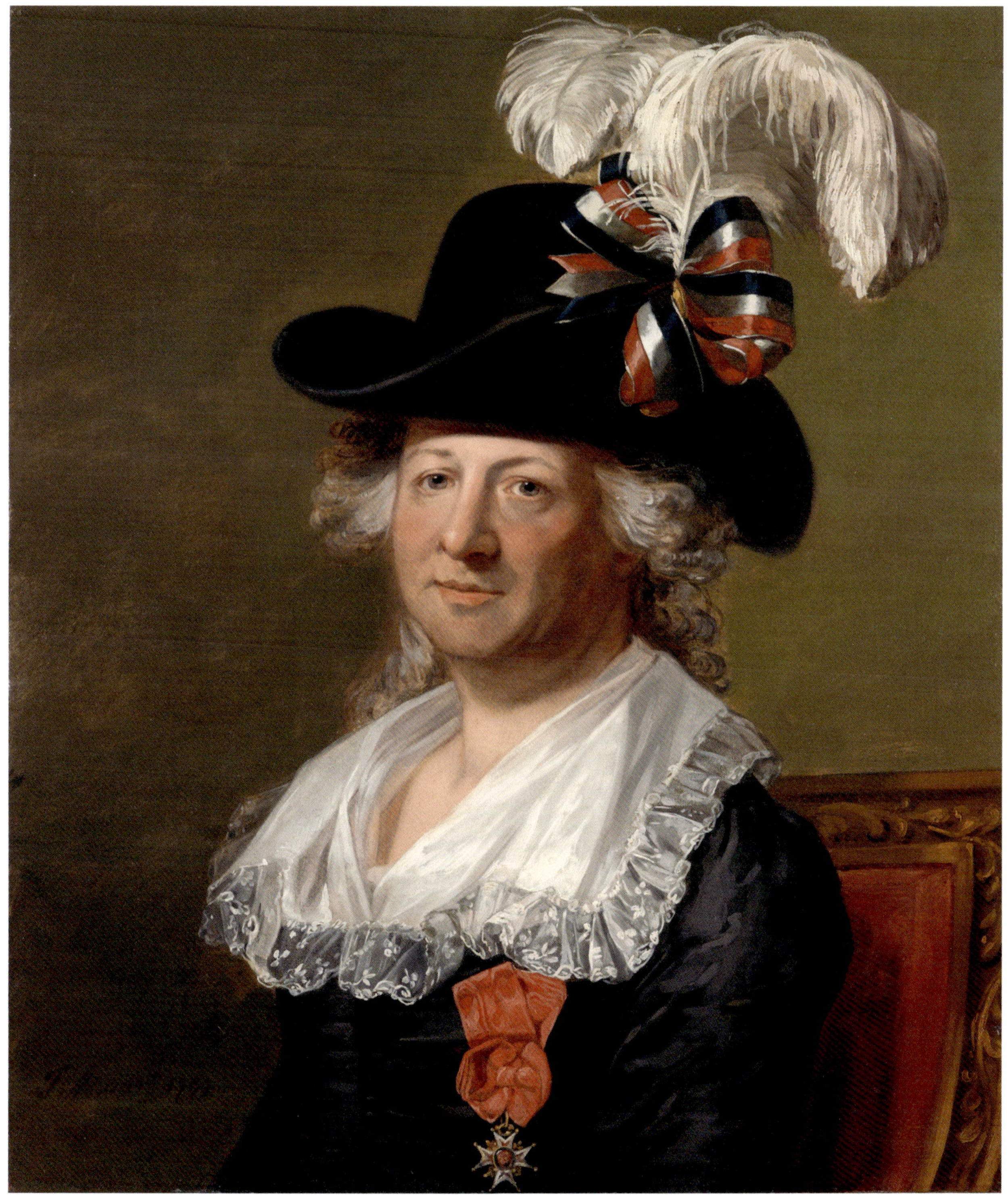

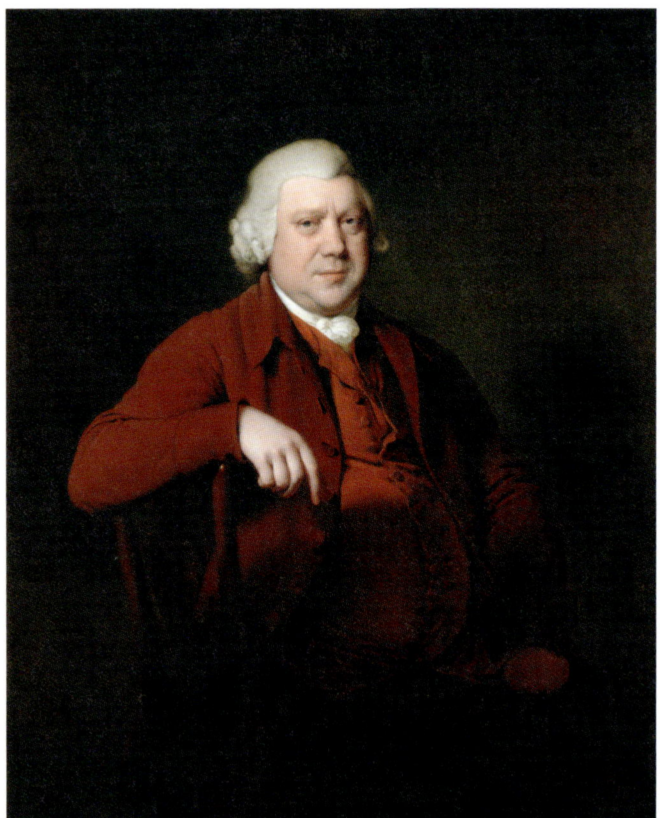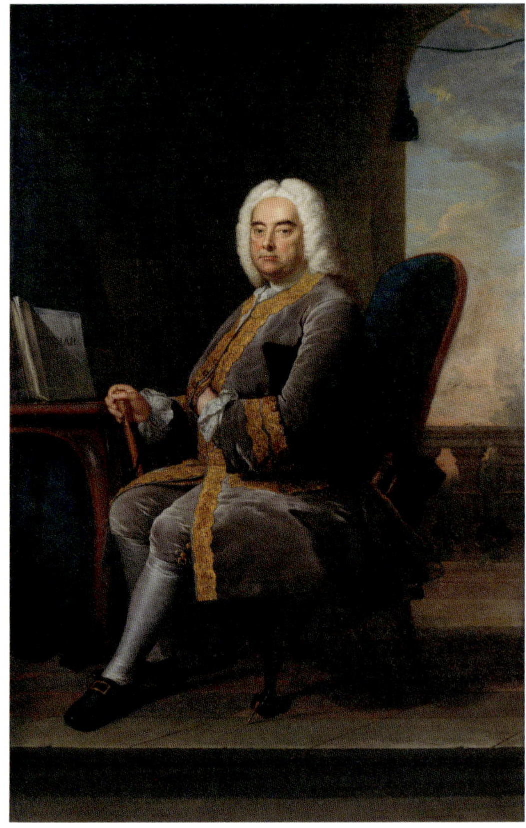

Sir Richard Arkwright
(1732–92)
Joseph Wright, *c*.1783–5
Oil on canvas, 1260 × 1020mm
NPG 6848

The inventor and manufacturer
Arkwright patented a spinning
frame for creating yarn in 1769.
His factories pioneered the
largescale mechanisation of the
cotton industry, which had a
profound social and economic
impact on Britain and the world.

George Frideric Handel
(1685–1759)
Thomas Hudson, 1756
Oil on canvas, 2388 × 1461mm
NPG 3970

German-born Handel is one of
the most famous composers
ever to work in Britain. Arriving
in 1710, he composed operas
and worked for the court and
the church. His most celebrated
work, *Messiah* (1742), became a
national phenomenon.

Sarah Siddons (*Mrs Siddons
with the Emblems of Tragedy*)
(1755–1831)
Sir William Beechey, 1793
Oil on canvas, 2456 × 1537mm
NPG 5159

Siddons is one of the greatest
actors in the history of British
theatre. Born into the thespian
Kemble family, she made her
London debut in 1782 and
dominated the theatre for three
decades playing tragic roles.

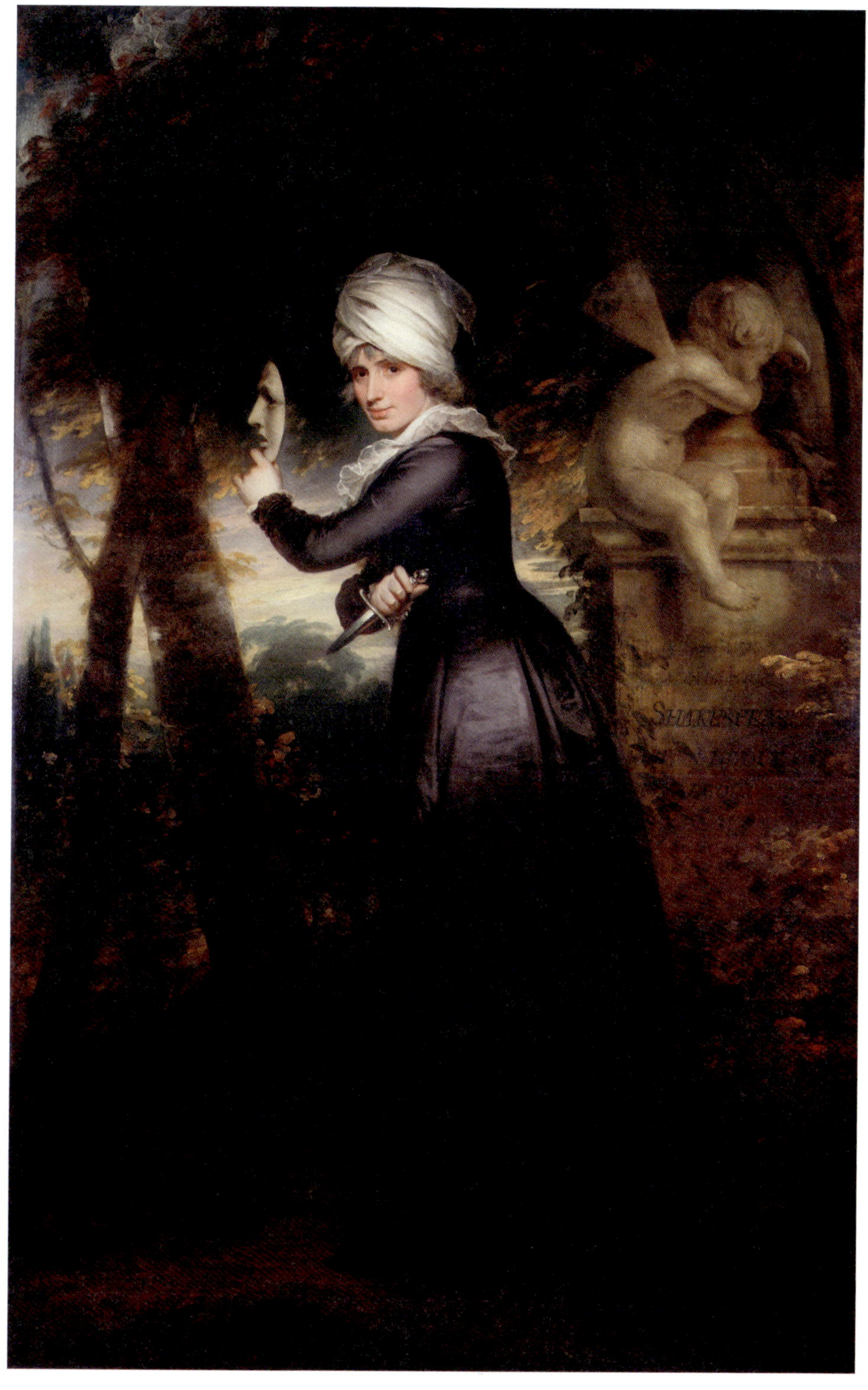

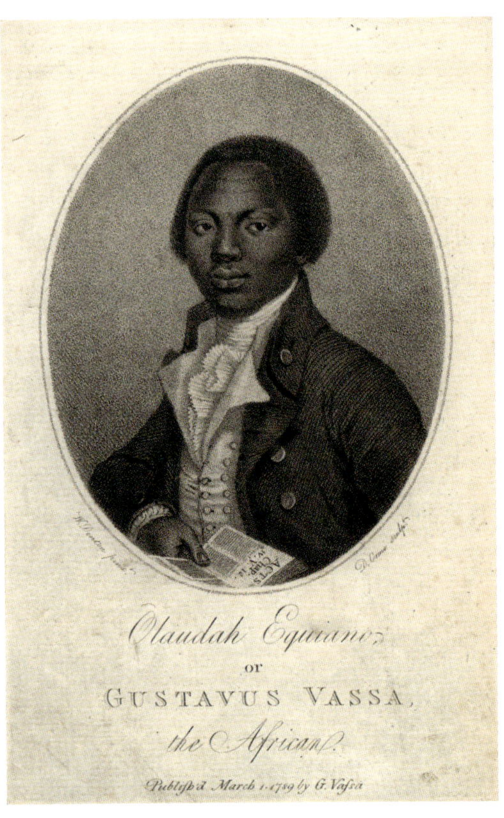

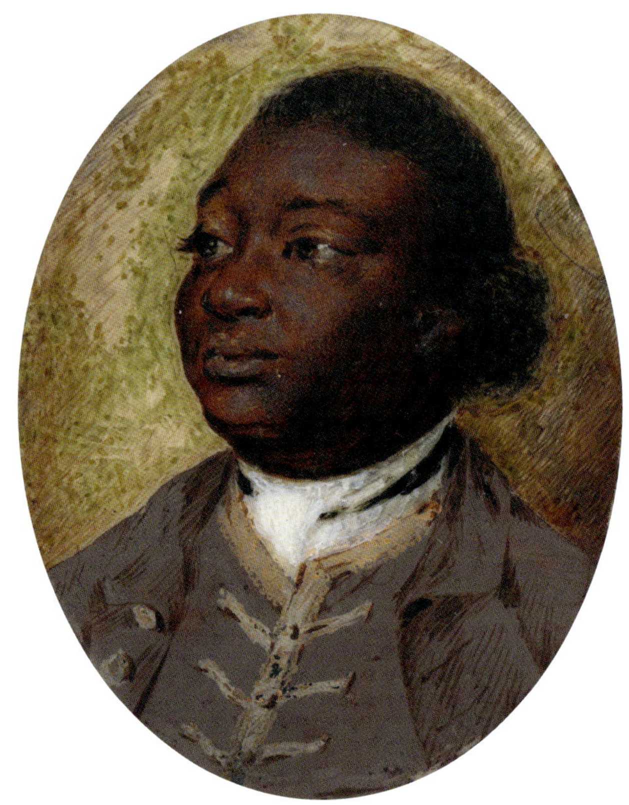

Olaudah Equiano
(*c*.1745–97)
D. Orme, after W. Denton, 1789
Stipple engraving, 156 × 95mm
NPG D8546

———

The writer Equiano was a political activist committed to the abolition of the slave trade and justice for black people in Britain. He experienced enslavement but was able to purchase his freedom and travel to Britain. His autobiography, *Interesting Narrative* (1789), had a powerful influence on the abolition movement.

Ignatius Sancho
(1729–80)
Unknown artist, after Thomas Gainsborough, *c*.1802–20
Watercolour and bodycolour on ivory, 61 × 42mm
NPG 7063

———

Born into slavery, Sancho was brought to Britain at the age of 2. Eventually gaining freedom, he opened a grocery shop in Westminster where he wrote, composed music and, in 1774, appears to have become the first black Briton to vote. His collected letters were published after his death to great acclaim.

Mai (Omai), Sir Joseph Banks and Daniel Solander
(*c*.1753–*c*.1780; 1743–1820; 1736–82)
William Parry, *c*.1775–6
Oil on canvas, 1525 × 1525mm
NPG 6652

———

Mai was a Polynesian man from Ra'iatea who came to Britain with Captain Cook's second voyage in 1774, hoping to obtain weaponry and social advancement. He is shown with his London hosts, the wealthy scientist Banks, who points to Mai's tattooed hands, and the Swedish scientist Solander.

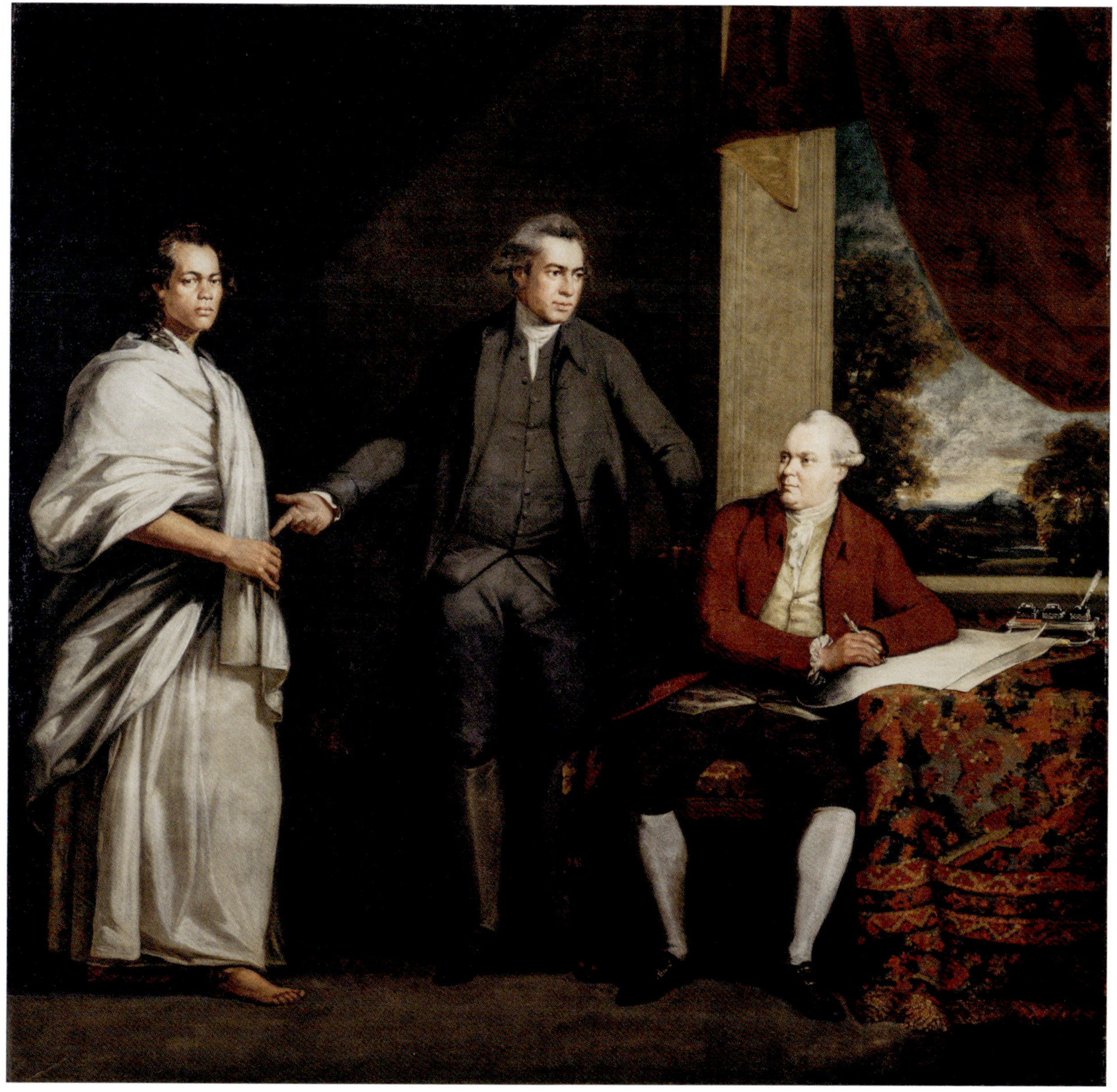

William Wilberforce
(1759–1833)
Sir Thomas Lawrence, 1828
Oil on canvas, 965 × 1092mm
NPG 3

Wilberforce was an evangelical Christian MP from Hull, England, who dedicated himself to the 'suppression of the slave trade and the reformation of manners'. He was renowned for his high principles and great personal charm. A prominent member of the Clapham Sect, an influential group of evangelicals, Wilberforce was the parliamentary leader of the campaign to abolish the slave trade and slavery from 1787. He campaigned tirelessly for 20 years, declaring to parliament in 1791 that 'never, never will we desist until we … extinguish every trace of this bloody traffic'. Wilberforce's bill was eventually passed in 1807. He then campaigned for the total abolition of slavery, dying just three days after the Slavery Abolition Bill was passed in the Commons in 1833.

This portrait was begun in 1828, after Wilberforce retired from parliament on account of his ill health. He suffered from a spinal condition, which made sitting for the portrait excruciating. This explains his unusual pose in a formal painting and also why he never returned for further sittings. This left the artist, Lawrence (1769–1830), with an unfinished canvas. Even with only one sitting, Lawrence, the most brilliant portraitist of the era, managed to capture 'the intellectual power and winning sweetness of the veteran statesman', as described by Wilberforce's friend John Harford. The portrait was the third work to enter the National Portrait Gallery upon its foundation in 1856.

'Whatever they might do, the people of Great Britain, I am confident, will abolish the slave trade … For myself, I am engaged in a work I will never abandon … Let us persevere and our triumph will be complete.'

William Wilberforce, 1791

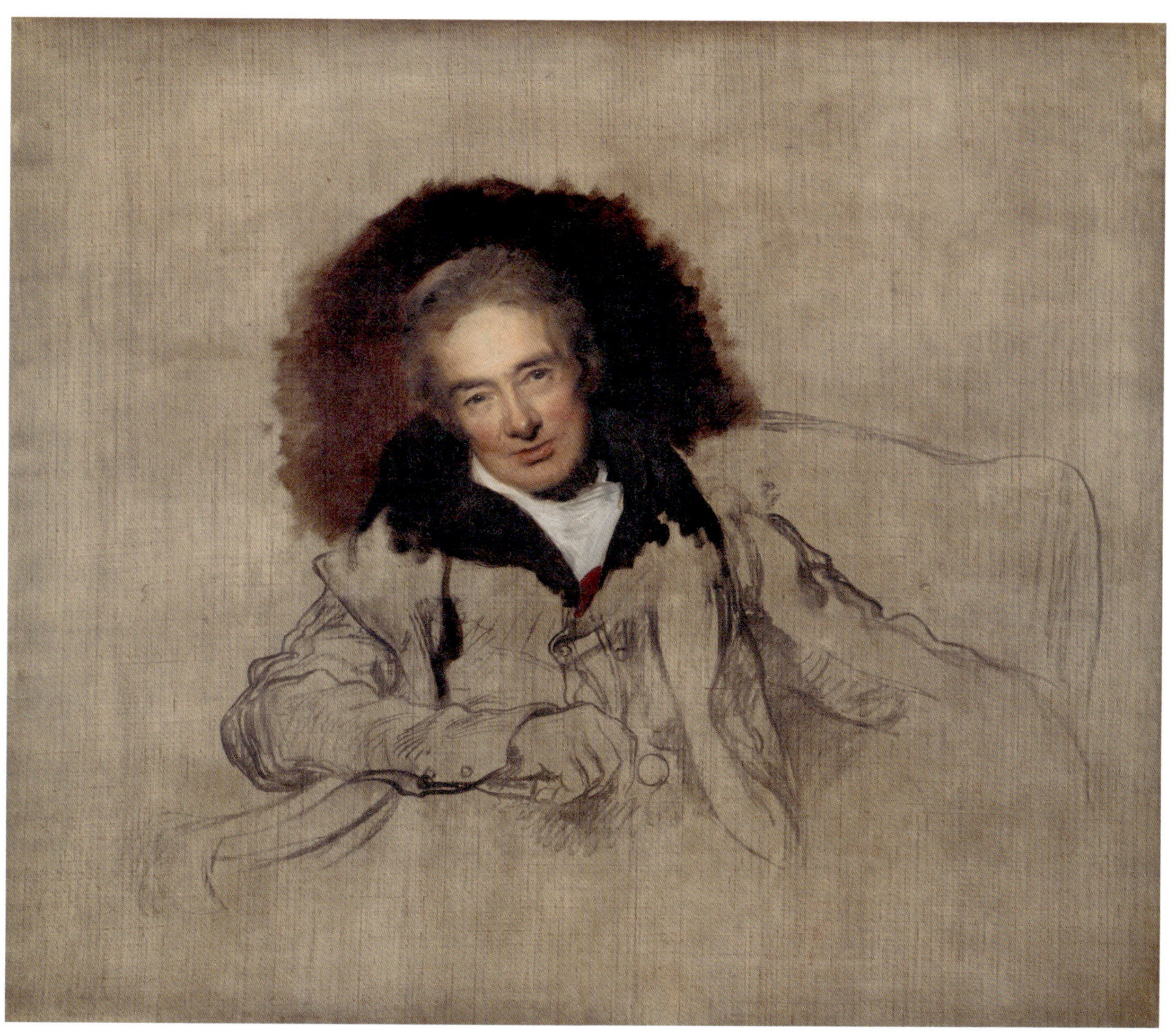

The Nineteenth Century

The United Kingdom became the world's leading industrial, commercial and imperial power during the nineteenth century. British society was transformed by innovations in engineering, science and technology, while popular movements for political reform gathered pace.

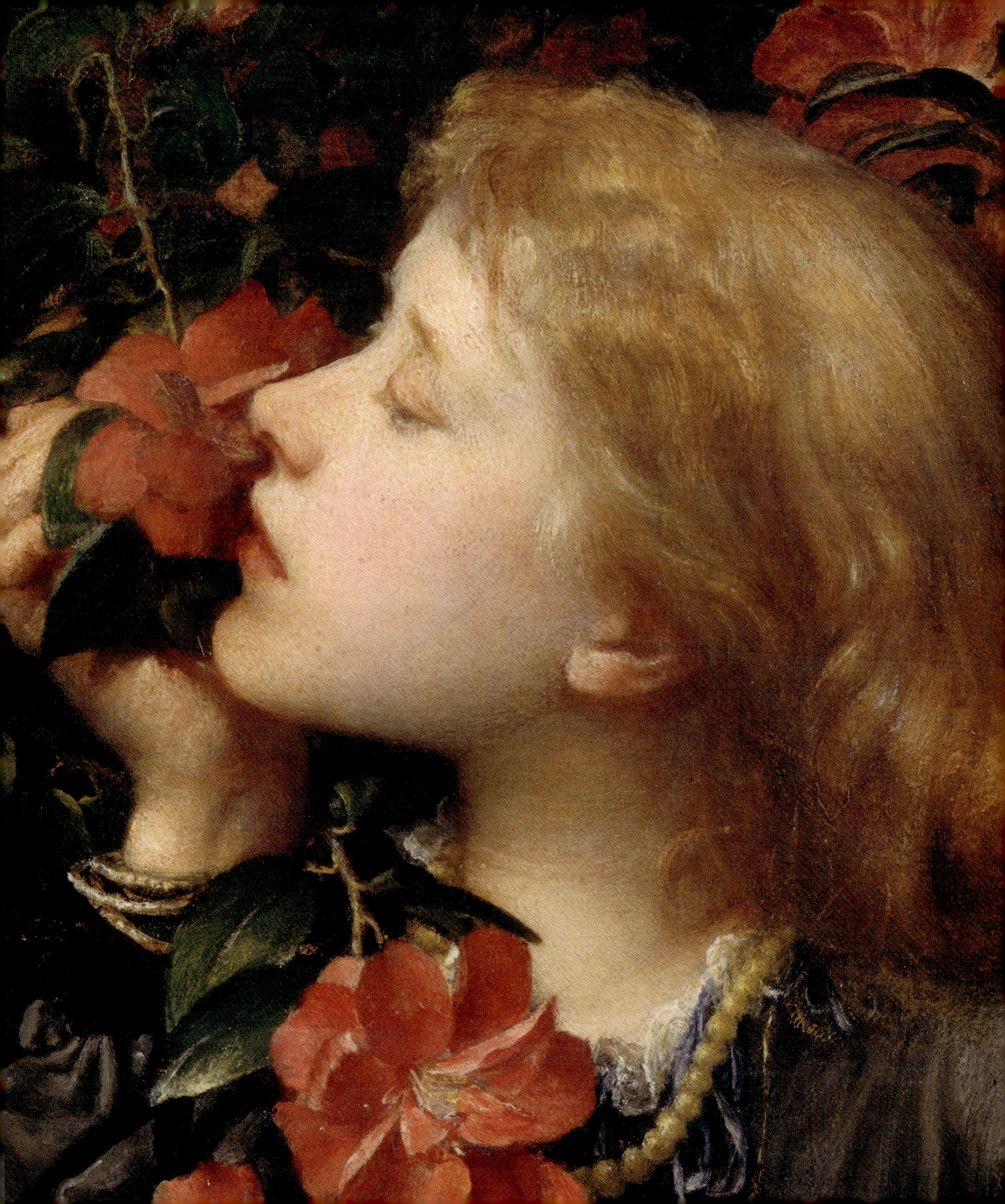

Reform and Empire

British victories over France in the Napoleonic Wars of 1803 to 1815 established the UK as the dominant naval and economic power in the world. Through wars and conquest, Britain's colonies and interests abroad were gradually transformed into an empire with Queen Victoria at its head, following her accession to the throne in 1837. At its peak, the British Empire ruled over almost a quarter of the world's land and peoples. Natural and human resources in colonised lands were exploited to create unprecedented levels of wealth for the British elite. High levels of inequality and deprivation were also experienced within Britain and Ireland, where communities suffered famine, mass displacement and emigration.

Calls for political and social reform intensified during the course of the century. The abolition of slavery within the British colonies in 1833 brought little immediate change to the conditions endured by enslaved people, but granted millions of pounds in compensation to plantation owners. In Britain, the Reform Act of 1832 increased the number of male voters but women and working-class activists continued to demand the right to vote. Incremental reforms helped Britain to avoid the revolutions that swept across Europe but a fully inclusive democracy was not achieved until 1928, when women finally gained equal voting rights with men.

Developments in science and industry revolutionised people's lives. The experimental scientist Michael Faraday helped to lay the foundations of modern chemical and electrical technologies. Engineers such as Isambard Kingdom Brunel designed the railways and ships that transformed commercial trade and expanded the horizons of millions of people. In the natural sciences, Charles Darwin's theory of evolution challenged traditional notions of the development of life on earth and led many people to question the biblical account of Creation.

In literature, the Romantic poets inspired people to explore themselves and the world around them. Their belief in self-expression, wild flights of the imagination and empathy with the everyday remain influential to this day. Writers Jane Austen, the Brontë sisters, Charles Dickens and Oscar Wilde were among the authors who defined their age, often with compelling social commentary that helped to bring about change. Many female writers achieved success at a time when women were denied access to most professions.

The visual arts saw an ebb and flow between new ideas and Victorian convention. Among the most enduring and powerful art produced during this period were the paintings by the Romantic artists and the work of the Pre-Raphaelite Brotherhood and the Arts and Crafts Movement, which promoted fine craftsmanship in a rejection of the new age of industrialised mass production. The most radical development in portraiture was the invention of photography. With its unique union of science, technology and art, photography democratised the means by which people could make, view and own portraits. It extended the possibilities of portrait making and there followed a period of creative cross-fertilisation between traditional and new media that continues to this day.

Ira Aldridge
(1807–67)
After James Northcote, *c.*1826
Oil on canvas, 763 × 632mm
NPG L251

The American Aldridge was the first black actor to perform on the British stage. This portrait probably shows him as Othello, the role in which he made his West End debut in 1833. He undertook several successful European tours and became one of the highest paid actors in the world.

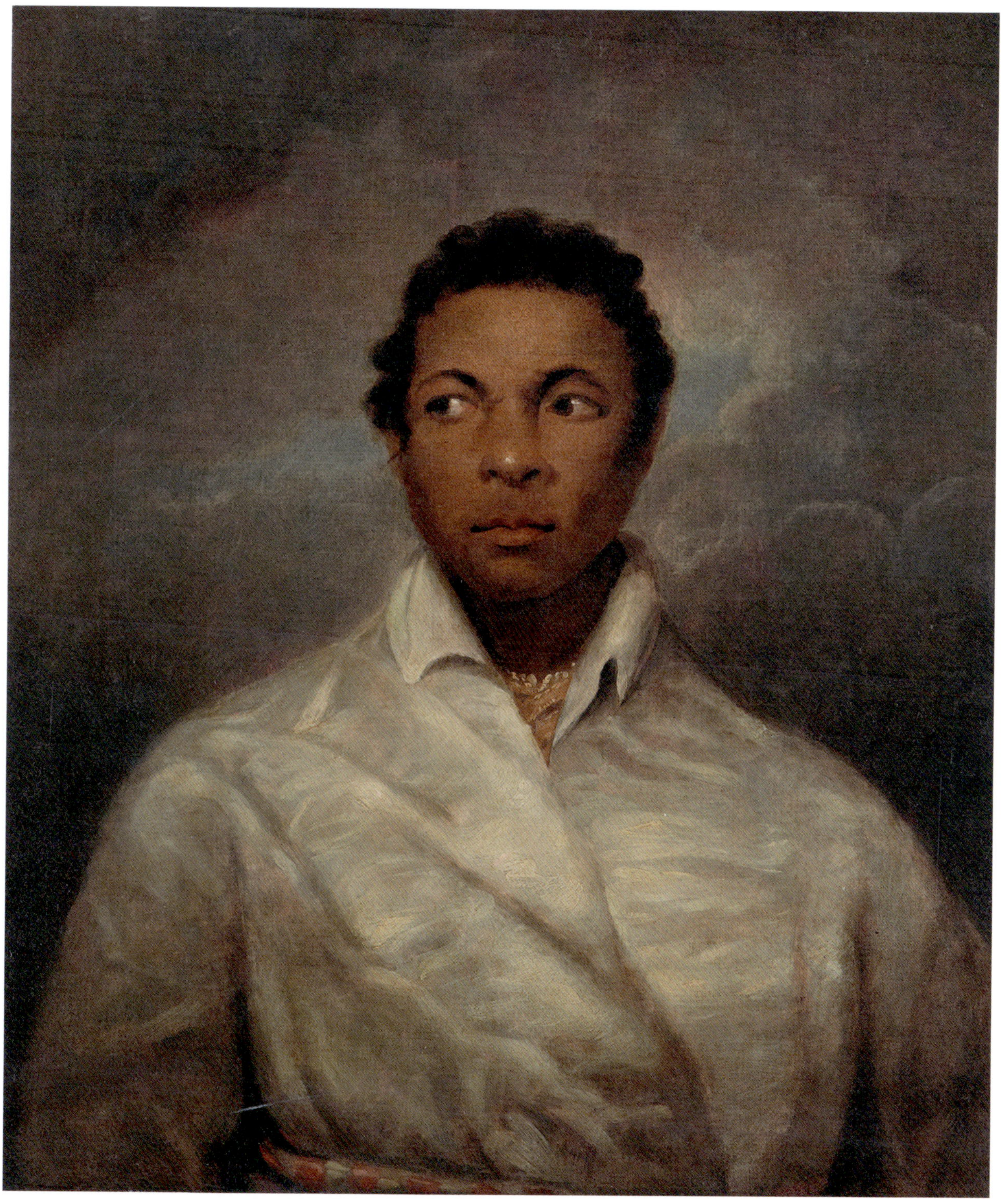

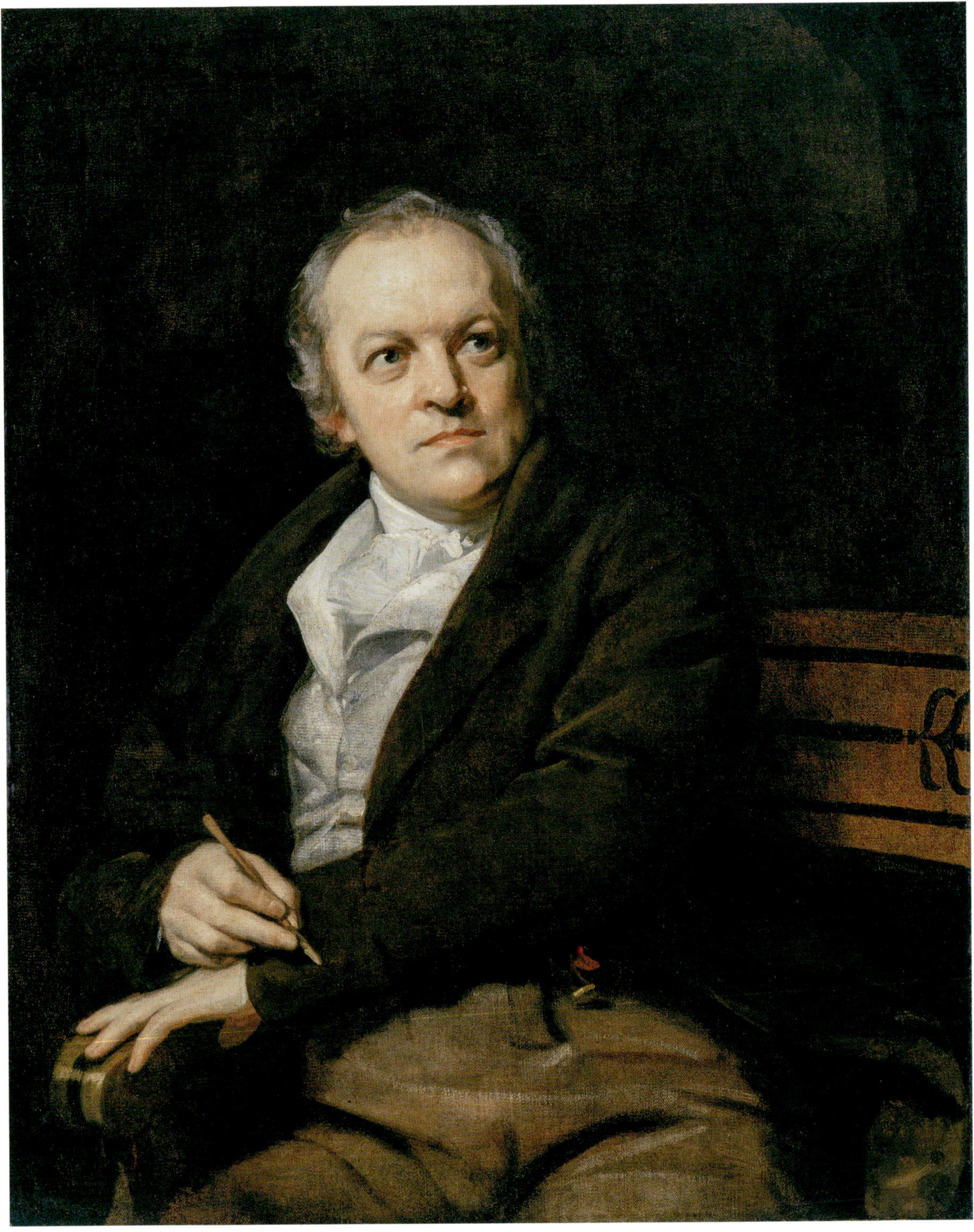

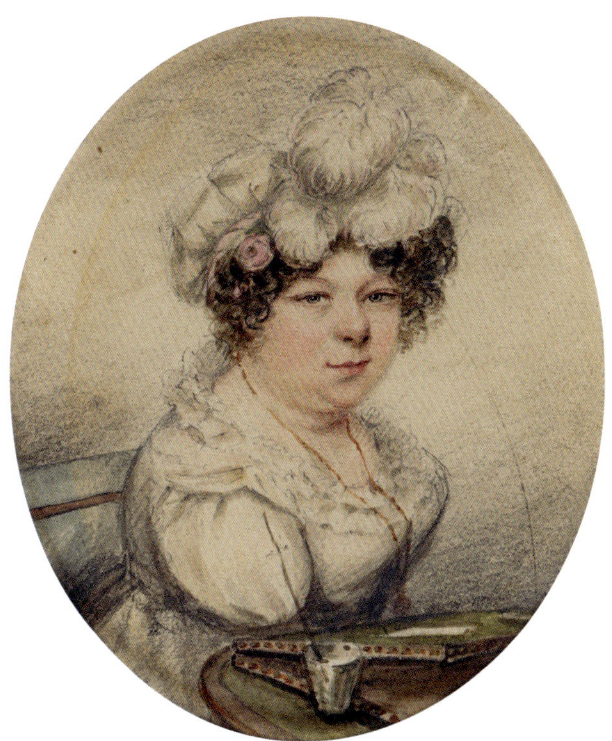 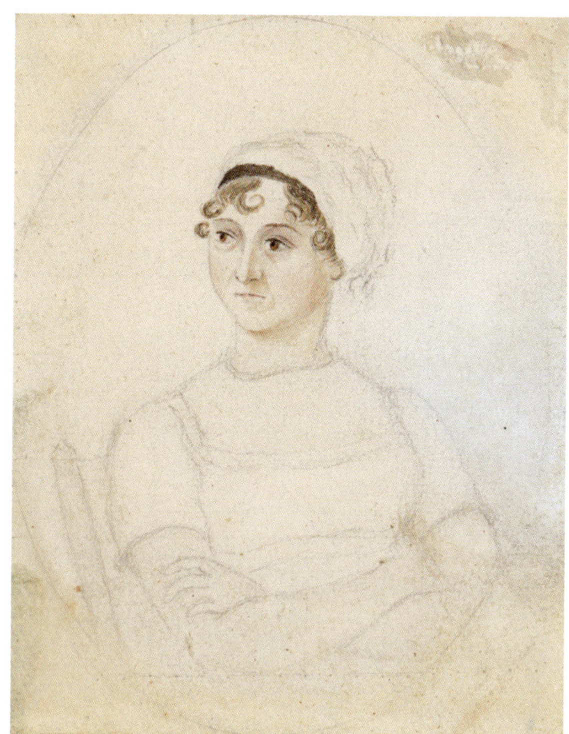

William Blake
(1757–1827)
Thomas Phillips, 1807
Oil on canvas, 921 × 720mm
NPG 212

A poet and artist, Blake was one of the most original and creative minds of his time. He grew up 'conversing with angels' and remained a visionary. In works such as *Songs of Innocence and Experience* (1794), his words and images came together in an innovative form of engraved and illustrated poetry.

Sarah Biffin
(1784–1850)
Probably a self-portrait, *c.*1825
Watercolour and graphite on card, 100mm high
NPG 7110

Biffin was born with no arms or legs and taught herself to paint using her mouth. After working as an attraction in a travelling show for 16 years, she established herself as an independent artist. She received commissions from royalty, exhibited at the Royal Academy and taught miniature painting.

Jane Austen
(1775–1817)
Cassandra Austen, *c.*1810
Pencil and watercolour on paper, 114 × 80mm
NPG 3630

This sketch by Austen's sister is the only certain portrait of the novelist. Her work was published anonymously during her lifetime, as it was widely considered inappropriate for women to have public careers. Today, she is celebrated for the witty social commentary and sharp accounts of everyday life in her novels.

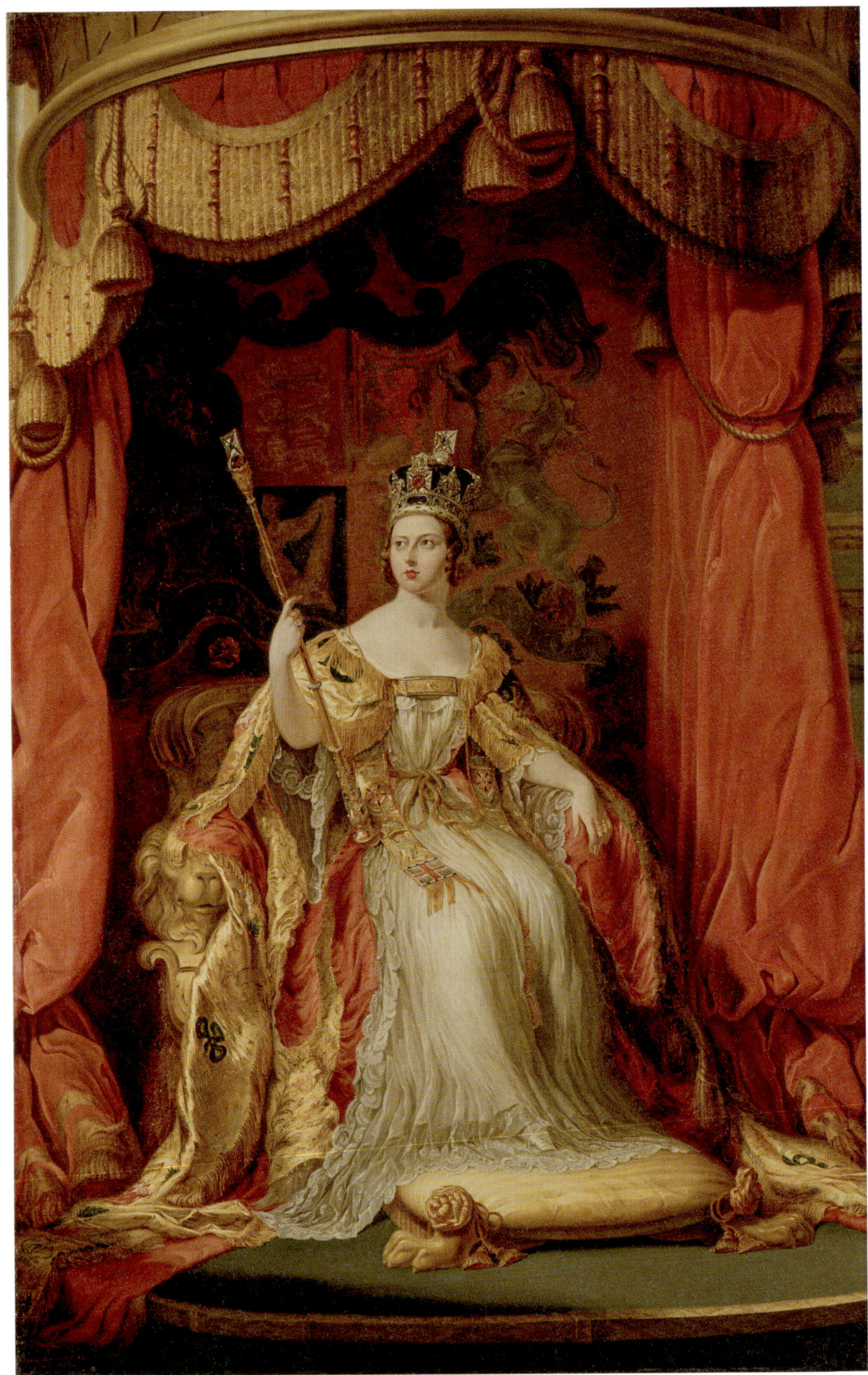

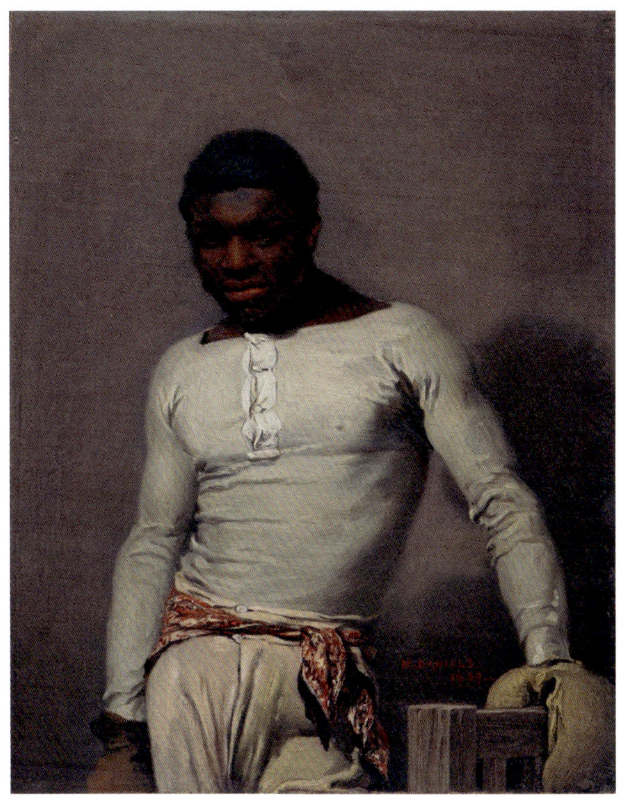

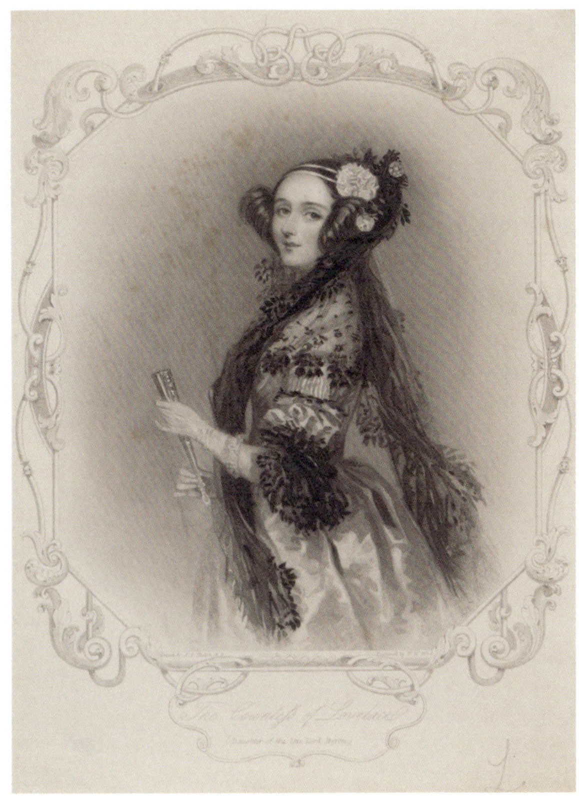

Queen Victoria
(1819–1901)
Sir George Hayter, 1863,
based on a work of 1838
Oil on canvas, 2858 × 1790mm
NPG 1250

Victoria succeeded to the
throne shortly after her 18th
birthday in July 1837. Her
63-year reign was longer than
any previous British monarch
and she held great influence
over the foreign and domestic
policies of the governments
she oversaw.

Jem Wharton
(1813–56)
William Daniels, 1839
Oil on canvas, 352 × 273mm
NPG L259

Wharton was one of the most
successful boxers in Britain in
the early nineteenth century.
He won his first bout in 1833
and retired undefeated in 1840,
later working as a trainer and
running a tavern in Liverpool.
This is one of the earliest
depictions of boxing gloves
in portraiture.

Ada Lovelace
(1815–52)
William H. Mote, after
Alfred E. Chalon, 1839
Stipple engraving,
315 × 227mm
NPG D5124

Daughter of the poet Lord
Byron and Annabella Milbanke,
Lovelace was a pioneering
mathematician at a time
when few women received
an education. Working with
Charles Babbage, she is widely
regarded as the world's first
computer programmer.

Aina, named Sarah Forbes Bonetta

(1843–80)
Camille Silvy, 1862
Albumen print, 102 × 112mm
NPG Ax61384

Caught up in Britain's imperial ambitions, Aina existed on the boundaries of different worlds. Born in modern-day south-west Nigeria, she was captured aged 3 by King Ghezo of Dahomey, a central figure in the transatlantic slave trade. In 1850, she was given to British naval captain Frederick Forbes as a gift during a diplomatic mission to persuade Ghezo to end the Dahomey slave trade. Forbes accepted Aina in the name of Queen Victoria and had her baptised Sarah Forbes Bonetta after his own name and that of the ship on which they returned to England, HMS *Bonetta*.

Aina was presented to the queen, who received her as her goddaughter. However, rather than being educated in Britain, Aina was sent to the Church Missionary Society School in Freetown, Sierra Leone. Four years later, she was brought back to England and, by her late teens, her status as a protégée of the queen made her a celebrity in Victorian high society.

When the leading photographer Silvy (1834–1910) took this photograph, Aina had recently married James Pinson Labulo Davies, a merchant from Sierra Leone. Her married name can be seen written above the image in Silvy's 'daybook', which recorded each of his portrait sittings. In 1862, Aina and her husband returned to live in West Africa and named their first daughter Victoria after the queen, who also became her godmother. After Aina's death from tuberculosis aged 37, the queen paid for the young Victoria to be educated in England.

'At the Midsummer and Christmas seasons, she often went either to Windsor or Osborne to stay in the family of one of the officers of Her Majesty's Household, and was frequently sent for by the Queen to see her privately.'

Annie Schoen, 1881

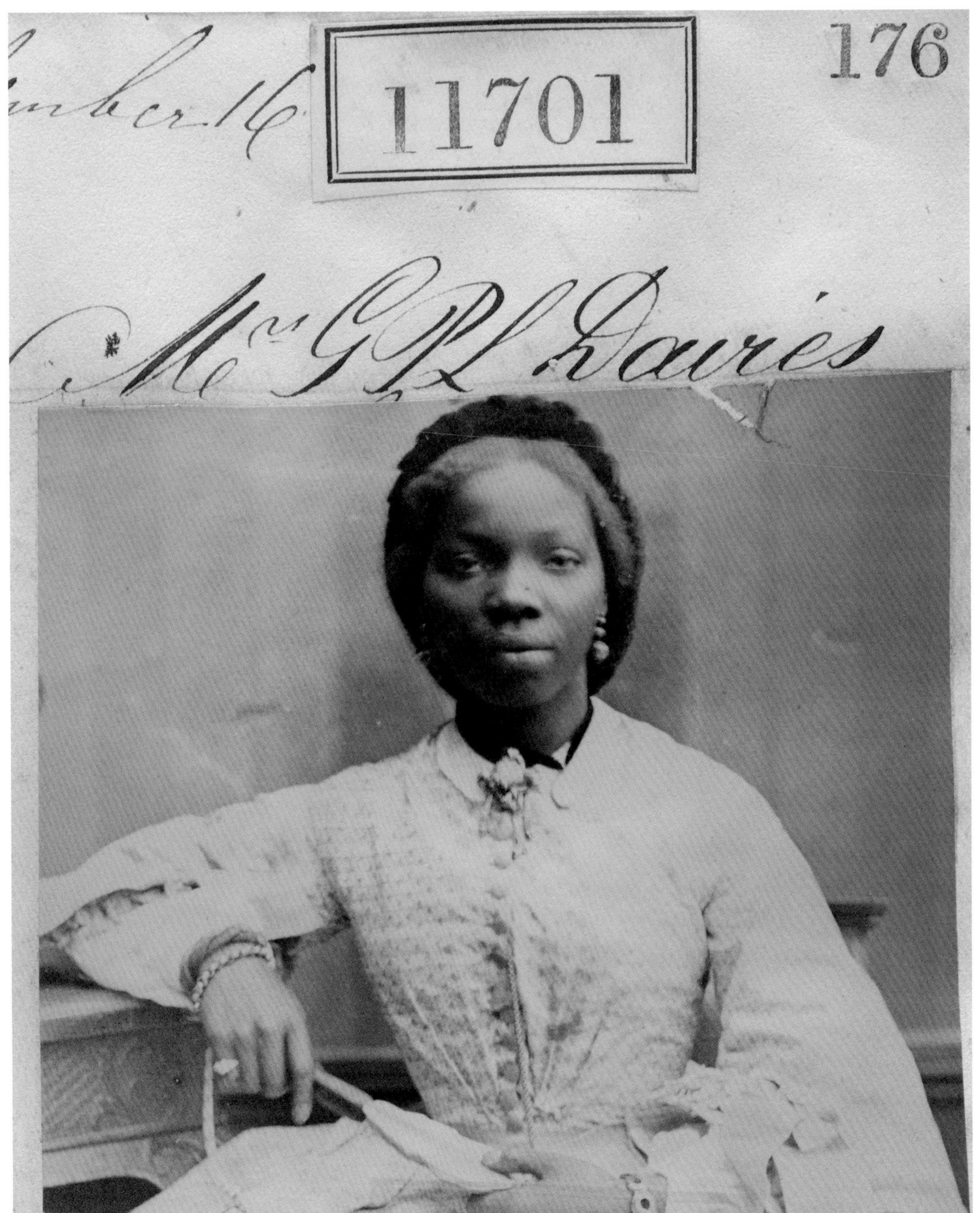
176
11701
...mber 16
Mrs G.P.R. Davies

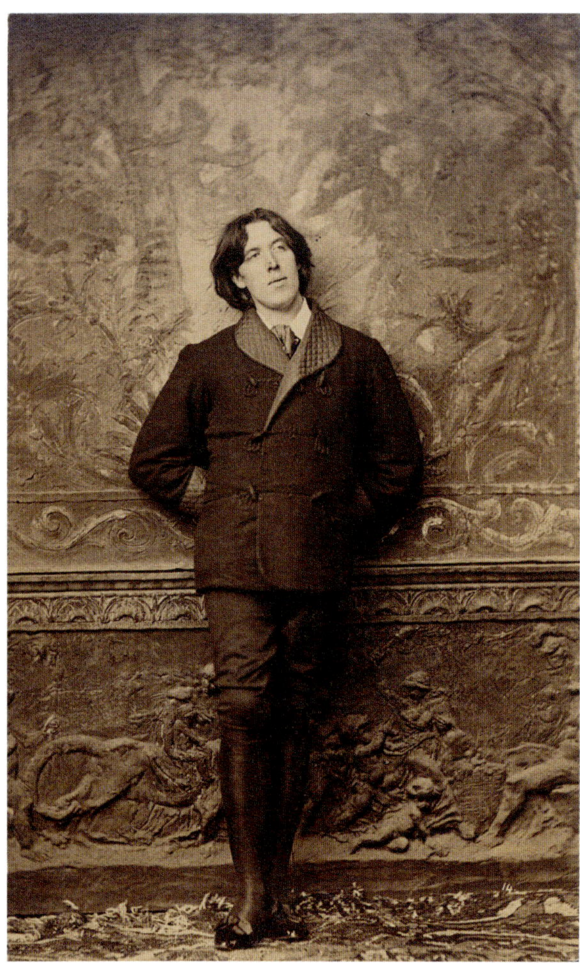

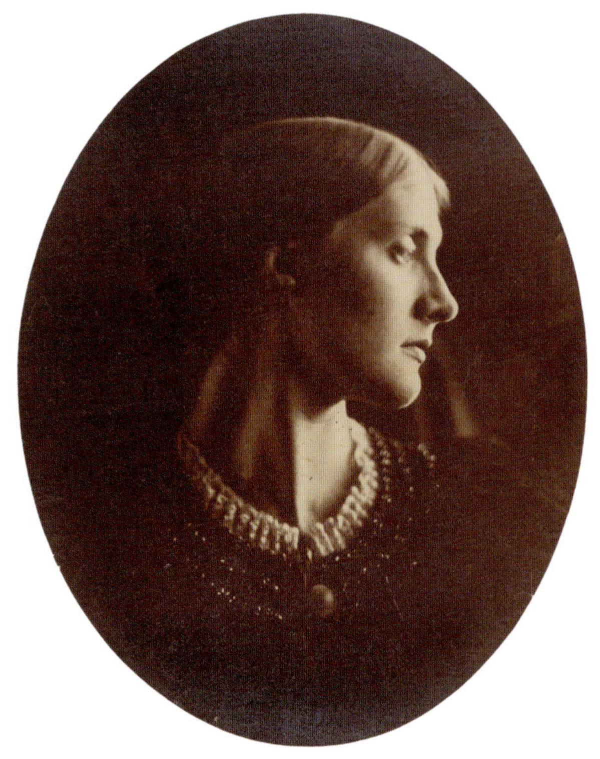

Oscar Wilde
(1854–1900)
Napoleon Sarony, 1882
Albumen panel card,
305 × 184mm
NPG P24

Wilde is a gay icon celebrated for his wit, books and plays, including *The Picture of Dorian Gray* (1891) and *The Importance of Being Earnest* (1895). In 1898, he wrote the poem *The Ballad of Reading Gaol*, having served a two-year prison sentence for homosexual offences.

Julia Prinsep Stephen
(1846–95)
Julia Margaret Cameron, 1867
Albumen print, 344 × 263mm
NPG x18018

Stephen was the niece and goddaughter of the pioneering photographer, Cameron, who took this photograph. She was a social activist and philanthropist, and a favourite model of the Pre-Raphaelite painters. Among her children were the writer Virginia Woolf and the artist Vanessa Bell.

Isambard Kingdom Brunel
(1806–59)
Robert Howlett, 1857
Albumen print, 286 × 225mm
NPG P112

Brunel was a central figure in Britain's industrial revolution. He was made engineer of the Great Western Railway at just 26 and went on to design the Clifton Suspension Bridge in Bristol. In 1838, his first steamship, the *Great Western*, became the first purpose-built steamship to carry passengers to America.

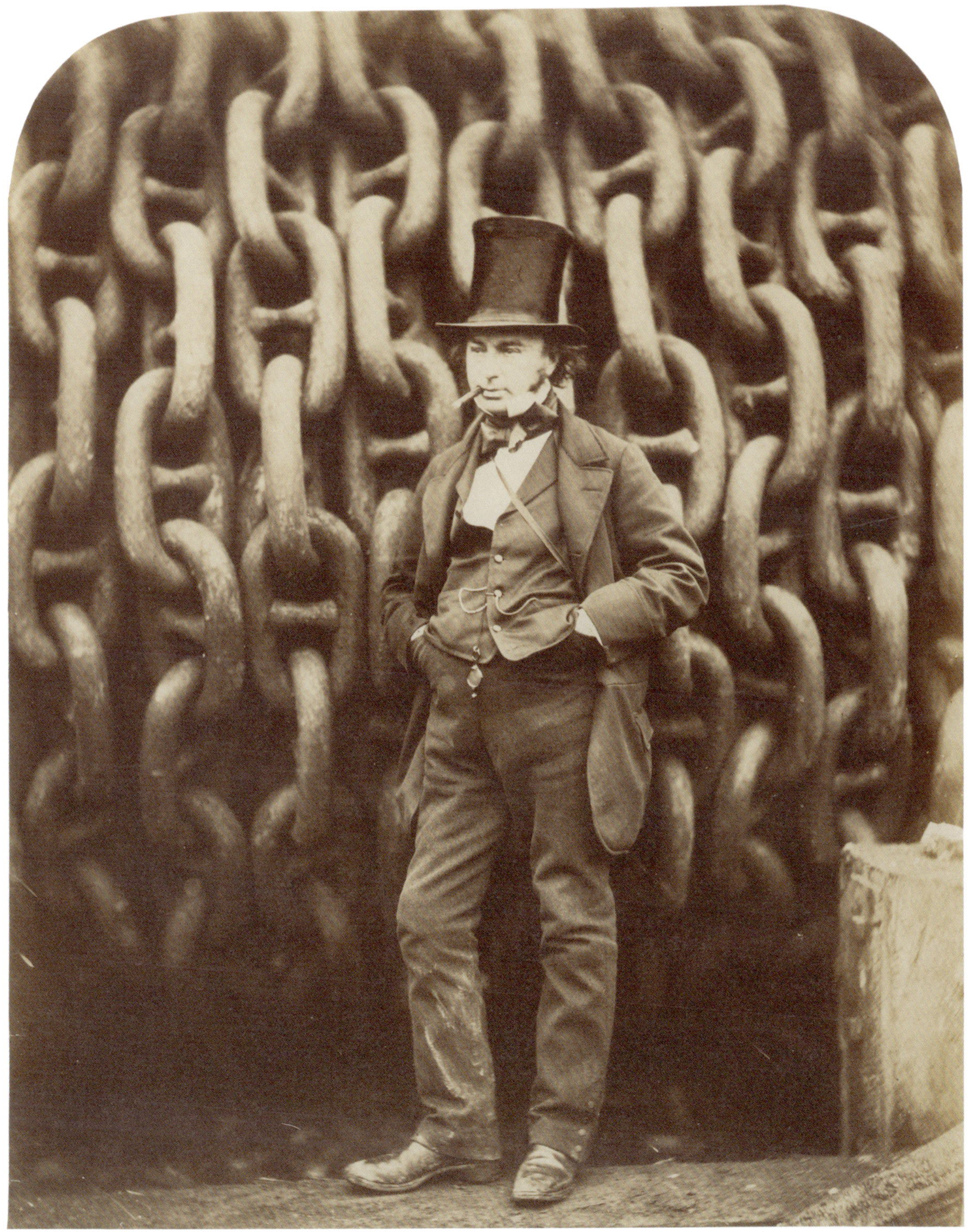

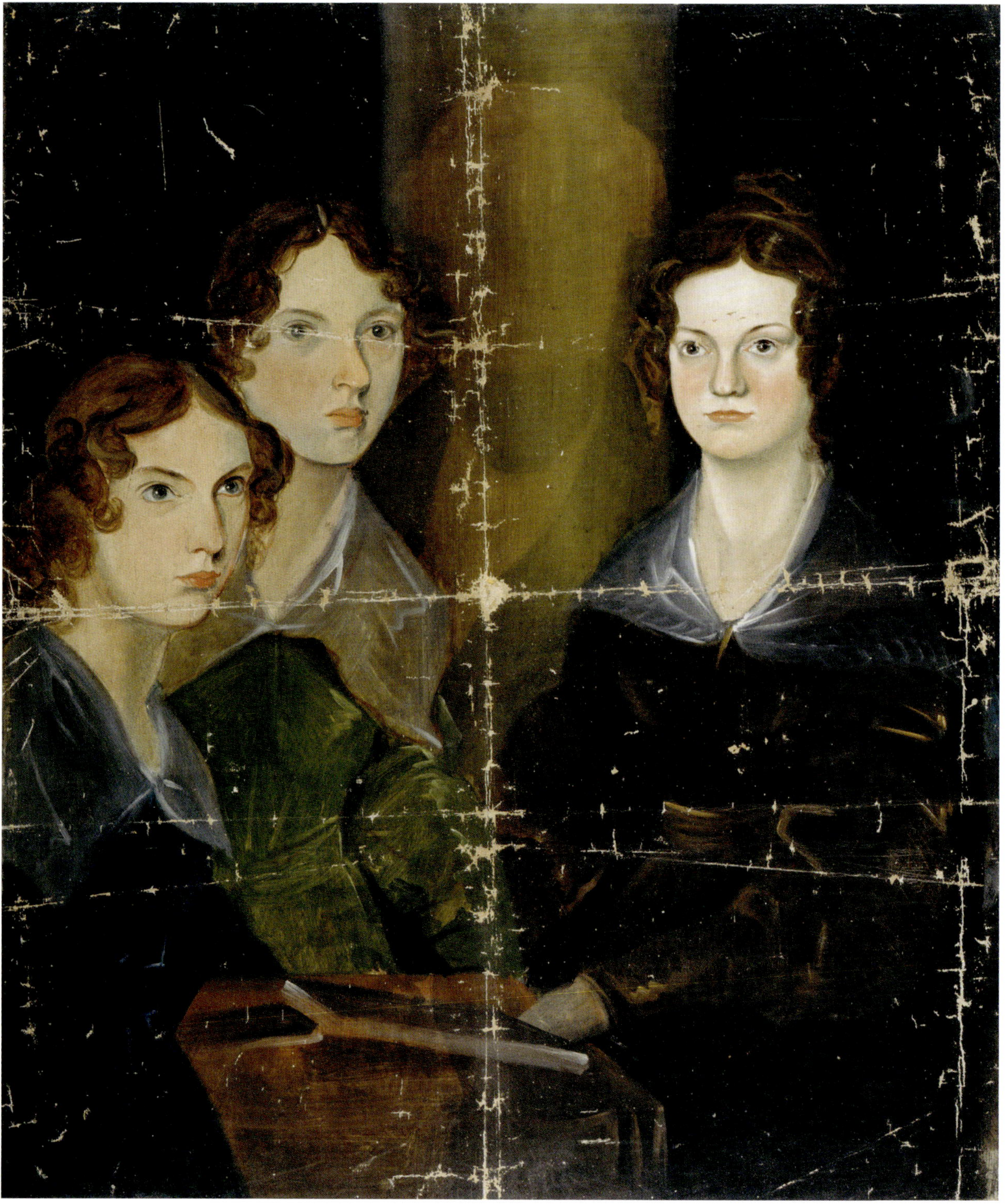

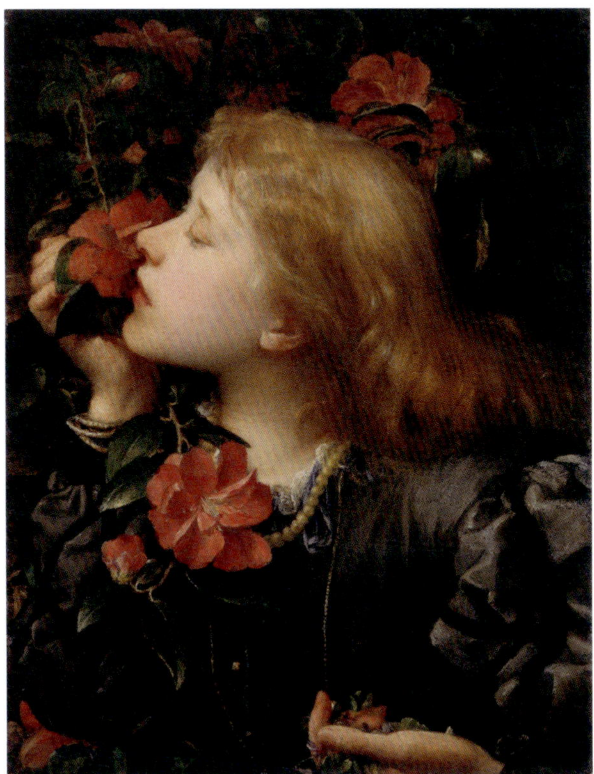 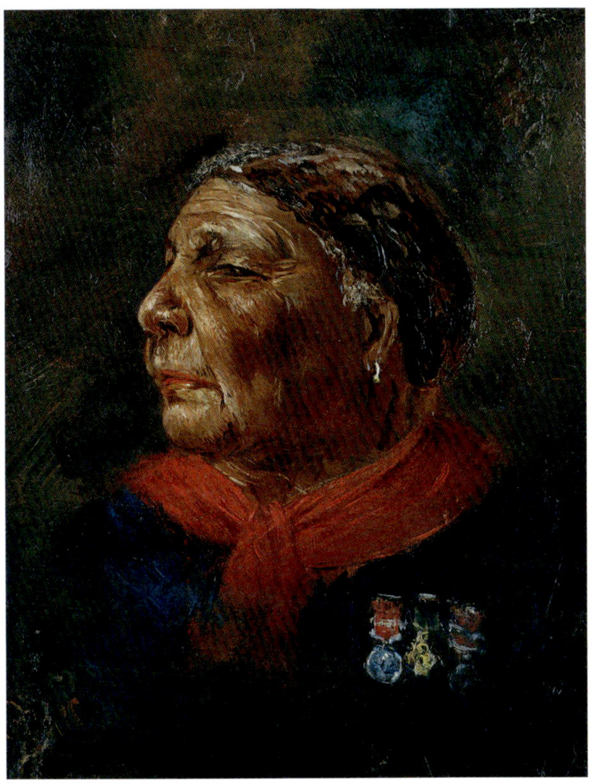

**Anne Brontë, Emily Brontë
and Charlotte Brontë**
(1820–49; 1818–48; 1816–55)
Patrick Branwell Brontë, *c*.1834
Oil on canvas, 902 × 746mm
NPG 1725

This portrait was believed lost
until it was discovered on top
of a cupboard in 1914. It is the
only known surviving portrait
of the great writers Anne, Emily
and Charlotte Brontë, and
was painted by their teenage
brother, Branwell. Fading paint
has revealed that he painted
over a self-portrait.

Ellen Terry (*Choosing*)
(1847–1928)
George Frederic Watts, 1864
Oil on board, 472 × 352mm
NPG 5048

Regarded as the greatest
English female actor of the
period, Terry played many
leading roles in Henry Irving's
productions, such as Portia in
Shakespeare's *The Merchant
of Venice*. This portrait was
painted by Watts at the time
of his short-lived marriage to
Terry, when he was 46 and
she was 16.

Mary Seacole
(1805–81)
Albert Charles Challen, 1869
Oil on panel, 240 × 180mm
NPG 6856

Seacole was a Jamaican-British
nurse who became a hero to
British military forces during
the Crimean War (1853–6).
Overcoming racial discrimination
and rejection as a nurse by
the official military hospitals,
Seacole opened the British
Hotel near the battlefields,
which served as a base for
nursing and catering.

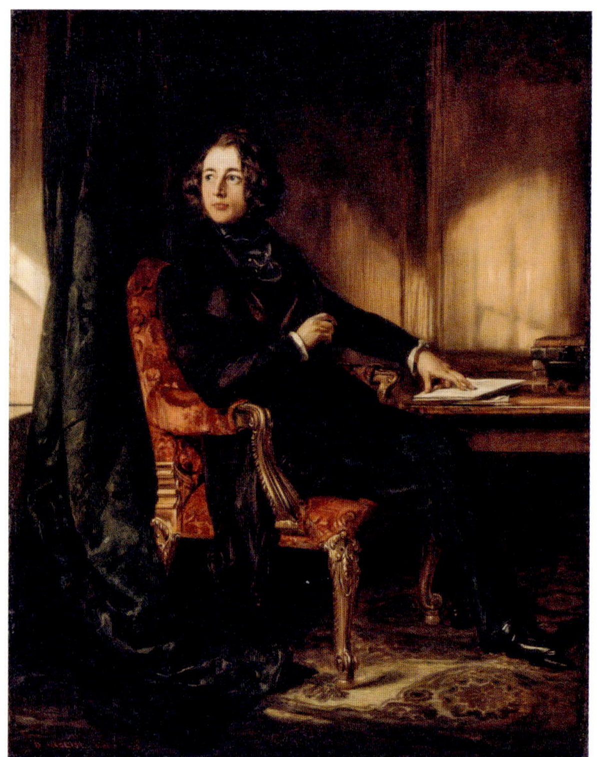

Charles Dickens
(1812–70)
Daniel Maclise, 1839
Oil on canvas, 914 × 714mm
NPG 1172

Dickens was one of the greatest
novelists of his age, with an
international reputation that
endures. Classics such as *Oliver
Twist* (1838), *A Christmas Carol*
(1843) and *Great Expectations*
(1861) are renowned for their
vivid portrayal of the Victorian
class system, and address
issues of social deprivation
and injustice.

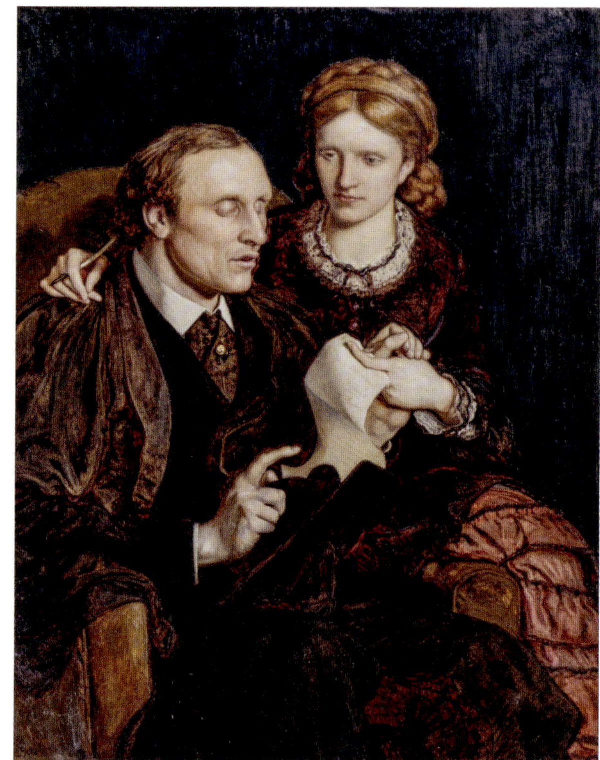

**Henry Fawcett and
Dame Millicent Fawcett**
(1833–84; 1847–1929)
Ford Madox Brown, 1872
Oil on canvas, 1086 × 838mm
NPG 1603

The Fawcetts were a married
couple dedicated to social
reform. Millicent's peaceful
suffrage campaign was critical in
winning women the right to vote.
The movement was supported
by her husband, Henry, a political
economist. Losing his eyesight in
an accident aged 25, he became
the first blind MP in 1865.

Frederick Burnaby
(1842–85)
Jacques Joseph Tissot, 1870
Oil on panel, 500 × 610mm
NPG 2642

The British army officer Burnaby
is shown relaxing off duty in this
portrait by the French painter
Tissot, but the large map on the
wall behind grounds him firmly
in the business of the British
Empire. Burnaby was famed for
the tales of his adventures in
Europe and Asia.

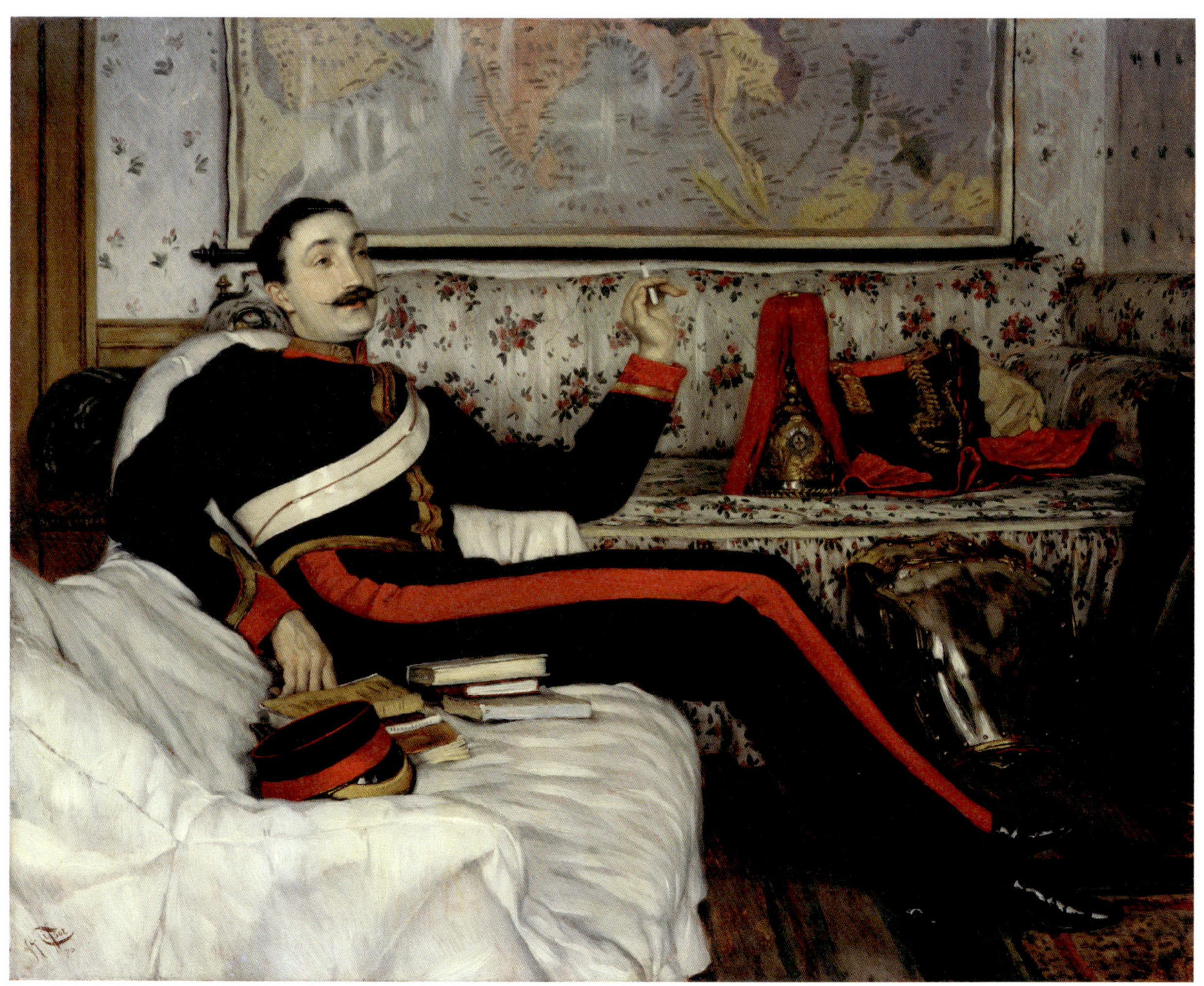

Charles Darwin
(1809–82)
John Collier, 1883,
based on a work of 1881
Oil on canvas, 1257 × 965mm
NPG 1024

Darwin is one of the world's most influential scientists. His theory of evolution by natural selection, first published in *On the Origin of Species* (1859), laid the foundation for all subsequent life sciences. His scientific career was largely based on his five-year round-the-world voyage on board HMS *Beagle*, during which he visited South America, the Galapagos Islands, Australia and South Africa. Darwin's experiences and the samples that he collected provided the foundations of his work on evolution. Although comprehensively accepted by the scientific community, Darwin's theory challenged the biblical account of Creation and has proved to be enduringly controversial to some religious groups.

This portrait shows Darwin as an old man in the year before his death. It is a copy by Collier (1850–1934) of a painting he made for the Linnean Society in 1881. Collier was the son-in-law of Thomas Huxley, Darwin's defender in the furore surrounding the publication of his work. The portrait was much admired. It was given to the Gallery by Darwin's eldest son, William Erasmus Darwin, who in 1896 wrote to the director, Lionel Cust, that 'as a likeness, it is an improvement on the original'.

'Many of those who knew his face most intimately, think that Mr Collier's picture is the best of the portraits and in this judgement the sitter himself was inclined to agree.'

Francis Darwin, 1887

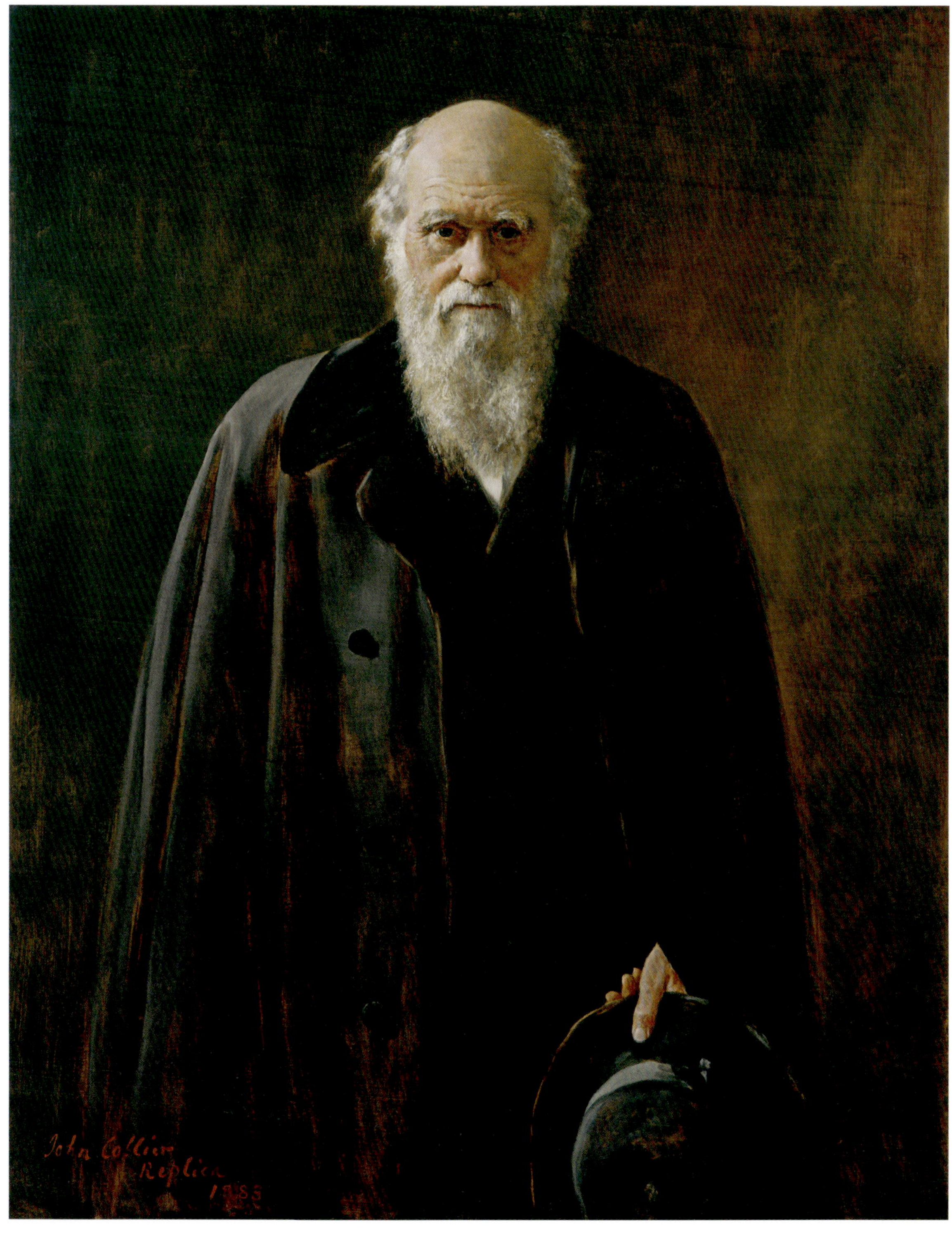

John Collier
Replica
1883

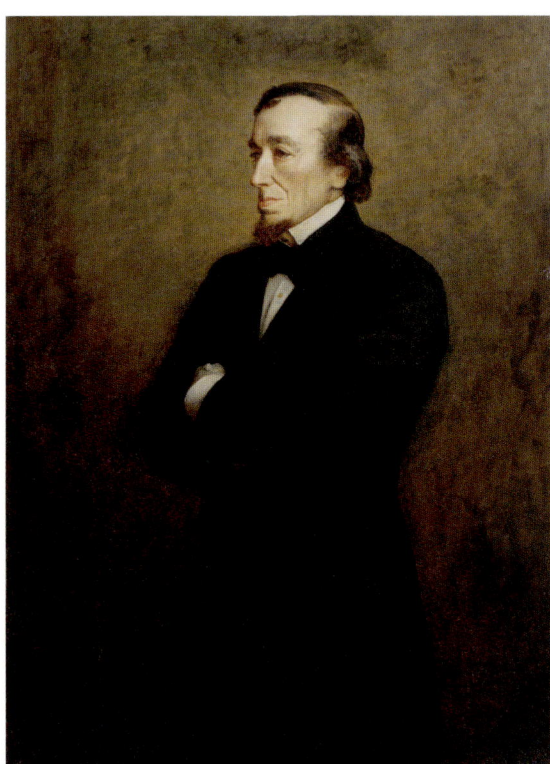

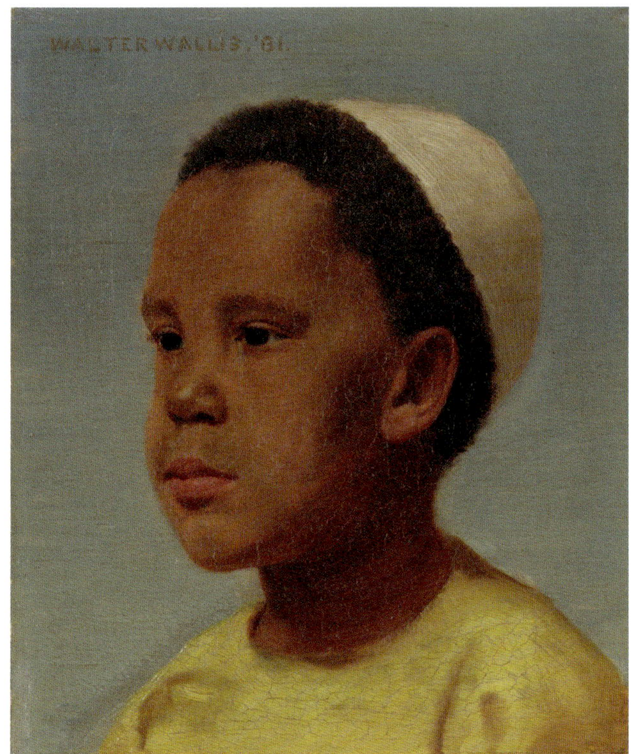

**Benjamin Disraeli,
Earl of Beaconsfield**
(1804–81)
Sir John Everett Millais, 1881
Oil on canvas, 1276 × 931mm
NPG 3241

Disraeli led the Conservative
Party during years marked by
intense rivalry with the Liberal
leader, William Gladstone. A
novelist as well as a politician,
he is the only British prime
minister to have been born
into a Jewish family. In 1877,
he proclaimed Queen Victoria
Empress of India.

Samuel Coleridge-Taylor
(1875–1912)
Walter Wallis, 1881
Oil on canvas, 256 × 205mm
NPG 5724

Coleridge-Taylor achieved
international fame as the
composer of *The Song of
Hiawatha* (1898) and used
his celebrity to promote black
rights. He sat for this work
while modelling at an art club
aged 7. In 1984, it became
the first painted portrait of an
identified black British sitter to
be acquired by the Gallery.

Edward Carpenter
(1844–1929)
Roger Fry, 1894
Oil on canvas, 749 × 438mm
NPG 2447

Carpenter, a socialist and poet,
was one of the foremost British
figures to call for law reform on
homosexuality. A co-founder of
the Independent Labour Party,
he promoted women's suffrage,
pacifism and anti-colonialism,
as well as environmentalism and
vegetarianism. In this portrait
Carpenter is wearing what Fry
called his 'anarchist overcoat'.

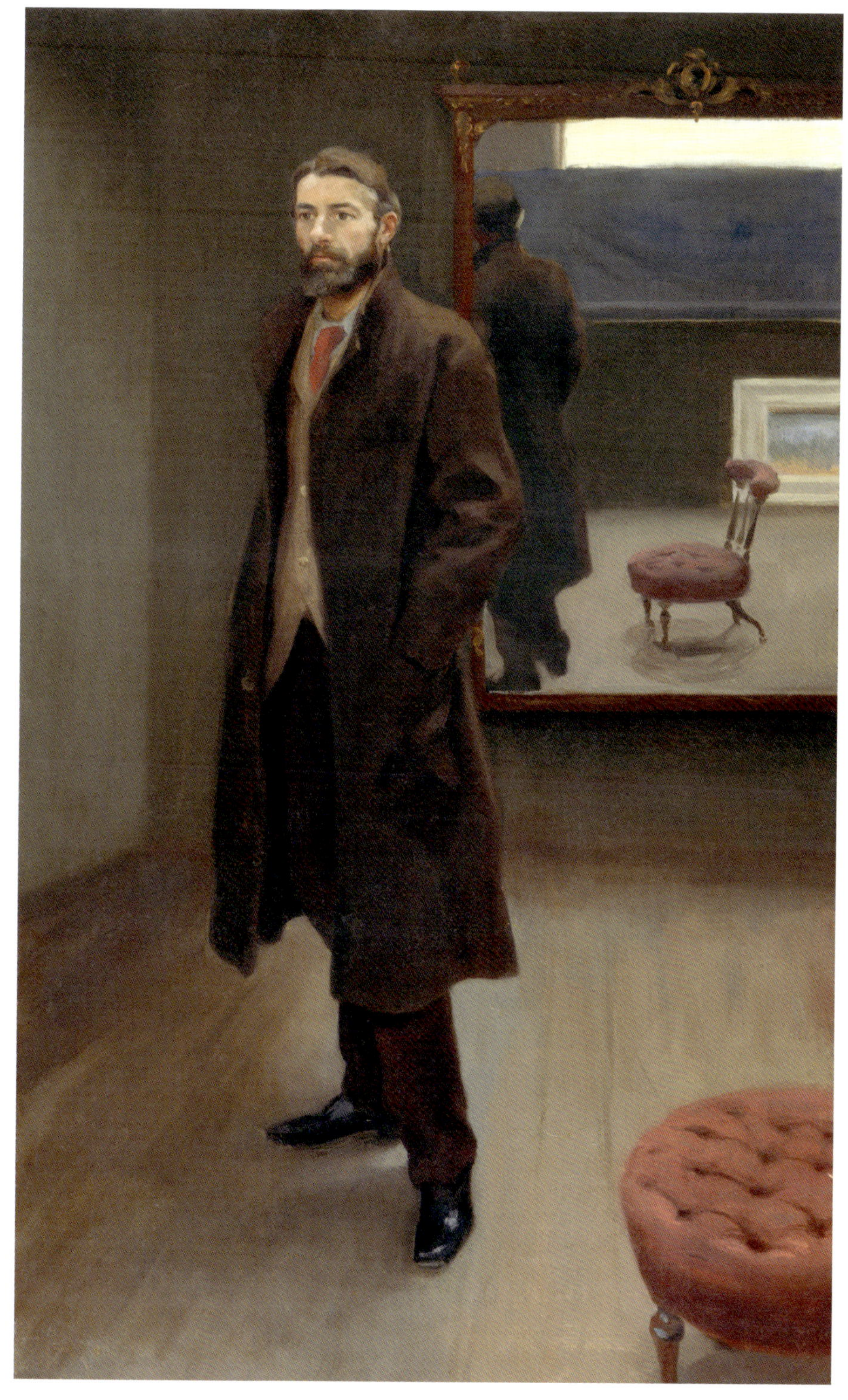

The Early Twentieth Century

The pace of social and economic change accelerated during the first half of the twentieth century. Progress was experienced in areas such as democratic representation, health and innovation but the era was dominated by the brutal impact of two world wars.

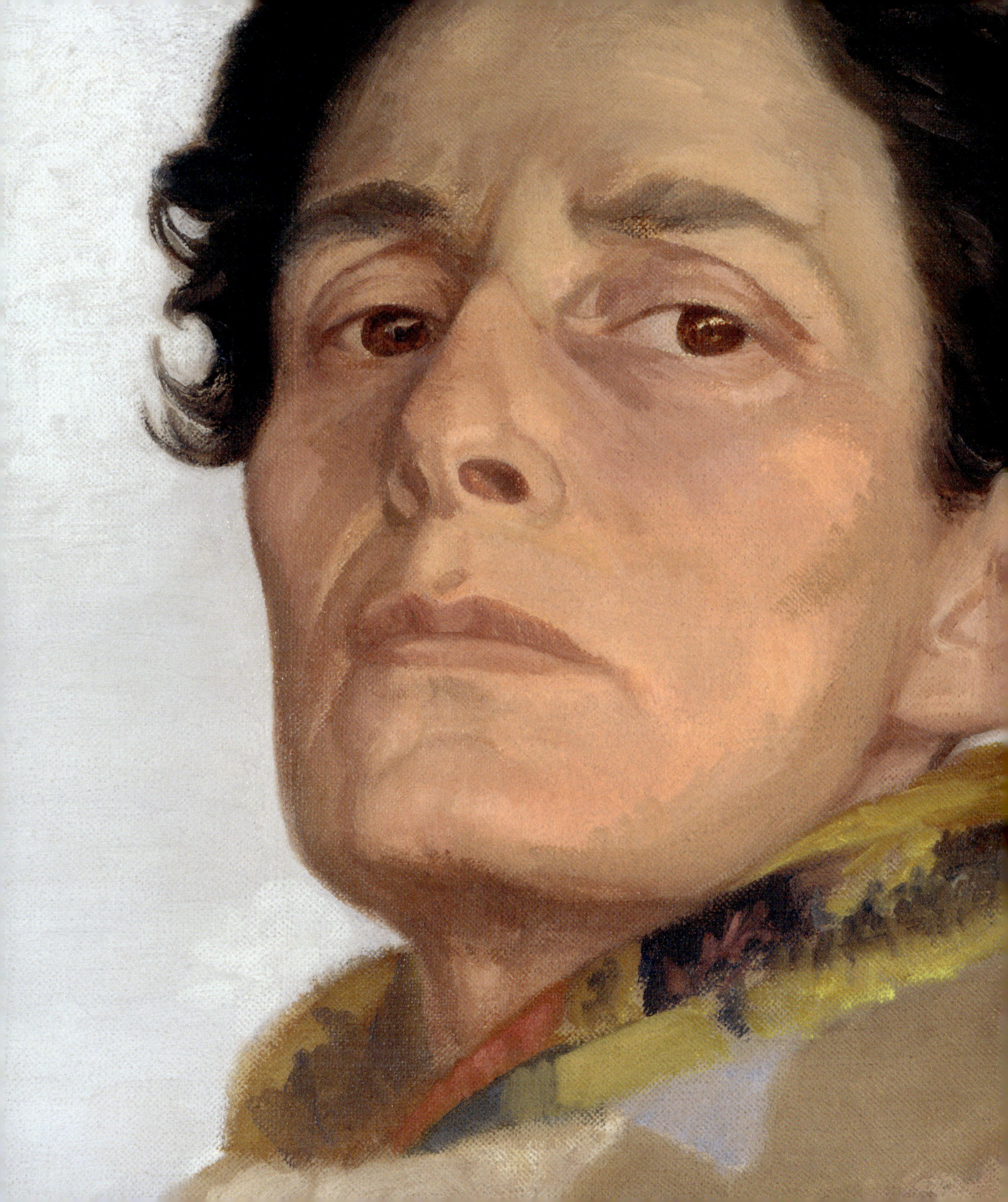

Modernity and War

The early twentieth century was a period in which long-established rules and sources of authority were contested by a broad spectrum of society. The death of Queen Victoria in 1901, after 63 years on the throne, was accompanied by a reassessment of many of the attitudes and social codes that had become associated with her reign. Political hierarchies were challenged by the growth of trade unions, the founding of the Labour Party, and the campaign for women's right to vote, which was partially realised in 1918 before voting equality with men was achieved in 1928. The role of government was also expanded by the Liberal Party, which laid the foundation of the welfare state through measures such as national insurance and pensions.

Cars and aeroplanes began to transform the way that people travelled, with profound social and environmental consequences. Communication, entertainment and the exchange of information were revolutionised by radio and cinema. The arts responded to the pace and proliferation of change by seeking new means of expression and breaking with past conventions. Portraiture remained largely dominated by artists working within the existing tradition, an outstanding exponent being John Singer Sargent. Increasingly, though, the genre was enriched by the emergence of new ideas and approaches, including the exploration of abstraction.

Widespread optimism about the progress of society was crushed by the horrors of the First World War (1914–18), a global conflict that claimed more than 16 million lives. Battlefields laid waste to vast areas of Europe and, on the home front, British civilians were bombed by aeroplanes and zeppelins. The British Empire responded to the call to arms and more than 3 million soldiers and labourers served alongside the British Army. The Treaty of Versailles, which marked the end of the war, expanded Britain's empire to its greatest extent through the acquisition of former German colonies. However, there followed increased resistance to British rule and the retraction of the empire. The Irish War of Independence (1919–21) resulted in the loss of most of Ireland and the creation of Northern Ireland.

The 'Roaring Twenties' was a period of decadence and glamour for some but, for many more, financial hardship made life a struggle. The attempt by workers to improve wages and conditions led to the only general strike in British history in 1926. In the following decade, a global economic depression resulted in widespread industrial decline and mass unemployment. As social discontent and the threat of war with Nazi Germany grew, Britain experienced a constitutional crisis with the abdication of Edward VIII in 1936.

The Second World War (1939–45) erupted three years later. For the second time in a generation, Britain and the British Empire were once again immersed in a global war. The Battle of Britain (1940) and the Blitz bombing campaign brought the dreadful realities of war onto home soil. National joy at the victory in 1945 was swiftly followed by the horrific revelation of the scale of Nazi atrocities, as well as anxiety brought about by the beginning of the atomic age with the bombing of the Japanese cities of Hiroshima and Nagasaki.

Dame Laura Knight
(1877–1970)
Self-portrait, 1913
Oil on canvas, 1524 × 1276mm
NPG 4839

Knight shows herself painting a nude model, posed by her friend the ceramicist Ella Naper. It was a bold statement of her ambition at a time when female students were excluded from life-drawing classes. In 1936, Knight became the first female Royal Academician in more than a century.

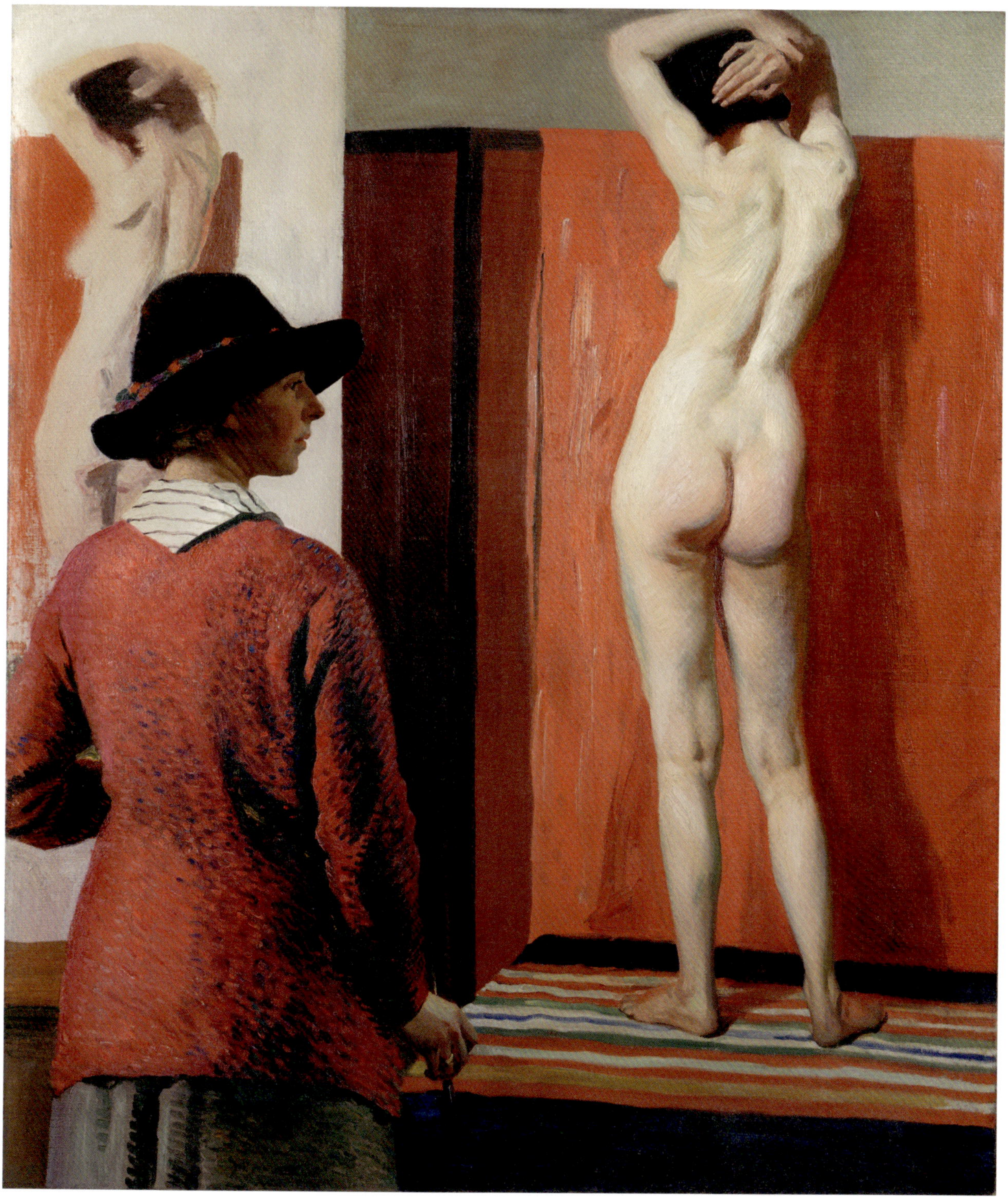

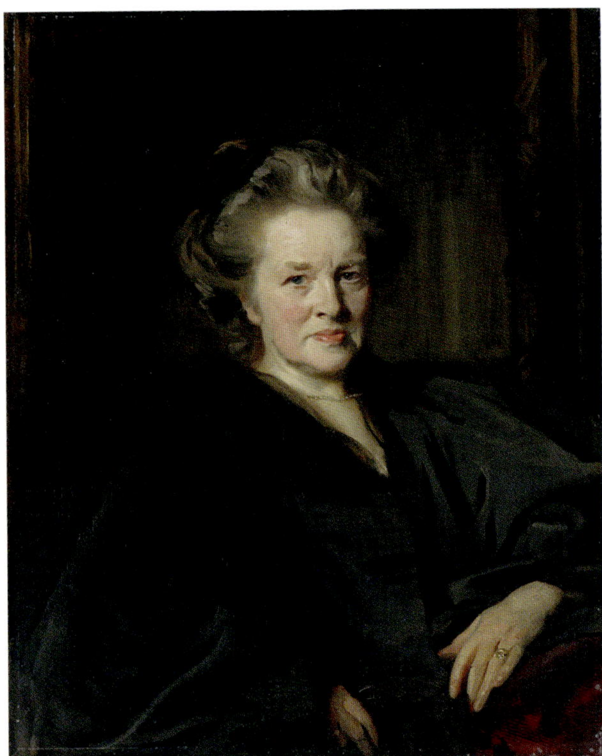 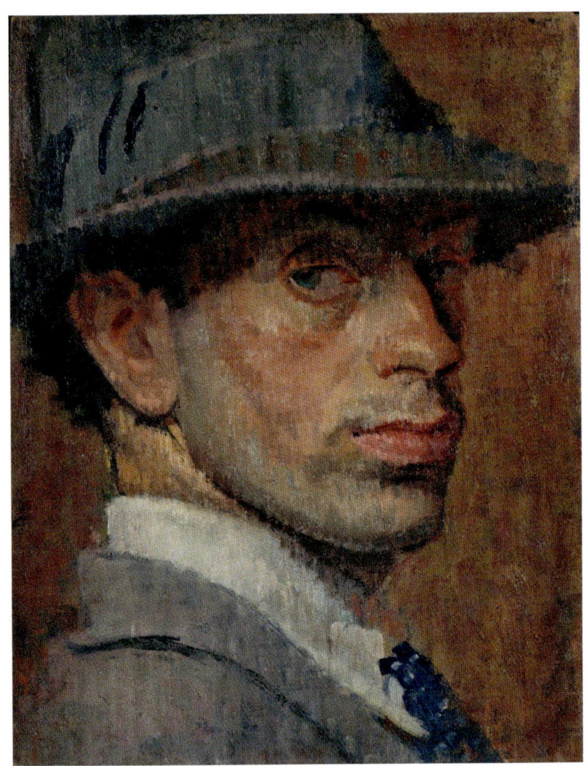

Elizabeth Garrett Anderson
(1836–1917)
John Singer Sargent, 1900
Oil on canvas, 838 × 660mm
NPG L254

In 1865, Garrett Anderson became the first English woman to qualify in medicine. During her life, she founded the New Hospital for Women, campaigned for women's suffrage and was England's first female mayor. This portrait was painted in 1900 by Sargent, the leading portrait artist of the time.

Isaac Rosenberg
(1890–1918)
Self-portrait, 1915
Oil on panel, 295 × 222mm
NPG 4129

Born to Jewish parents from Lithuania, the poet and artist Rosenberg grew up in poverty in London's East End. He is acclaimed for poetry communicating his experiences of the First World War. Despite being a pacifist, he joined the army in 1915 and was killed on the Western Front in 1918.

Virginia Woolf
(1882–1941)
Vanessa Bell, 1912
Oil on board, 400 × 340mm
NPG 5933

Woolf was a member of the Bloomsbury Group of artists and writers and is one of the major writers of English fiction. In novels such as *Mrs Dalloway* (1925) and *To the Lighthouse* (1927) she shunned conventional literary approaches to structure, plot and characterisation. This portrait is by her sister, Vanessa Bell.

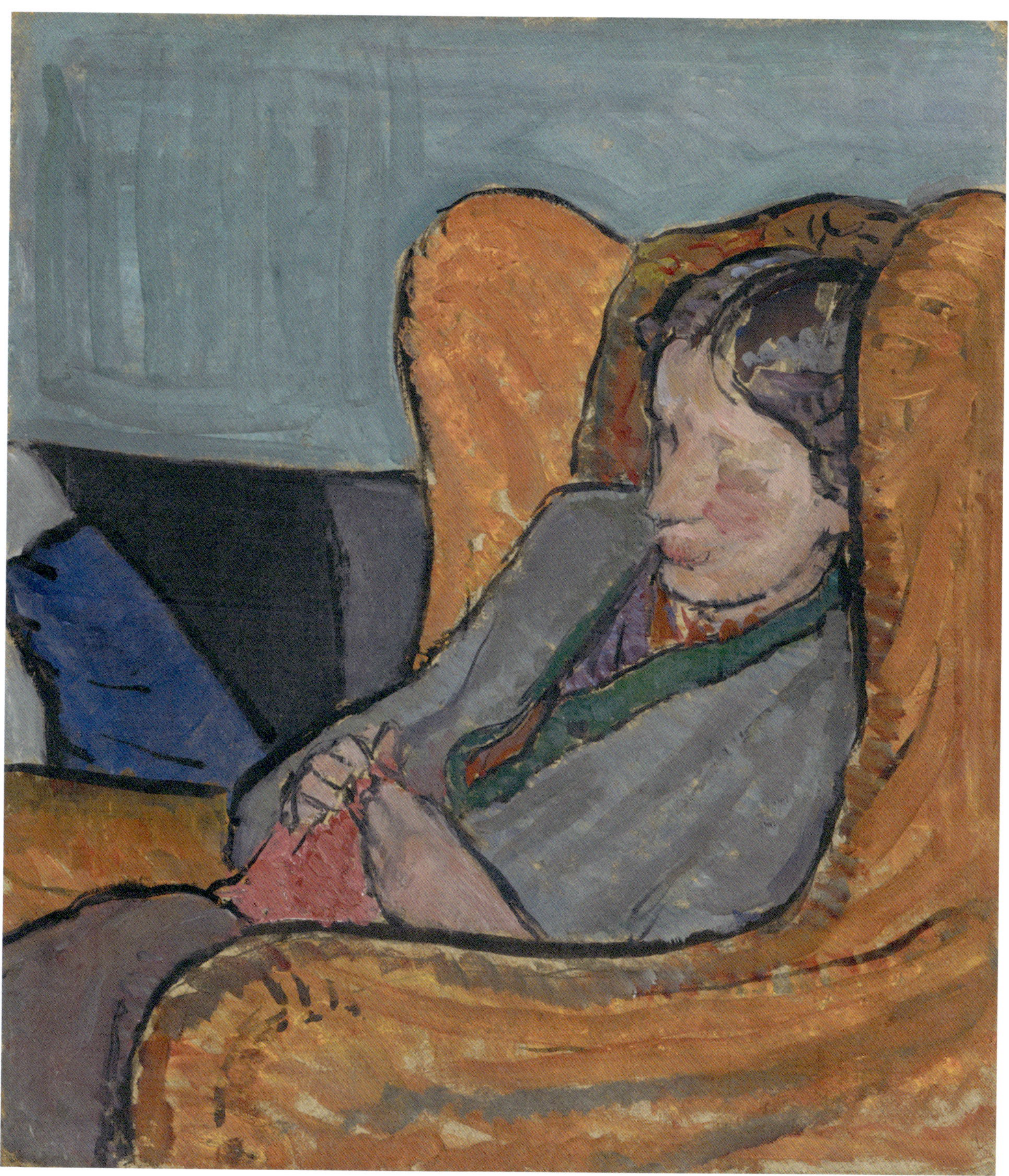

Gwen John
(1876–1939)
Self-portrait, *c.*1900
Oil on canvas, 610 × 378mm
NPG 4439

John is one of the most important British artists of the twentieth century. Although she only had one exhibition devoted to her work during her lifetime, today she is especially celebrated for her sensitive paintings of solitary, introspective women. This self-portrait, with her hand on her hip and direct gaze, shows her as a confident young woman in an art world that was dominated by men.

Born in Haverfordwest, Wales, John studied at the Slade School of Fine Art with her brother, fellow acclaimed artist, Augustus, and at James McNeill Whistler's Académie Carmen in Paris. She exhibited at the New English Art Club, London, before permanently moving to France in 1903. Initially, she earned a meagre living as an artists' model in Paris, most notably for Auguste Rodin, with whom she had a passionate relationship. Having established herself as an artist, she stayed in France throughout the First World War and then began to exhibit in New York. In 1926, a solo exhibition of her work was held at the Chenil Galleries, London.

Increasingly reclusive in later life, John died in Dieppe in 1939. She had been overshadowed by her extrovert brother during her lifetime but, as Augustus predicted, today she is the more critically lauded of the siblings.

'As to me, I cannot imagine why my vision will have some value in the world – and yet I know it will.'

Gwen John, 1910

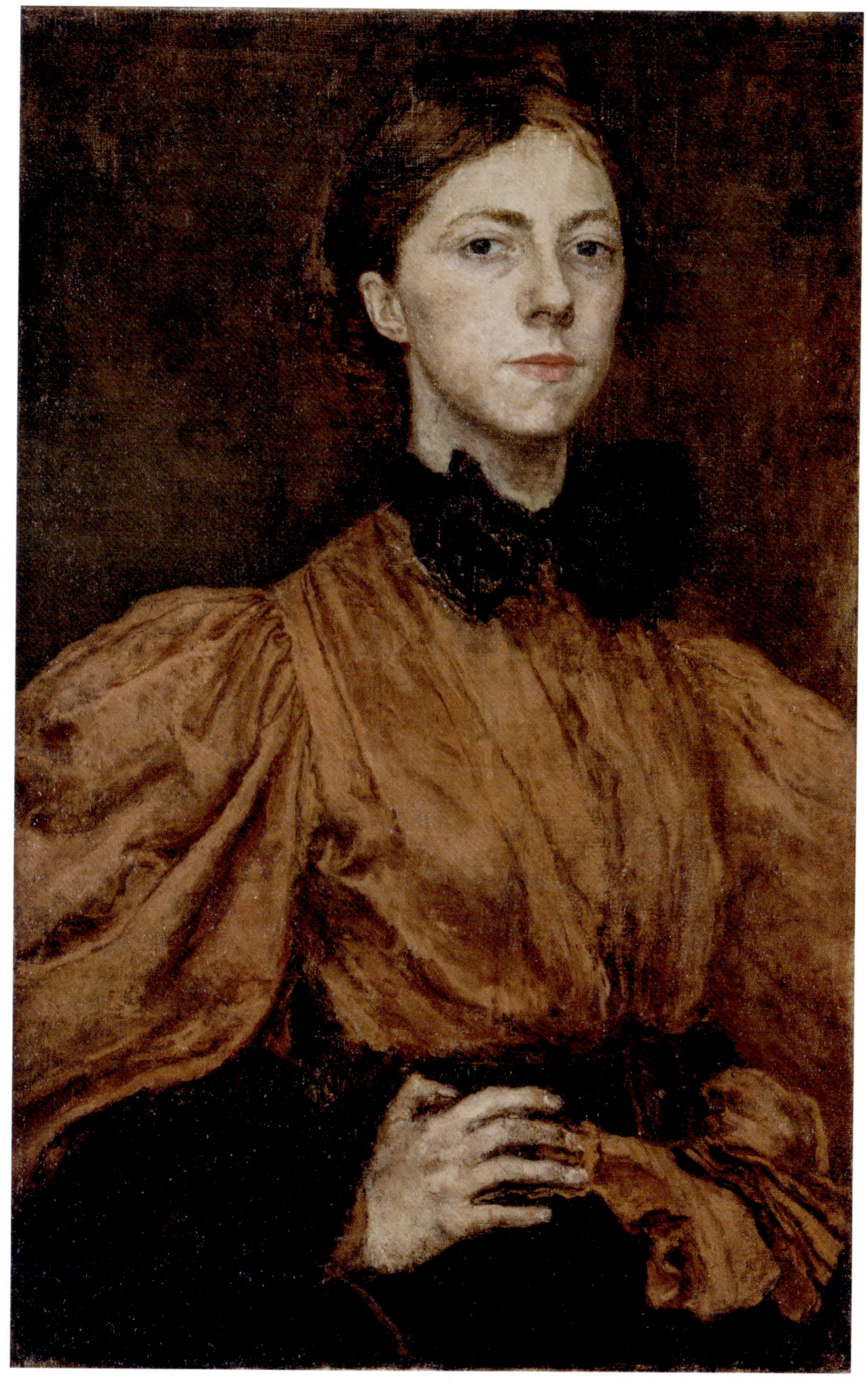

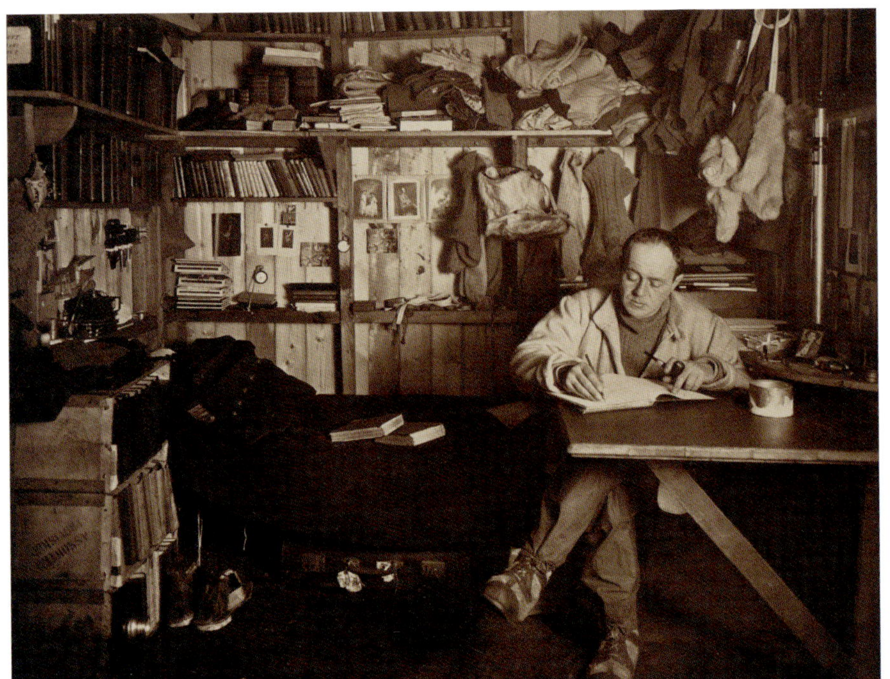

Robert Falcon Scott
(1868–1912)
Herbert Ponting, 1911
Carbon print, 356 × 457mm
NPG P23

Captain Scott is the most famous British explorer of the twentieth century, renowned for his expeditions to the Antarctic. His death, along with four of his crew, on the return journey from the South Pole, has made Scott a controversial figure as well as an icon of heroism and courage.

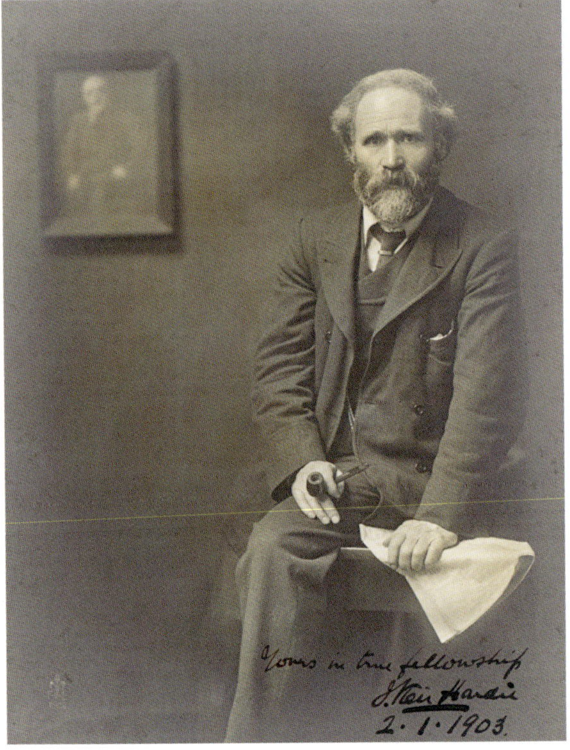

Keir Hardie
(1856–1915)
Furley Lewis, 1902
Gelatin silver print,
209 × 156mm
NPG P1091

A Scottish politician, trade unionist and former miner, Hardie was largely responsible for creating the modern Labour Party and was its first leader (1906–8). He championed equality, particularly in the cause of women's suffrage, and was an advocate of free schooling, pensions and Indian self-rule.

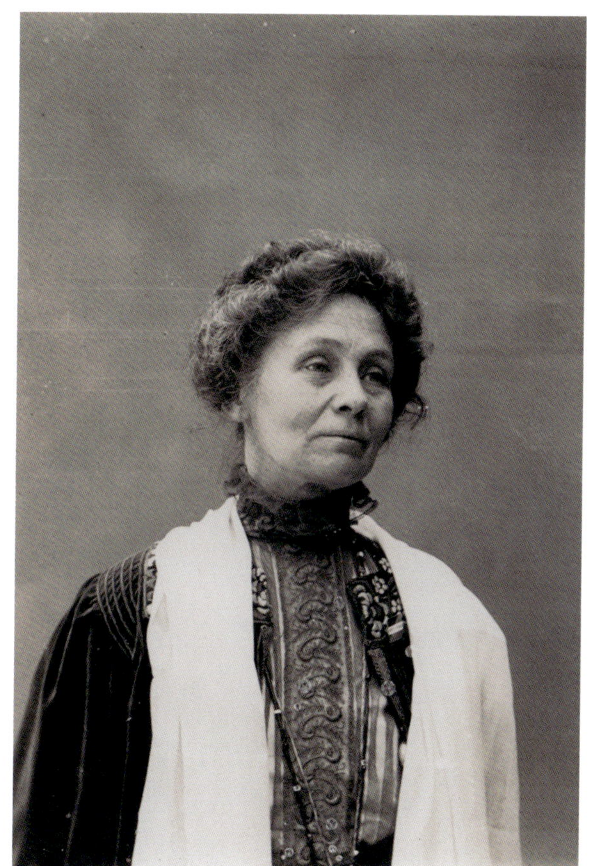

Emmeline Pankhurst
(1858–1928)
Christina Broom, 1910s
Gelatin silver print,
106 × 70mm
NPG x6194

In 1903, Pankhurst founded the
Women's Social and Political
Union. With their motto 'deeds
not words', the suffragettes
stood apart from members of
the wider suffrage movement,
pioneering a militant campaign
of civil disobedience, which
helped to secure votes for
women in 1918.

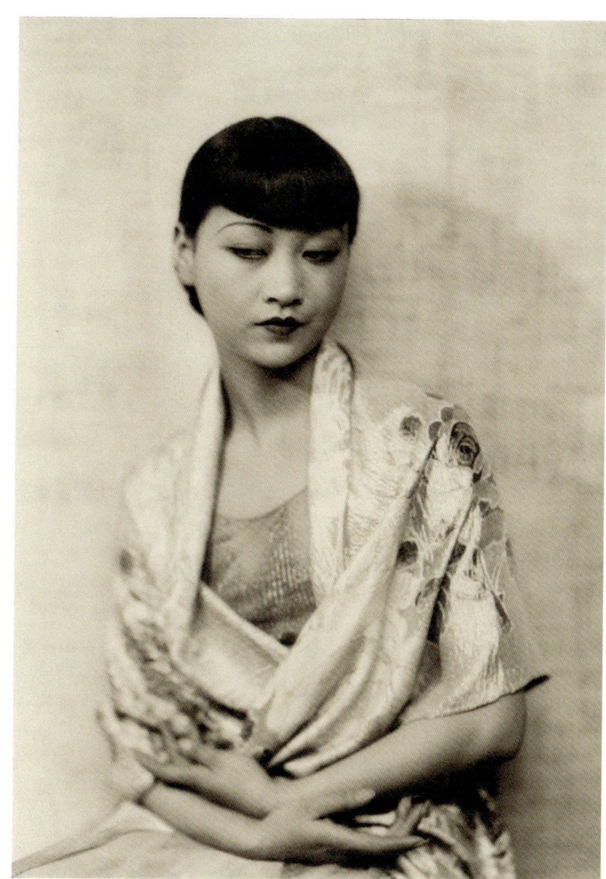

Anna May Wong
(1905–61)
Dorothy Wilding, 1929
Gelatin silver print,
265 × 182mm
NPG x27480

One of Hollywood's first
Chinese-American stars, Wong
appeared in more than 50 films
of the silent and early sound
era and opposed biased racial
casting. After relocating to
Europe in 1928, she starred in a
number of notable productions,
such as *Piccadilly* (1929), which
was filmed in London.

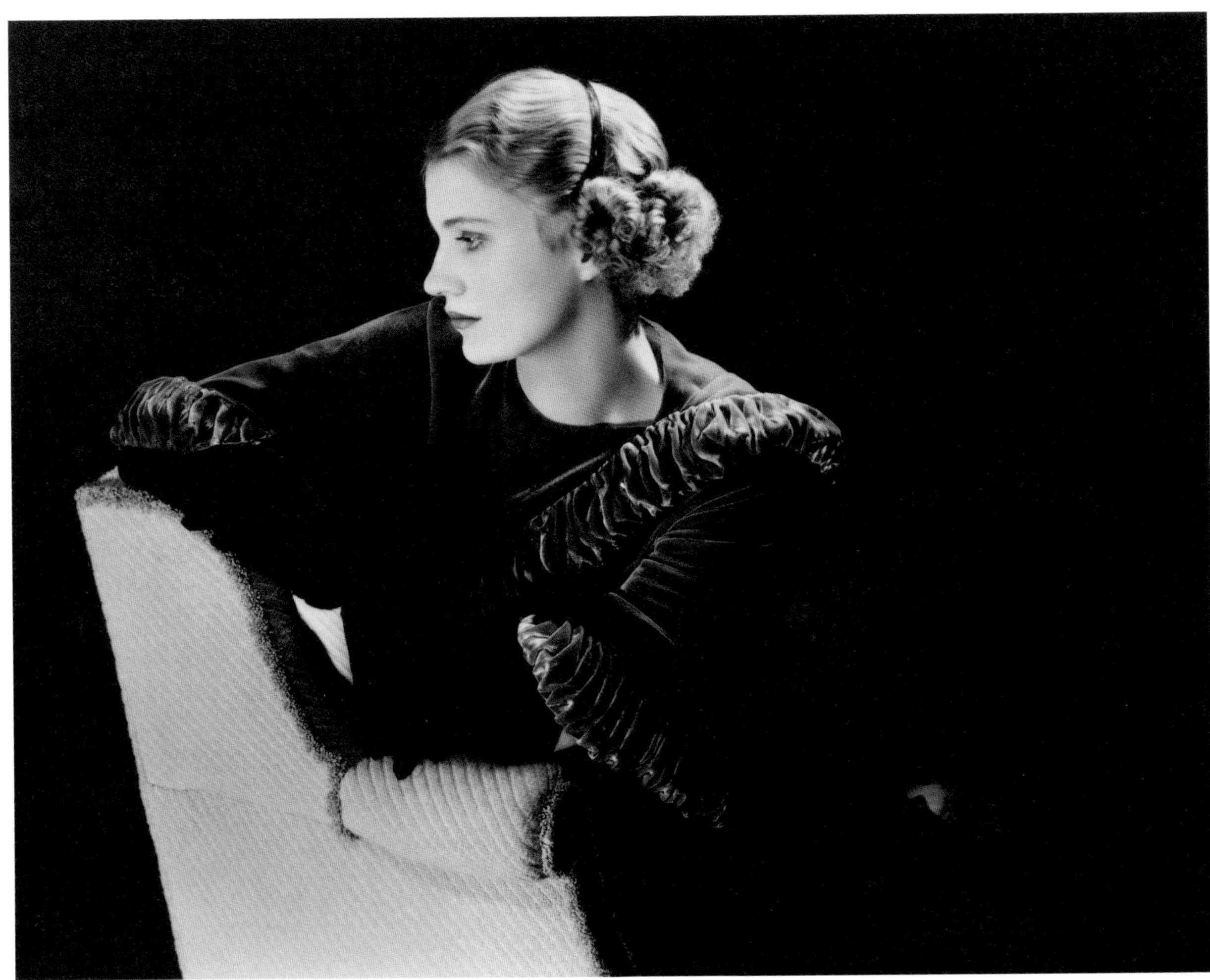

Lee Miller
(1907–77)
Self-portrait, 1932
Gelatin silver print, 153 × 191mm
NPG P1081

American-born Miller is
celebrated for her Surrealist and
fashion photography. After a
period living and working with
the artist Man Ray in Paris, she
moved to London in 1937. She
was employed by *Vogue* as a
war correspondent and travelled
through Europe in the final
months of the Second World War.

Sir Winston Churchill
(1874–1965)
Yousuf Karsh, 1941
Gelatin silver print,
604 × 503mm
NPG P1368

____

Churchill's charismatic
leadership as prime minister
during the Second World War
was the high point in a long and
varied political career. Dubbed
'The Roaring Lion', this became
one of the most enduring of his
portraits and is among the most
widely reproduced photographs
of all time.

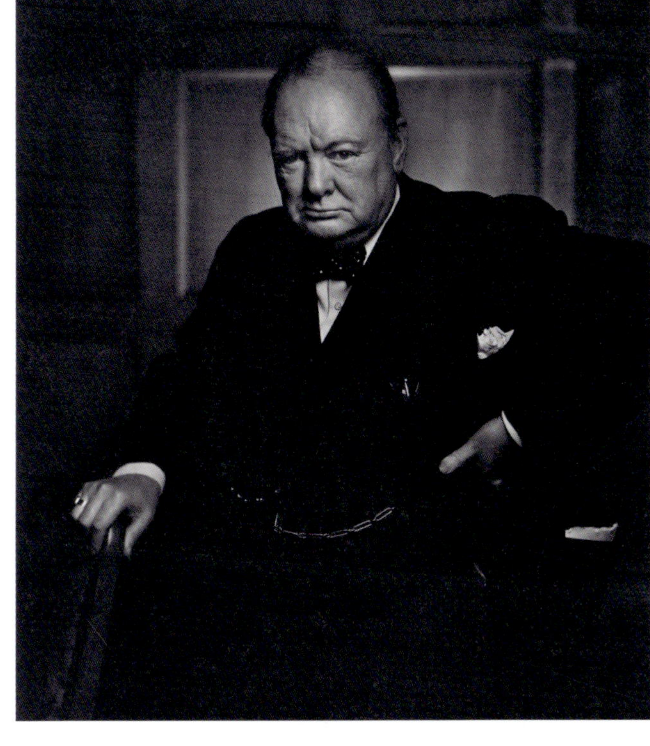

Harold Moody
(1882–1947)
Ronald Moody, 1997,
based on a work of 1946
Bronze head, 420 × 220mm
NPG 6380

____

Harold Moody was an influential
doctor who moved to south
London from Jamaica in 1904.
He fought racial discrimination in
Britain, founding the pioneering
civil-rights organisation the
League of Coloured Peoples
in 1931. This bronze head was
cast from the original plaster
made by his brother, the artist
Ronald Moody.

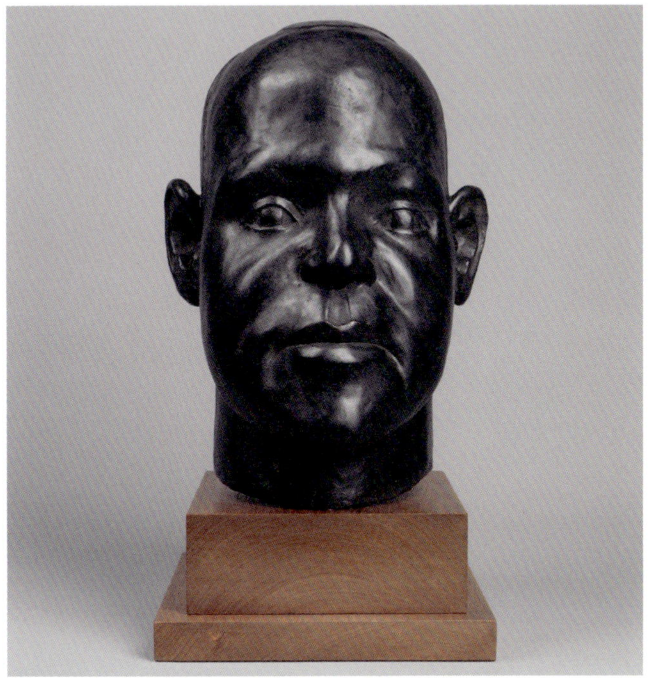

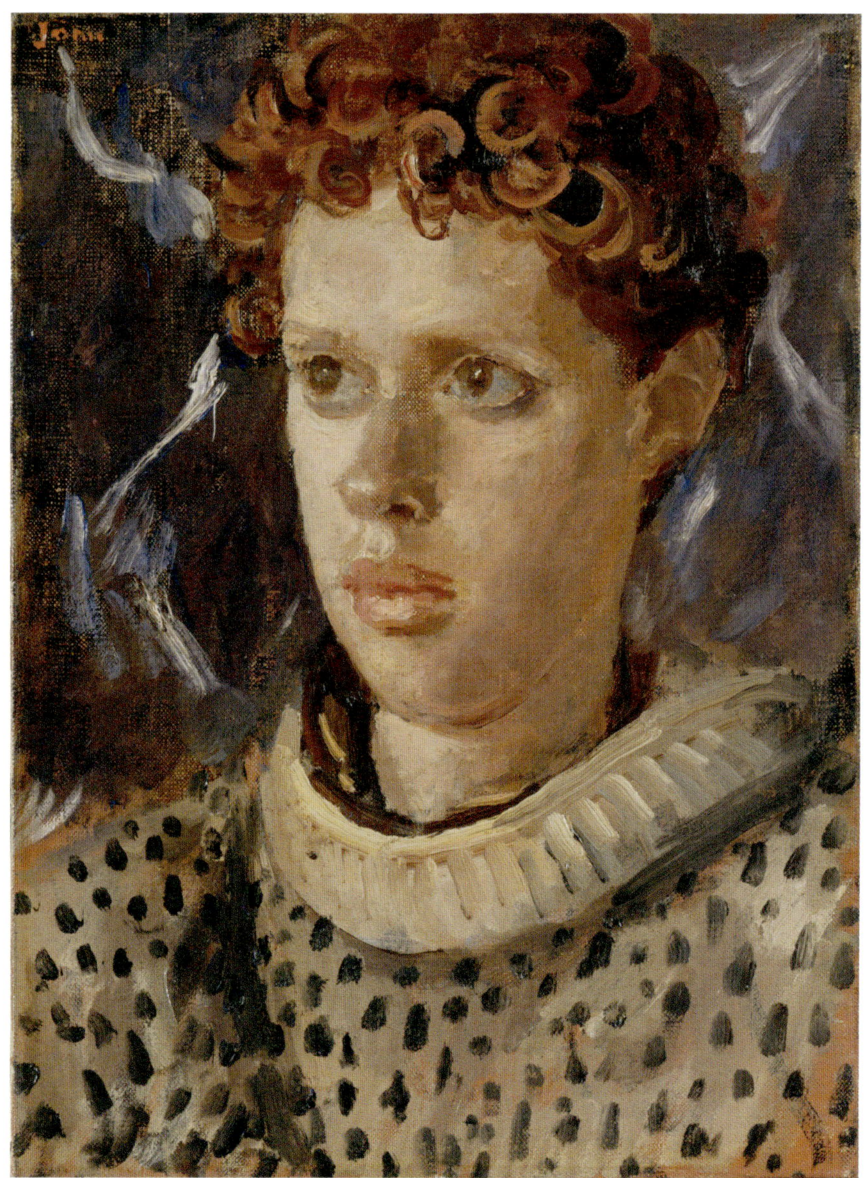

Dylan Thomas
(1914–53)
Augustus John, *c.*1937–8
Oil on canvas, 457 × 337mm
NPG 7049

This portrait resulted from a close friendship between the painter and the poet, both of whom were Welsh, after they met at the Fitzroy Tavern in London. Thomas's works include the play for voices *Under Milk Wood* (1954) and 'Do not go gentle into that good night' (1951).

**Sir Peter Pears and
Benjamin Britten**
(1910–86; 1913–76)
Kenneth Green, 1943
Oil on canvas, 715 × 969mm
NPG 5136

Britten is one of the most
distinguished British composers
of the twentieth century. His
life-partner, Pears, performed
the lead role in *Peter Grimes*
(1945), the first of Britten's ten
operas. *Billy Budd* (1951) was
commissioned for the Festival of
Britain, and his *War Requiem* for
the consecration of Coventry
Cathedral in 1962.

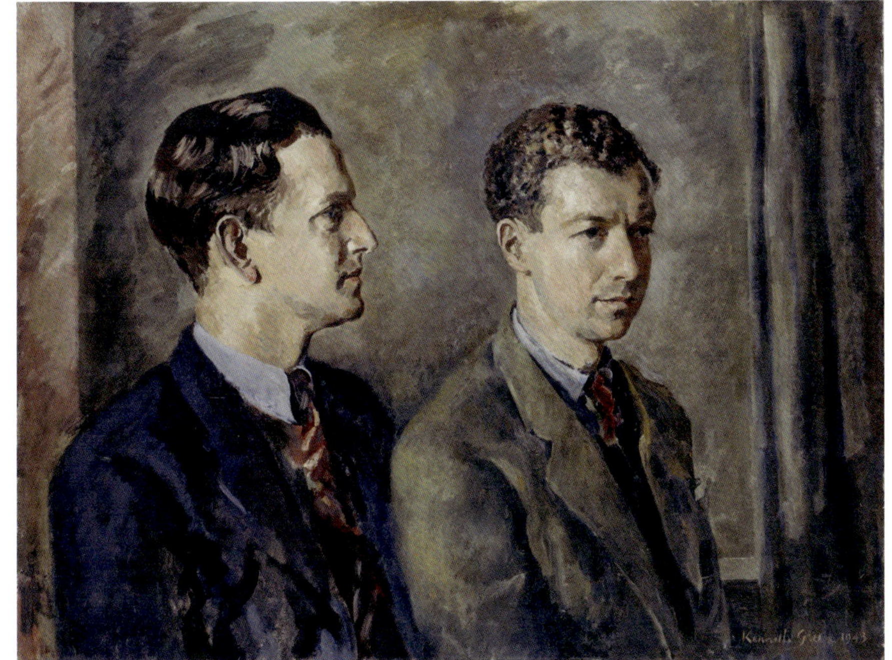

Beatrix Potter
(1866–1943)
Delmar Banner, 1938
Oil on canvas, 749 × 622mm
NPG 3635

Potter is one of the world's most
popular children's writers. *The
Tale of Peter Rabbit* (1901) was
followed by many further tales
featuring celebrated animal
characters. She lived in England's
Lake District and bequeathed
more than 4,000 acres of land
to the National Trust.

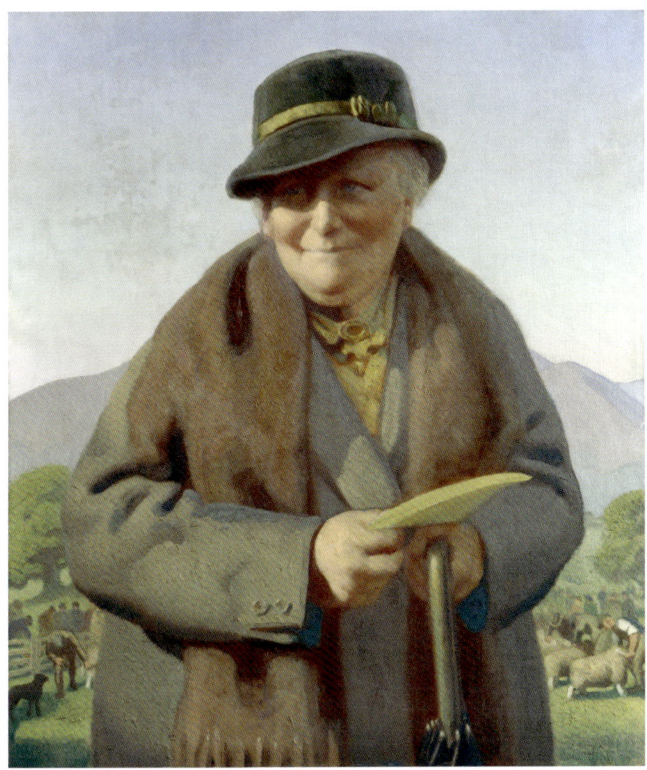

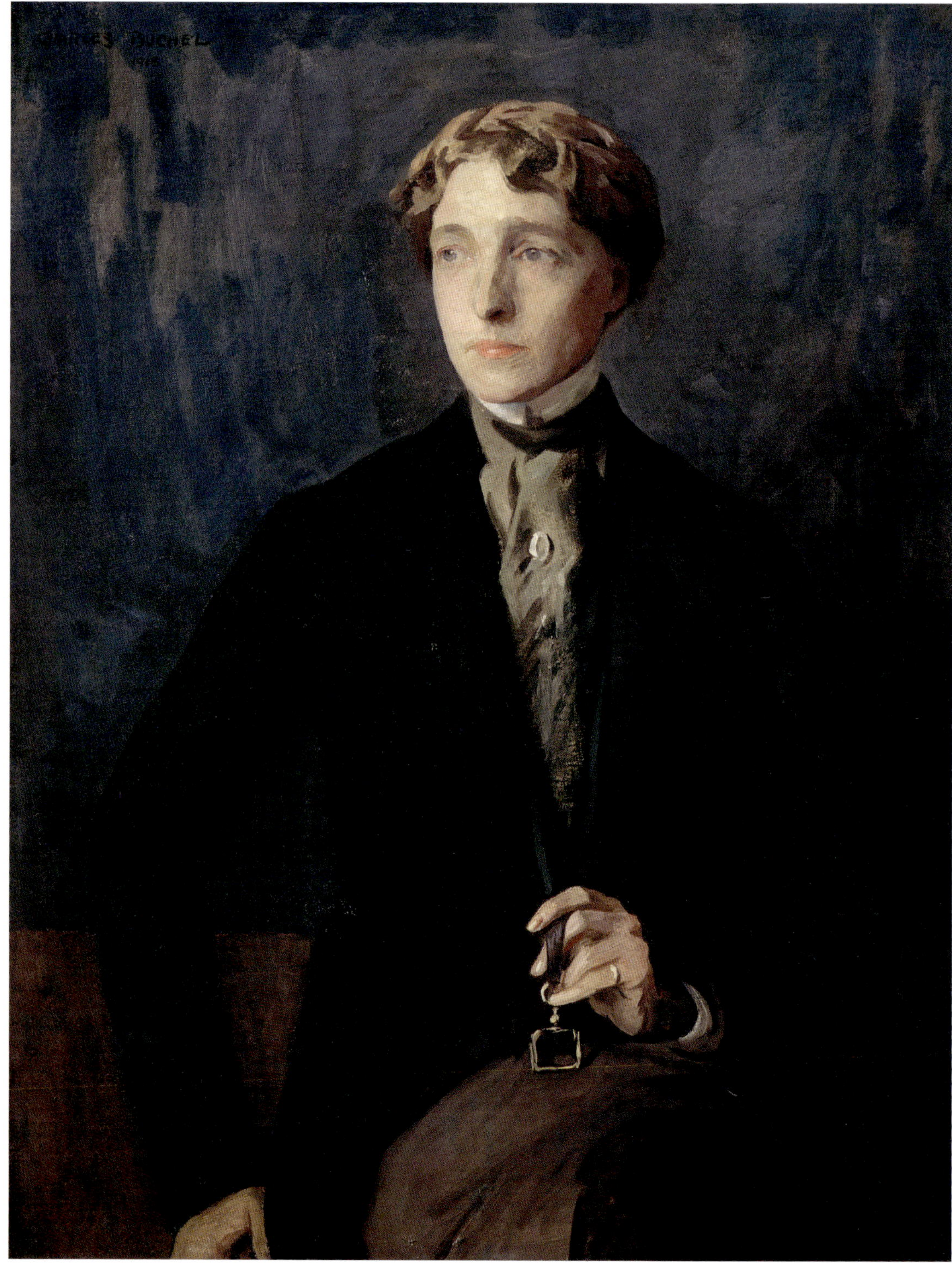

Radclyffe Hall
(1880–1943)
Charles Buchel, 1918
Oil on canvas, 914 × 711mm
NPG 4347

———————————————

Hall is famed for the pioneering
novel *The Well of Loneliness*
(1928), which portrays a lesbian
relationship. Believing herself to
be a man trapped in a woman's
body, the writer cultivated
a sophisticated masculine
appearance and stopped using
her birth name, Marguerite.

Gluck
(1895–1978)
Self-portrait, 1942
Oil on canvas, 306 × 254mm
NPG 6462

———————————————

Born Hannah Gluckstein, Gluck
adopted a gender-neutral name
in 1918. By that point, Gluck
was wearing men's clothes,
smoking a pipe and entering
into relationships with women.
Gluck studied at St John's Wood
School of Art from 1913 to 1916
and spent time at an artists'
colony in Lamorna, Cornwall,
working alongside Laura Knight.

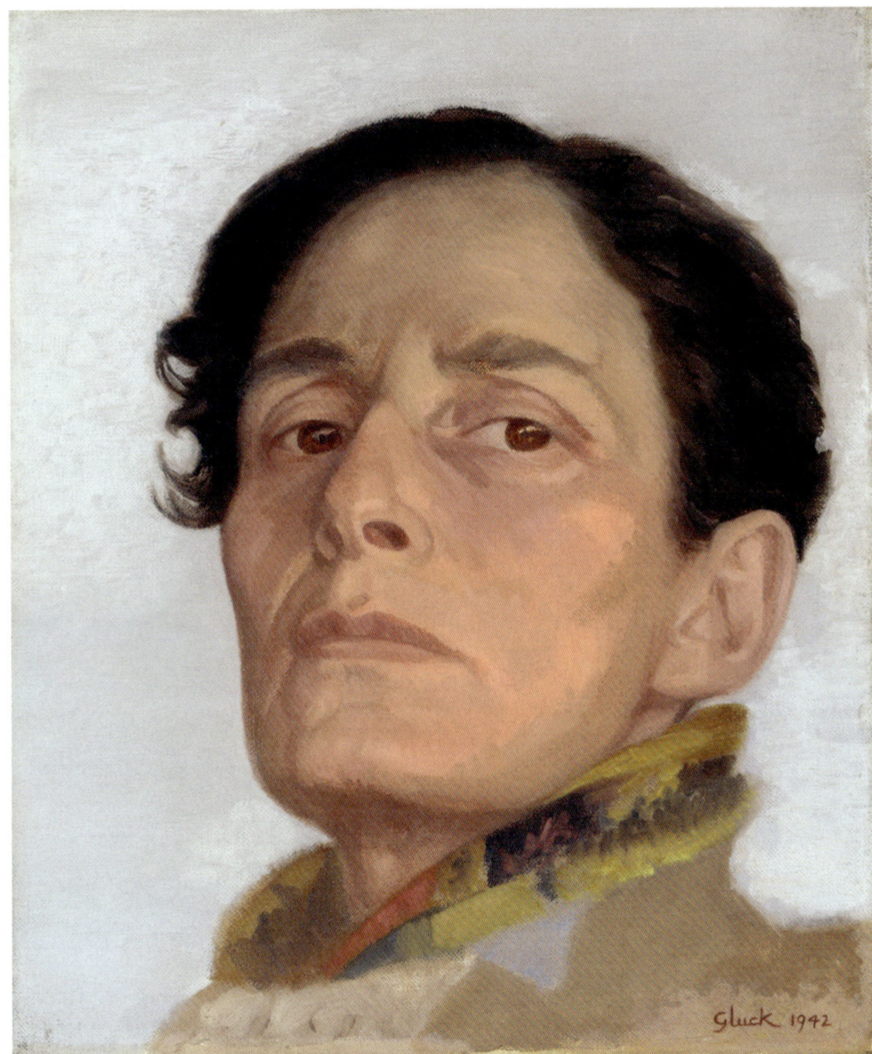

T.S. Eliot
(1888–1965)
Patrick Heron, 1949
Oil on canvas, 762 × 629mm
NPG 4467

The American-born Eliot was one of the twentieth century's
most important poets and a recipient of the Nobel Prize for
Literature in 1948. The genesis of this painting by Heron
(1920–99) was a drawing made from life on 4 March 1947.
Two months earlier, the young, relatively unknown painter
had written to Eliot asking whether he would be willing to
sit for a portrait. Encouraged by a positive response, Heron
visited Eliot in his office at the publishers Faber & Faber,
where Eliot was a director. An electricity crisis meant that
there was no heating, so Eliot wore a blue overcoat, which
can be seen in the completed painting.

Observing the writer of *The Waste Land* (1922) and *Four
Quartets* (1943), both landmarks in modern literature, Heron
recalled feeling that he was gazing 'into the very centre
of contemporary consciousness.' At that time, Heron's art
was influenced by Pierre Bonnard, Georges Braque, Henri
Matisse and Pablo Picasso, and their example is evident.
Subsequent drawings from life, and related experimental
studies, underpinned a progressively abstracted image
incorporating a double profile. The finished portrait drew
on observation but eventually was made, over a period of
nearly three years, from memory.

'I remember looking straight
into the grey eye of this
greatest of living writers, and
feeling that I was looking
into the most conscious eye
in the universe.'

Patrick Heron, 1988

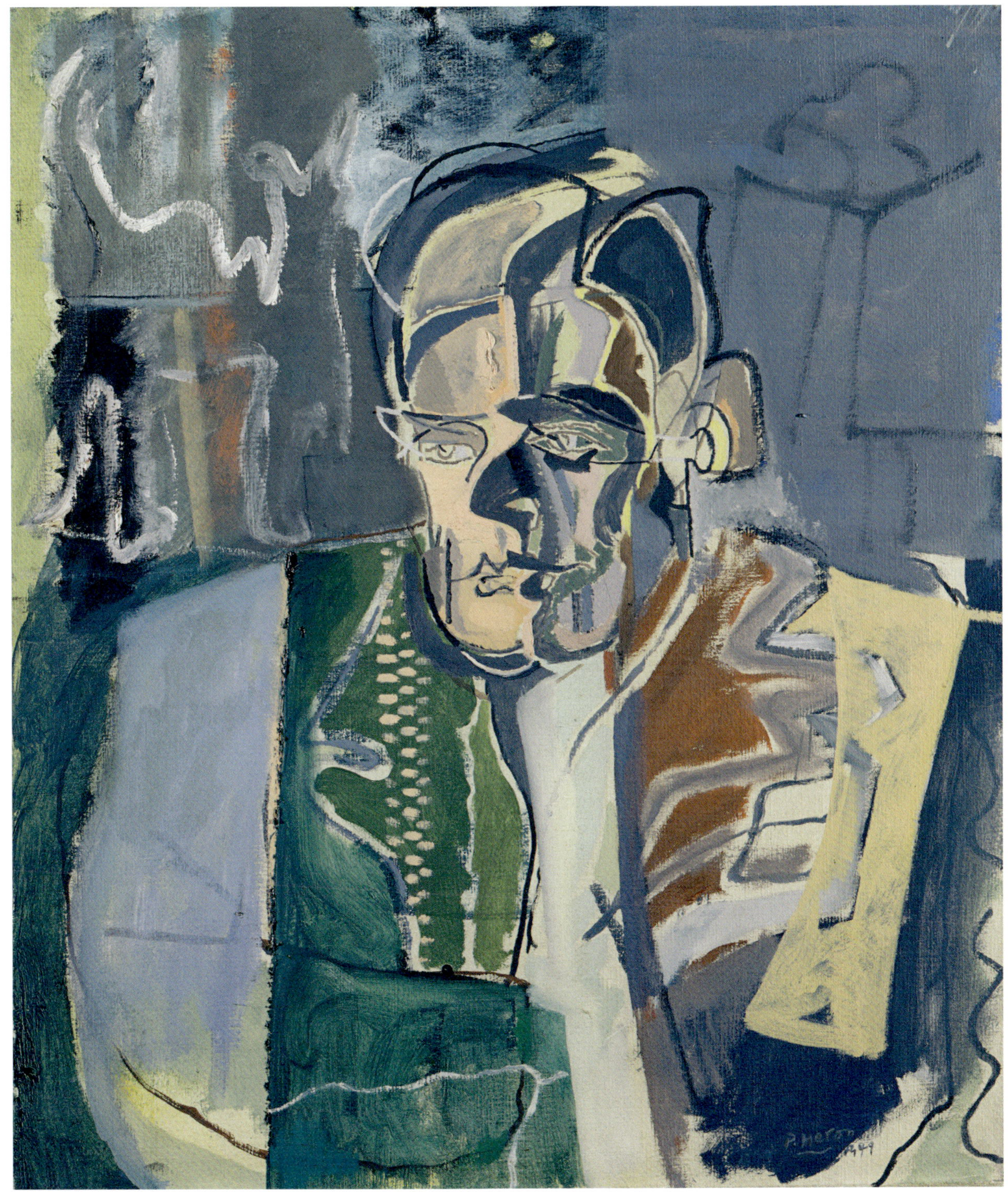

The Late Twentieth Century

The social and cultural transformation that took place in the decades following the Second World War continues to impact all aspects of life in the UK today, from the introduction of the National Health Service in 1948 to the invention of the World Wide Web in 1989.

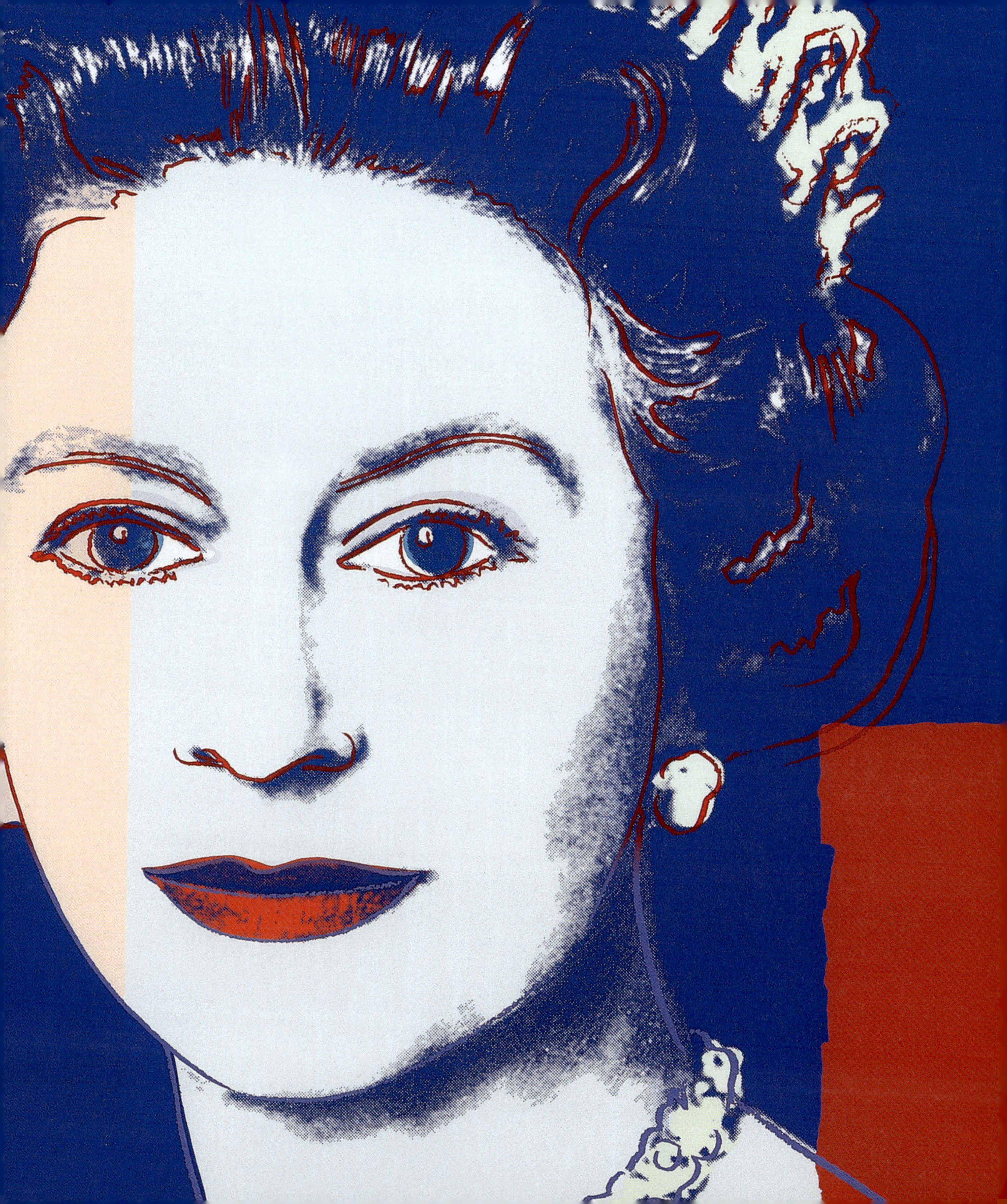

A New Britain

The UK emerged from the Second World War with victory but at a high social and economic cost. Post-war austerity saw an increase in rationing for some food products, which did not completely end until 1954, two years after the accession of Elizabeth II. The 1945 Labour government implemented the welfare state, founding the National Health Service and nationalising industries and transport. A broad political consensus about the role of the state continued until Britain's first female prime minister, Margaret Thatcher, initiated free-market reforms and privatisation in the 1980s.

The post-war period witnessed the dismantling of the British Empire as the demands of colonised peoples for independence became overwhelming in light of their vital role in the Allied victory. India secured independence in 1947 and was partitioned to create Pakistan, but brutal colonial conflicts continued. In some countries, the legacy of colonisation included further political instability and violence.

The shrinking of the UK's global power was underlined by the defeat against Egypt in the Suez Crisis of 1956. Although it was no longer a superpower, the UK developed an independent nuclear arsenal and was closely allied with the United States during the Cold War with the Soviet Union. Major British conflicts of the later decades include the Falklands War (1982) and Gulf War (1990–1). Within the British Isles, Northern Ireland suffered from decades of intense sectarian violence prior to the Belfast Agreement of 1998.

Migration to the UK from South Asia, Africa and the Caribbean increased following the 1948 British Nationality Act, which gave British citizenship to people from colonised nations. Encouraged by the government to boost the UK workforce, immigration enriched and challenged British cultural identity. Discrimination against immigrant communities began to be addressed through Race Relations Acts but racism and outbreaks of racial tension continued to be experienced.

In general, society became more liberal and tolerant, with the abolition of the death penalty, decriminalisation of male homosexuality and increased opportunities and freedoms for women. A changing society was reflected through creativity and culture, with new forms of expression in music, fashion and art. Portraiture was transformed by Pop artists such as Andy Warhol and David Hockney in the 1960s, and the Young British Artists of the 1990s. Photography enabled an ever-increasing saturation of imagery in daily life and photographers became crucial agents in turning actors, musicians and sports people into celebrities.

Immense scientific and technological developments included the discovery of the structure of DNA, which revealed the key building block of life, and the expansion of commercial aviation through the power of the jet engine. Computer pioneers from Alan Turing to Tim Berners-Lee revolutionised information and communication. By the century's end, the impact of human activity on the environment was increasingly understood. Acid rain, deforestation and the depletion of the ozone layer prompted public demands for stronger action to protect life on Earth.

Twiggy
(b.1949)
Barry Lategan, 1966
Gelatin silver print,
428 × 382mm
NPG x133189

Launched by a famous 'little-boy' haircut, Twiggy (born Lesley Hornby) was the most famous model of her era. As both 'British Woman of the Year' and the 'Face of 1966', Twiggy was the embodiment of the Sixties look. She was made a dame in 2019 for services to fashion, the arts and charity.

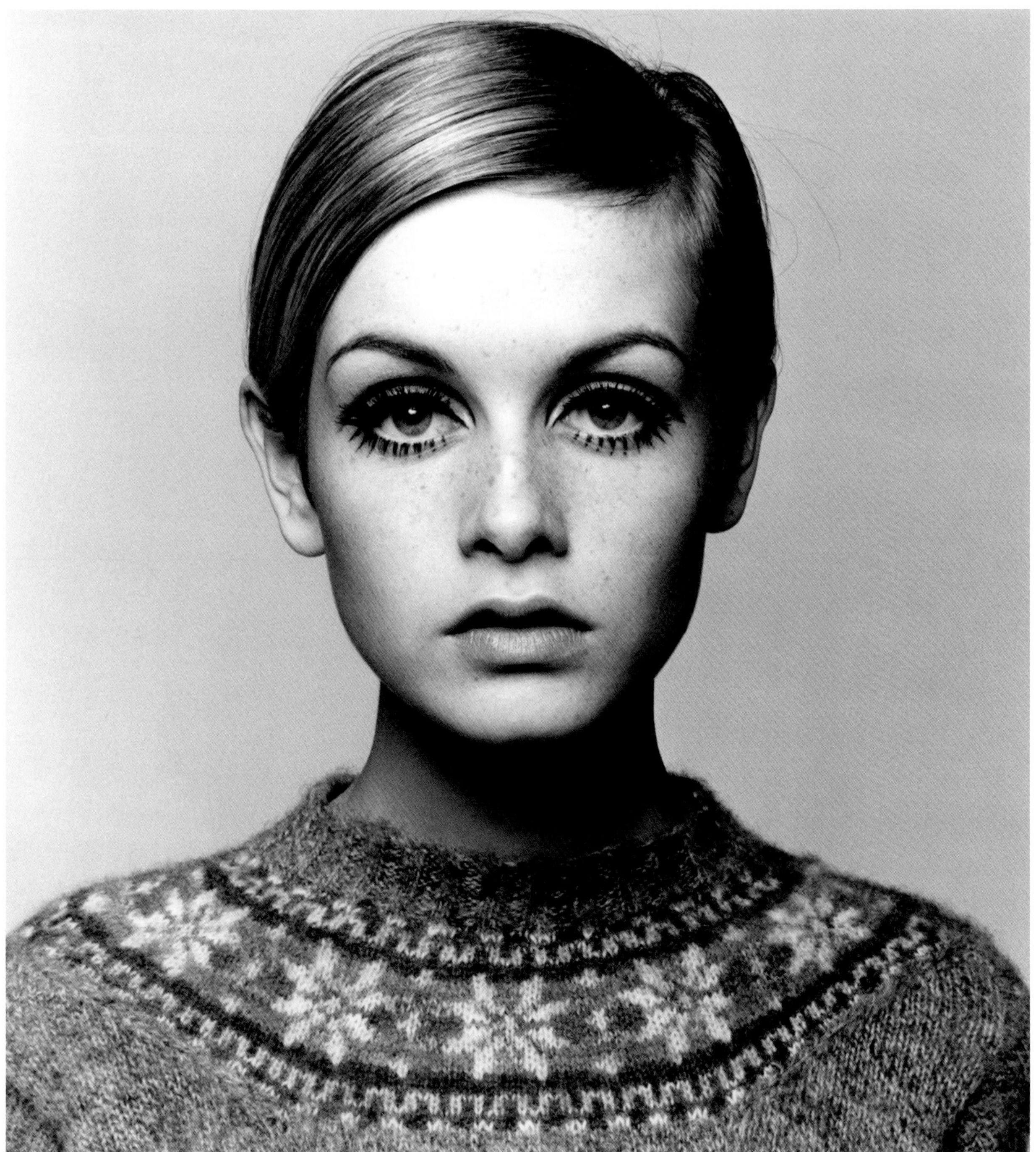

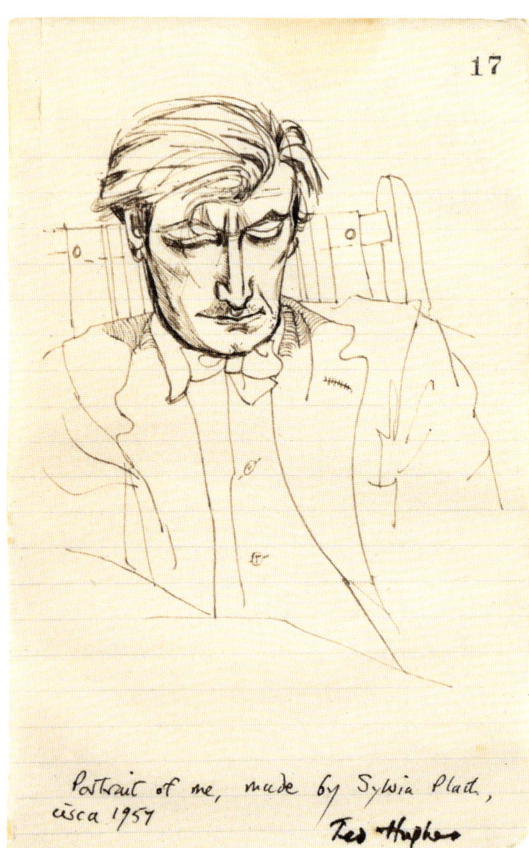

Ted Hughes
(1930–98)
Sylvia Plath, c.1957
Pen and ink on paper,
213 × 130mm
NPG 6739

———————————————

West Yorkshire-born Hughes wrote poems addressing humanity's connection with nature and animals, often intimating the violence of that relationship. This sketch was made by his first wife, the American writer Plath. The couple were married from 1956 until 1963, when Plath took her own life.

Audrey Hepburn
(1929–93)
Cecil Beaton, 1954
Gelatin silver print,
256 × 234mm
NPG x40179

———————————————

The Belgian-born actor made her first appearance on Broadway in 1951 and played small parts in British films before Hollywood stardom saw her become a beloved style icon. Hepburn's grace, charm and beauty were praised in films such as *Roman Holiday* (1953), *Breakfast at Tiffany's* (1961) and *My Fair Lady* (1964).

Alan Turing
(1912–54)
Elliott & Fry, 1951
Gelatin silver print, 161 × 117mm
NPG x27078

———————————————

Turing is considered to be the father of modern computing. He played a pivotal role in ending the Second World War by cracking the Enigma code used by the Germans. Turing's computing career was cut short when he was arrested for homosexuality in 1952. Having been forced to take hormonal treatment, he took his own life aged 41.

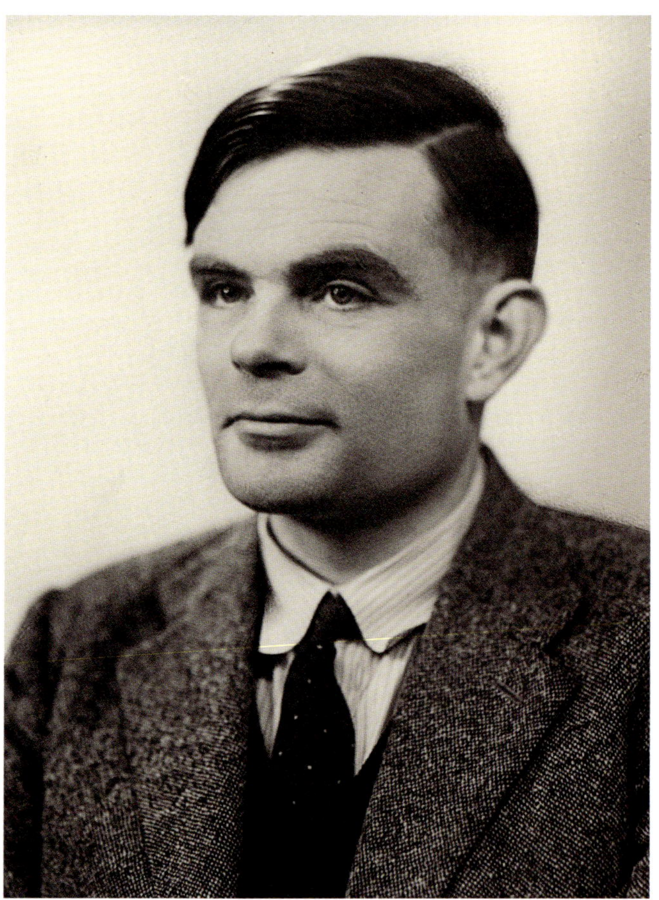

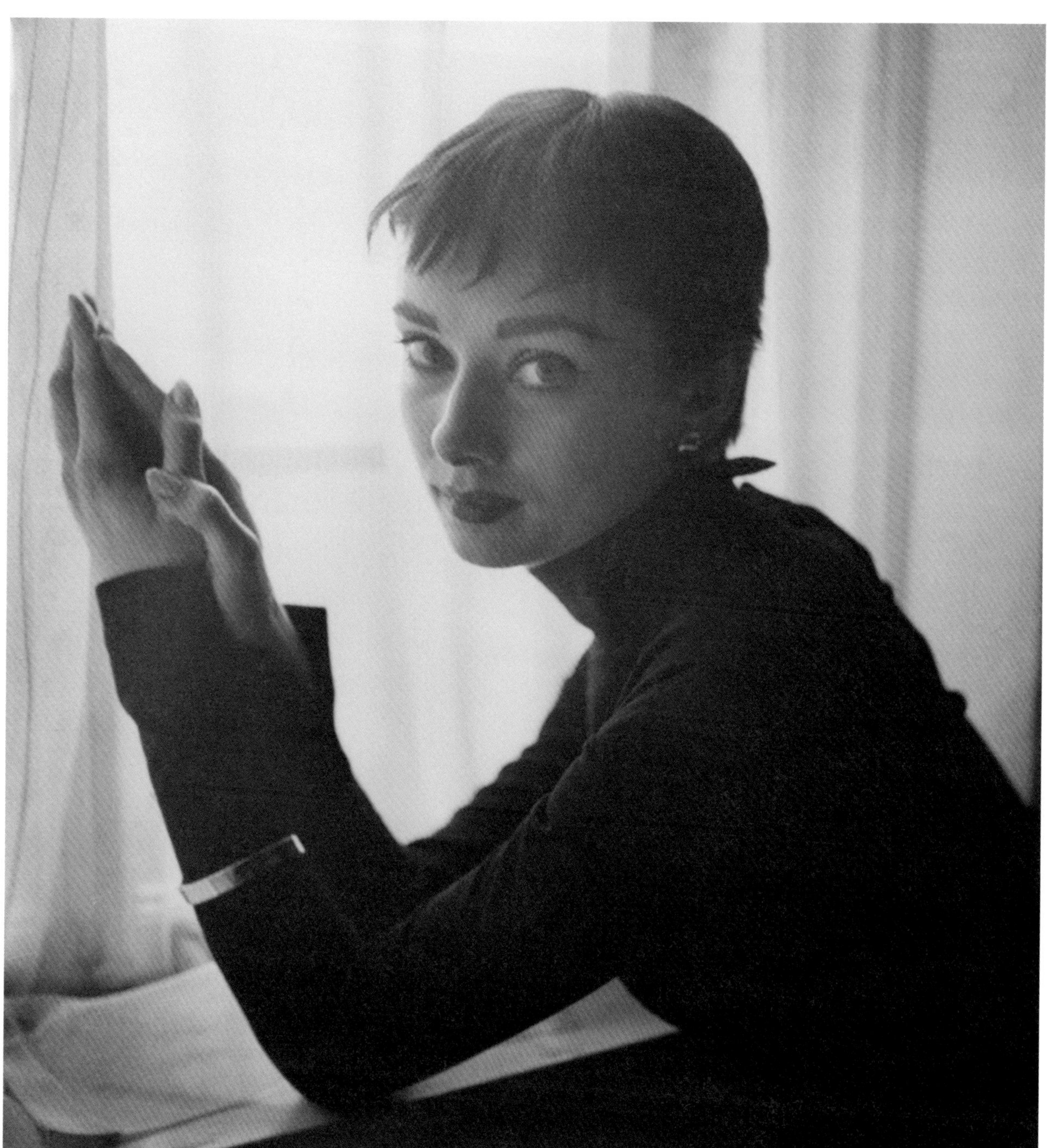

Lucian Freud
(1922–2011)
Self-portrait, 1963
Oil on canvas, 305 × 251mm
NPG 5205

Freud, grandson of the psychoanalyst Sigmund Freud, was
born in Berlin and emigrated to England with his family in
1933 to escape the rise of Nazism. He briefly attended the
Central School of Arts and Crafts in London and was also
taught for a period by Cedric Morris, who influenced Freud's
early precise style of painting.

In the late 1950s, he began to adopt a looser, more
animated style, using hog's hair brushes to build up a heavily
textured surface. The result of many hours spent with sitters,
his closely observed figurative works are unflinching in their
realism. The subjects are often naked and the scrutiny with
which Freud portrayed the human body distinguished him
amongst fellow artists in the twentieth century.

Freud produced many self-portraits, and this is the
last of three painted in quick succession in 1963. It is an
early example of the broadly painted, expressive style that
characterised his mature period. Turning his uncompromising
gaze upon himself, Freud stares out from the canvas with
arresting directness, but his features are abstracted,
almost mask-like.

The presence of the artist is implicit throughout his oeuvre,
which includes portraits of lovers, friends and children, all of
whom sat for him at his studio. As Freud himself stated, 'My
work is purely autobiographical.'

'My work is purely auto-
biographical. It is about
myself and my surroundings.
It is an attempt at a record.
I work from the people that
interest me and that I care
about, in rooms that I live in
and know.'

Lucian Freud, 1974

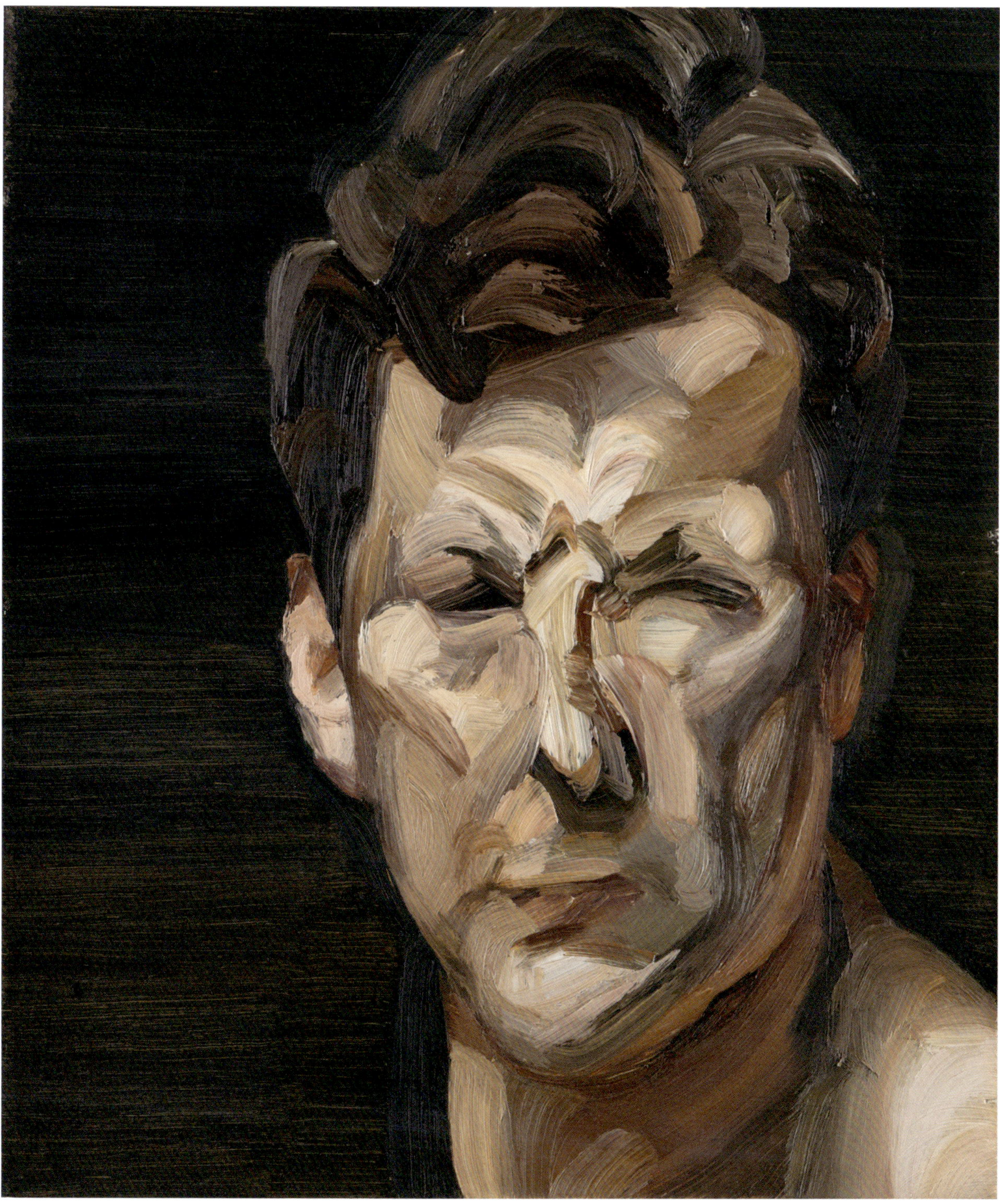

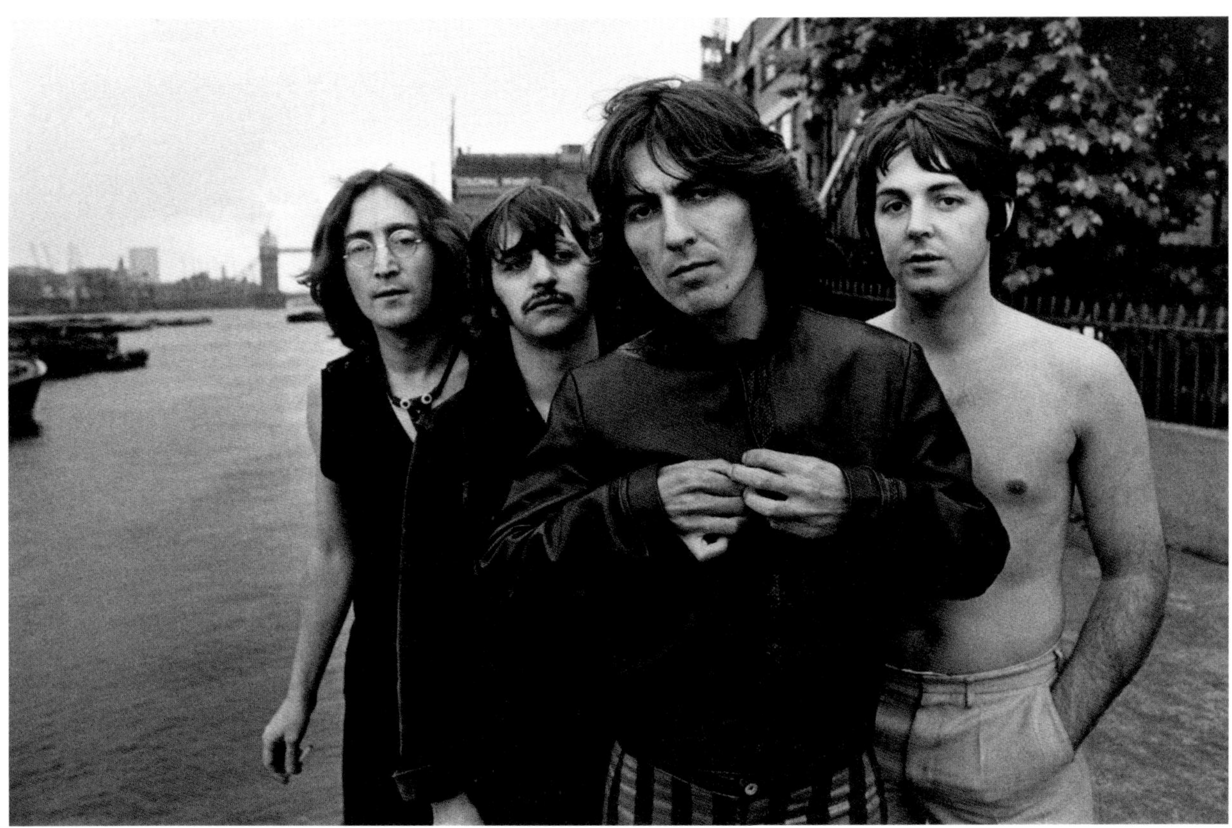

The Beatles
Don McCullin, 1968
Gelatin silver print,
320 × 480mm
NPG P1382

The Beatles were formed
in 1960 and dominated the
international music scene for
the next decade, becoming
arguably the most influential
band in the history of popular
music. This gritty photograph
was taken at Wapping Head
Pier in London by McCullin, an
esteemed war photographer.

Sonia Boyce
(b.1962)
Pogus Caesar, 1983
Gelatin silver print,
250 × 350mm
NPG x200717

Boyce became a pivotal figure
in the 1980s British black arts
movement, a radical group of
artists inspired by anti-racism
and feminism. Caeser admired
how 'her art transcends so
many boundaries'. In 2022,
Boyce won the Golden Lion
prize at the Venice Biennale.

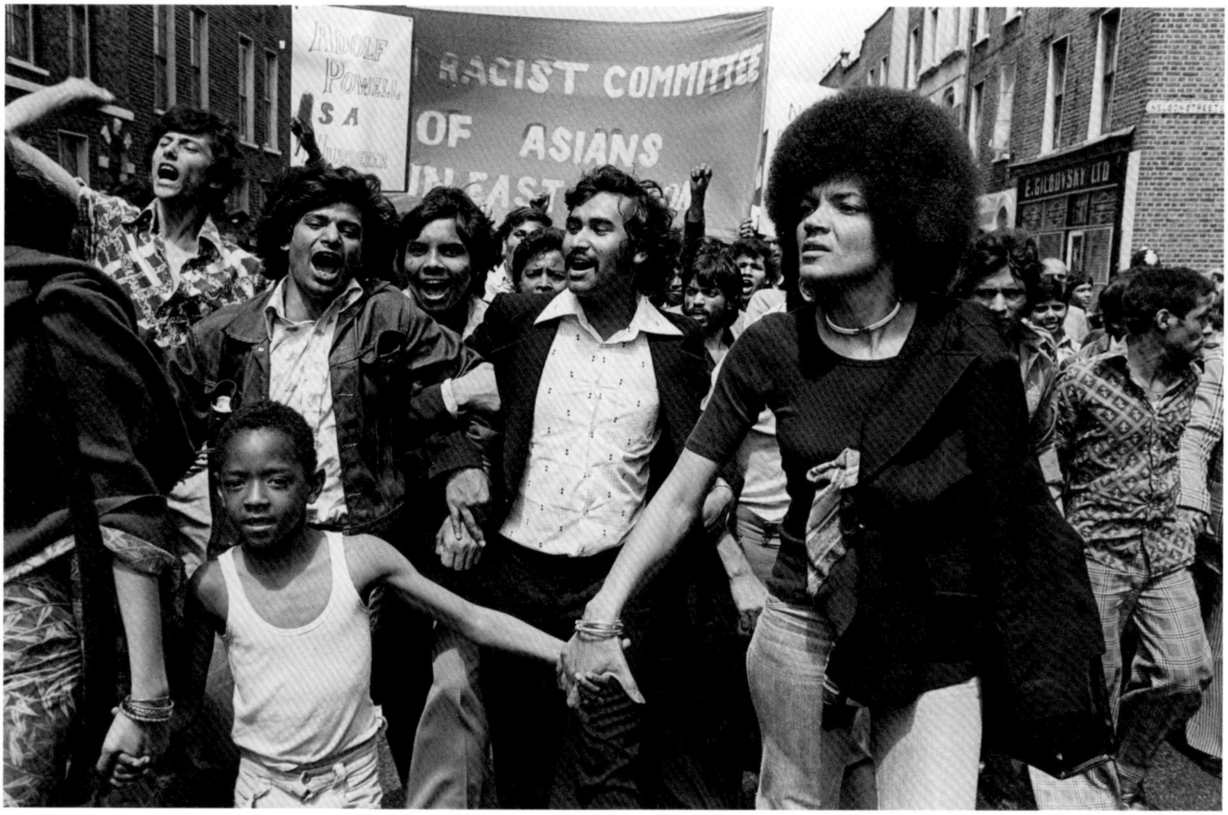

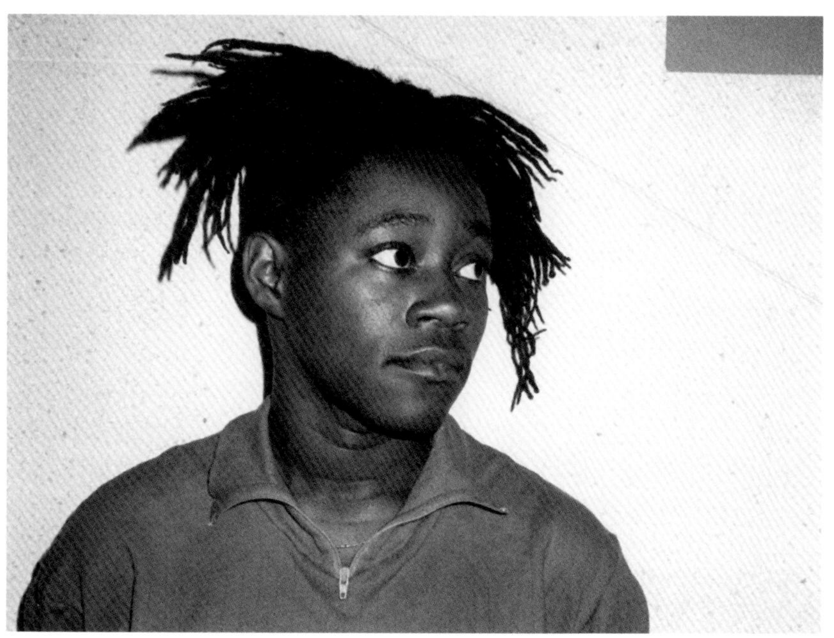

**Anti-racism demonstration,
Brick Lane, London**
Paul Trevor, 1976
Pigment print, 314 × 470mm
NPG x201507

In June 1976, the racially
motivated murder of Gurdip
Singh Chaggar sparked a series
of protests by British South
Asians. Trevor documented
the racial abuse endured by
the community, as well as
the activists who mobilised in
support of the protests, including
Barbara Beese, member of the
Mangrove Nine, who can be
seen here with her son Darcus.

David Bowie
(1947–2016)
Brian Duffy, 1973
Chromogenic print,
197 × 197mm
NPG x137463

Born David Robert Jones in Brixton, south London,
singer-songwriter Bowie is one of the most influential
figures in modern British popular culture. He gained
recognition with his single 'Space Oddity' (1969), the release
of which coincided with the first moon landing, and achieved
international fame with his rock albums *The Rise and Fall
of Ziggy Stardust and the Spiders from Mars* (1972) and
Aladdin Sane (1973). Bowie's music career spanned more
than five decades, with his final album, *Blackstar*, released
just two days before his death in 2016. He pioneered
an experimental approach to identity, characterised by
continual reinvention.

Renowned for his distinctive make-up, costumes and
theatrical performances, Bowie appeared as one of his
flamboyant stage alter-egos for the cover of his sixth album,
Aladdin Sane. A pose from the same shoot, showing Bowie
with his eyes closed, was used on the album cover. It has
become one of the most recognisable and celebrated of pop
images. Duffy (1936–2010), a fashion, music and advertising
photographer who came to prominence during the 1960s,
is one of the photographers who helped to define the era,
along with David Bailey and Terence Donovan. He also
photographed Bowie for the covers of his albums *Lodger*
(1979) and *Scary Monsters (and Super Creeps)* (1980).

'Tomorrow belongs to those
who can hear it coming.'

David Bowie, 1977

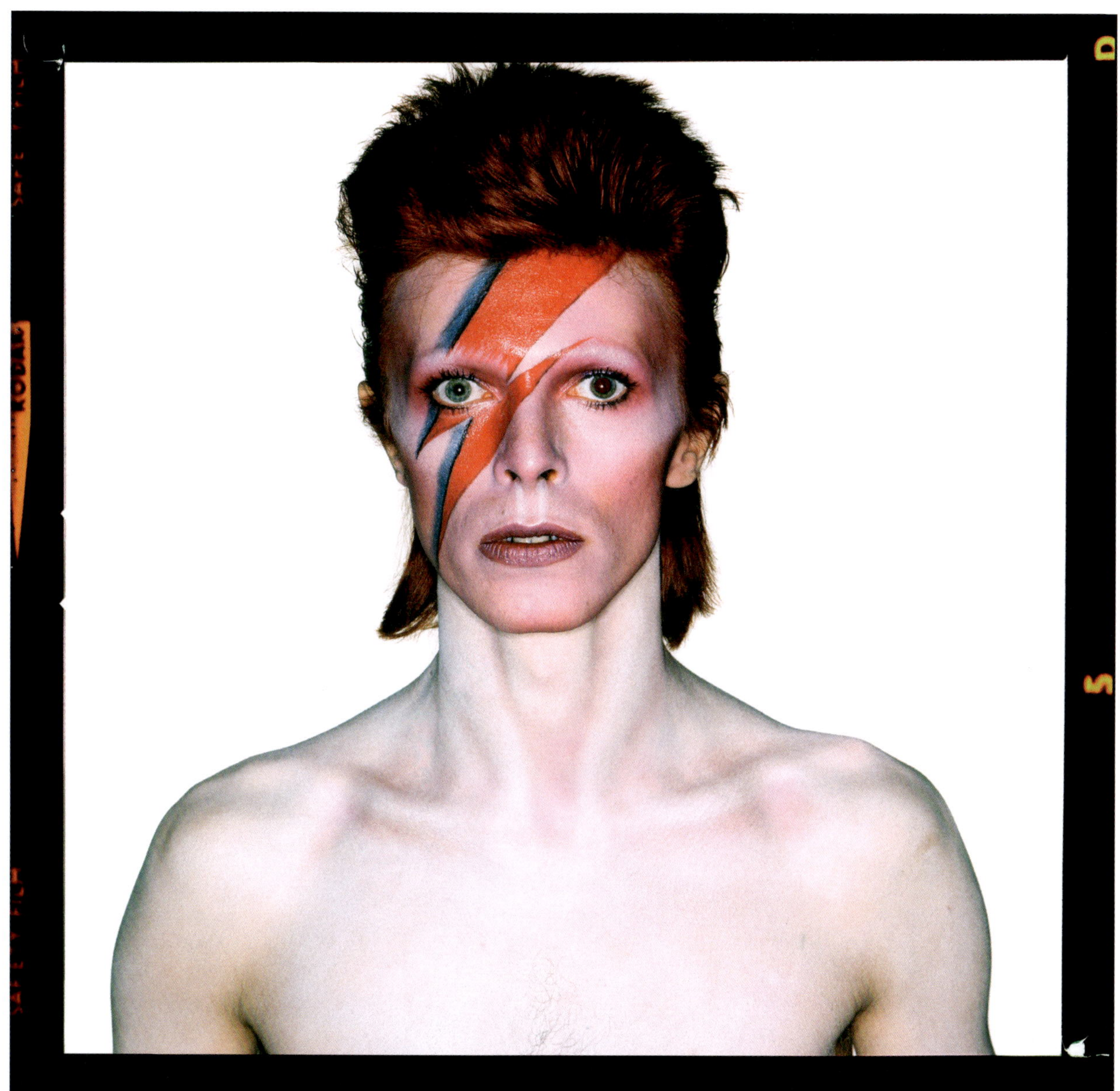

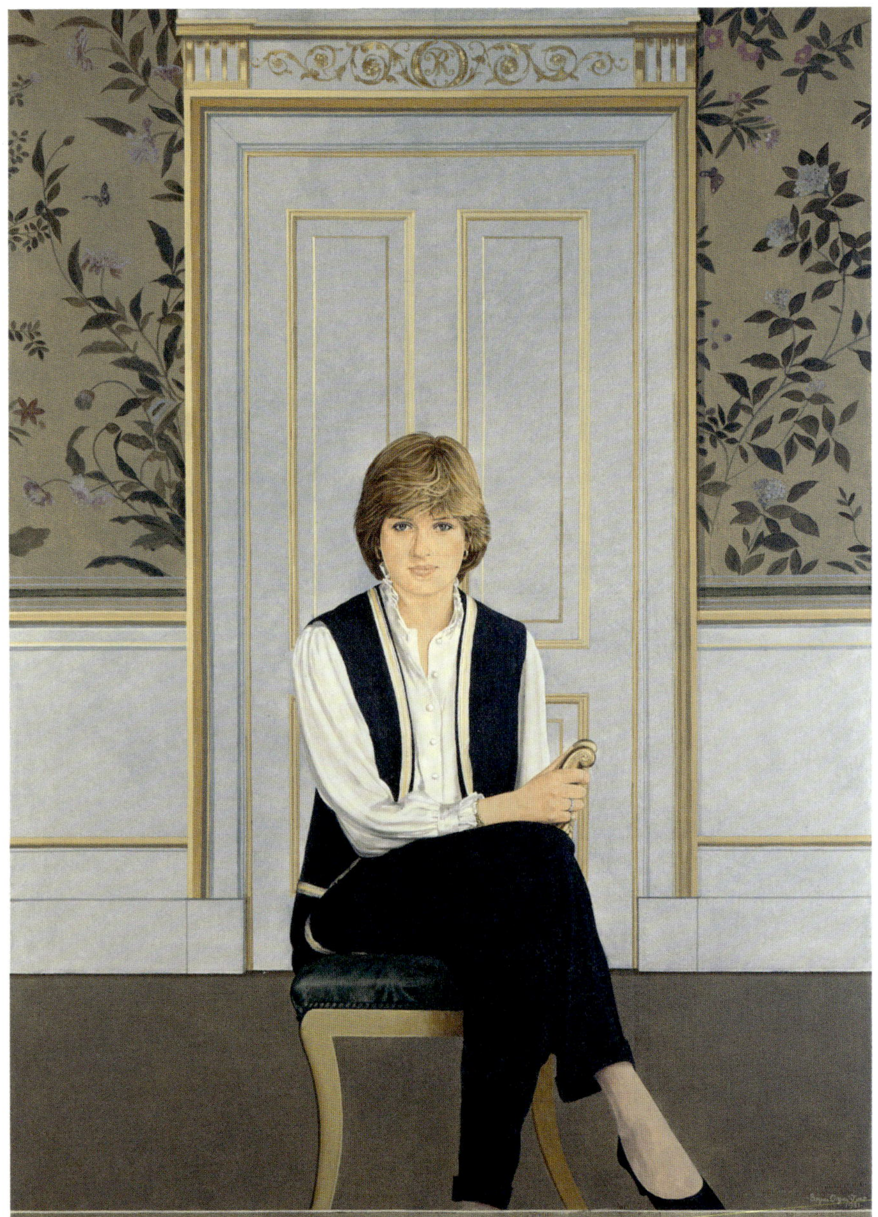

Diana, Princess of Wales
(1961–97)
Bryan Organ, 1981
Acrylic on canvas,
1778 × 1270mm
NPG 5408

Diana, Princess of Wales, brought a refreshing new image to the British royal family. Renowned for her charity work, she raised awareness of AIDS and the use of landmines. She had two sons, the princes William and Harry, with Charles, Prince of Wales, now King Charles III. Her tragic death in 1997 caused widespread mourning.

Queen Elizabeth II
(1926–2022)
Andy Warhol, 1985
Silkscreen prints,
1000 × 800mm each
NPG 5882(1–4)

Elizabeth II became queen aged 25 in 1952. Her 70-year reign, during a period of great social and technological change, was the longest in British history. This iconic set of portraits by the American artist Warhol reflects the sheer quantity of images that exist of the queen and emphasises the commodification of individual likenesses in a media-focussed world.

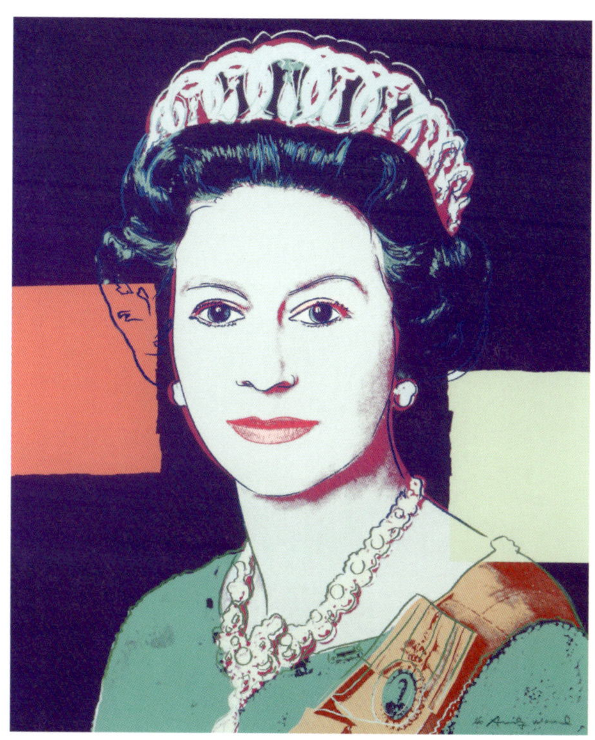
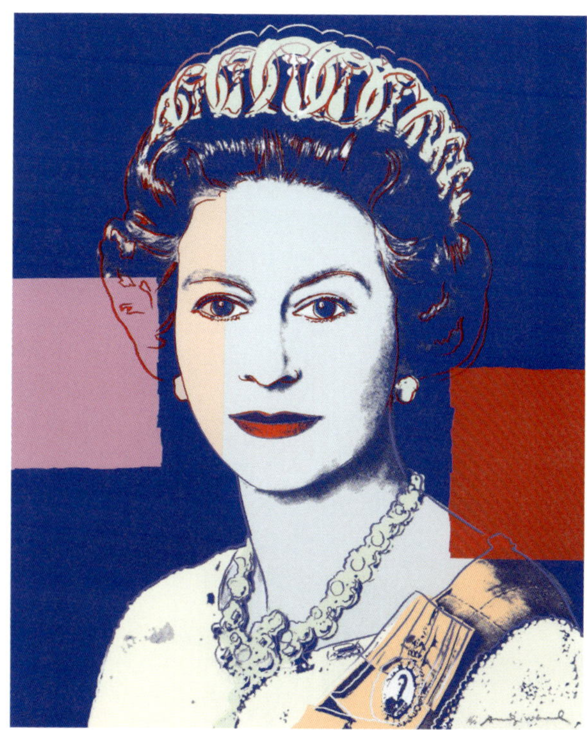
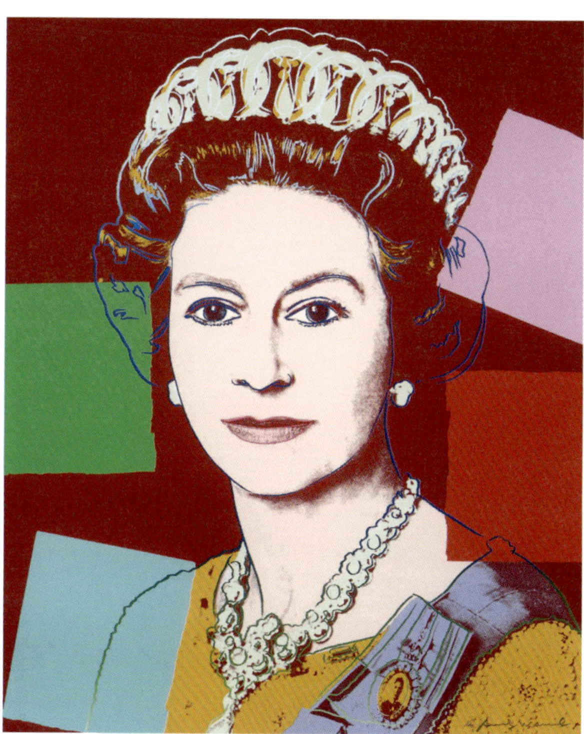
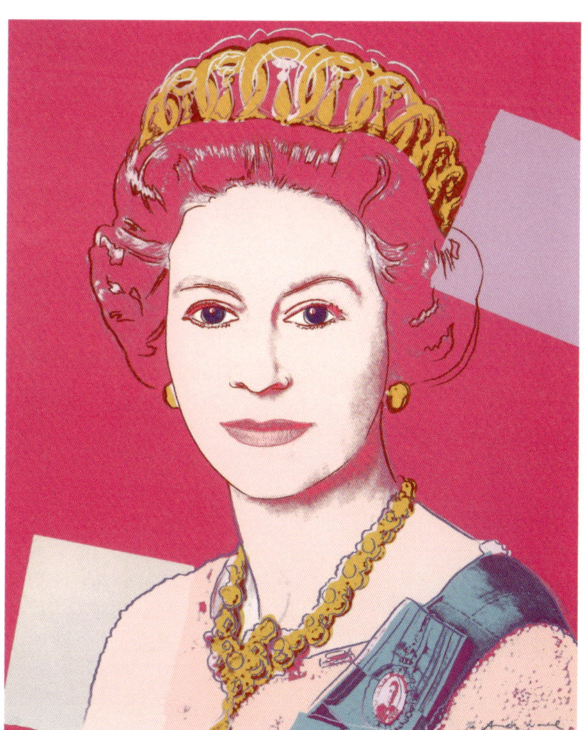

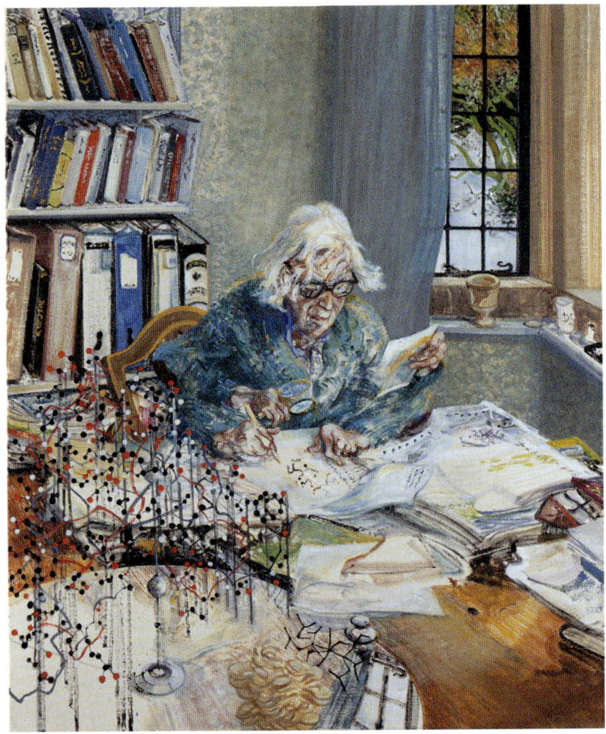

Dorothy Hodgkin
(1910–94)
Maggi Hambling, 1985
Oil on canvas, 932 × 760mm
NPG 5797

The first British woman to win the Nobel Prize for Chemistry (1964), Hodgkin was able to define the structure of penicillin (1949), Vitamin B12 (1956) and insulin (1969), transforming their therapeutic potential. Hambling's portrait conveys Hodgkin's energy and activity, and includes a structural model of insulin.

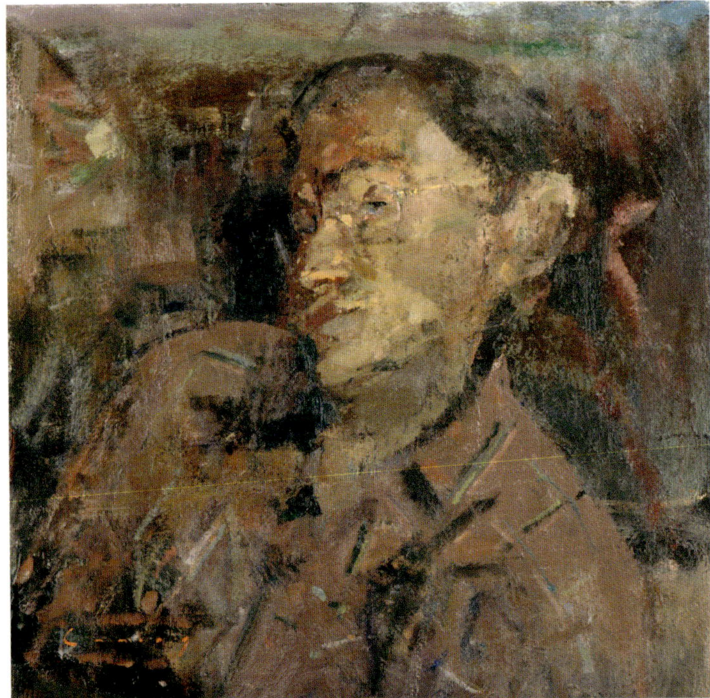

Stephen Hawking
(1942–2018)
Fred Cuming, 2005
Oil on board, 610 × 610mm
NPG 6764

A mathematician, theoretical physicist and cosmologist, Hawking made revolutionary contributions to science. His multiple publications include the best-selling *A Brief History of Time* (1988). He explained that his goal was to achieve 'a complete understanding of the universe, why it is as it is and why it exists at all'.

Germaine Greer
(b.1939)
Dame Paula Rego, 1995
Pastel on paper laid on
aluminium, 1200 × 1111mm
NPG 6351

Greer is an Australian-born
writer, broadcaster and critic,
whose book *The Female
Eunuch* (1970) is an important
feminist text. This portrait by
the internationally celebrated
artist Rego shows Greer
wearing her favourite dress,
designed by Jean Muir, and a
pair of worn-out shoes.

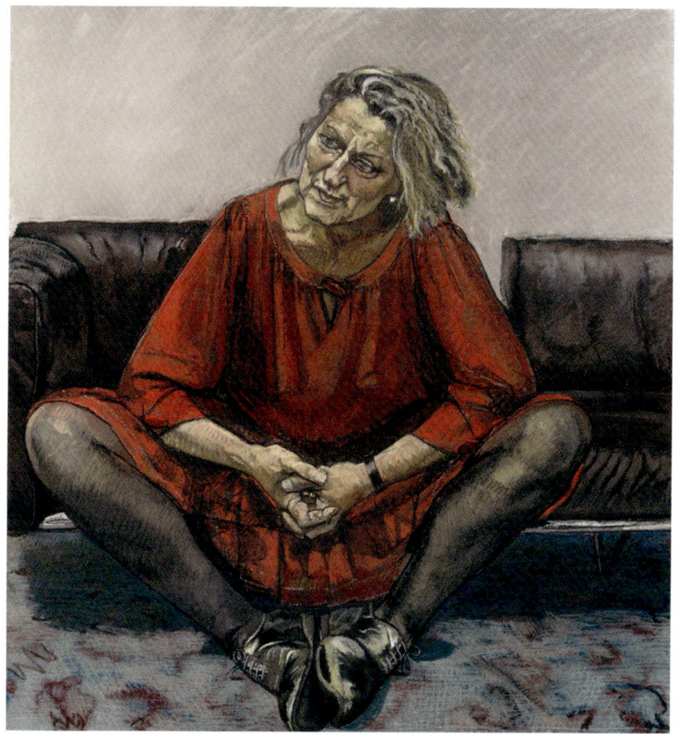

Salman Rushdie (*The Moor*)
(b.1947)
Bhupen Khakhar, 1995
Oil on linen, 1219 × 1219mm
NPG 6352

Rushdie is celebrated for
his novels set in the Indian
sub-continent, including
Midnight's Children (1981).
The Satanic Verses (1989)
is considered blasphemous
by some Muslims, which
has resulted in attempts on
Rushdie's life. This portrait
depicts scenes from his novel
The Moor's Last Sigh (1995).

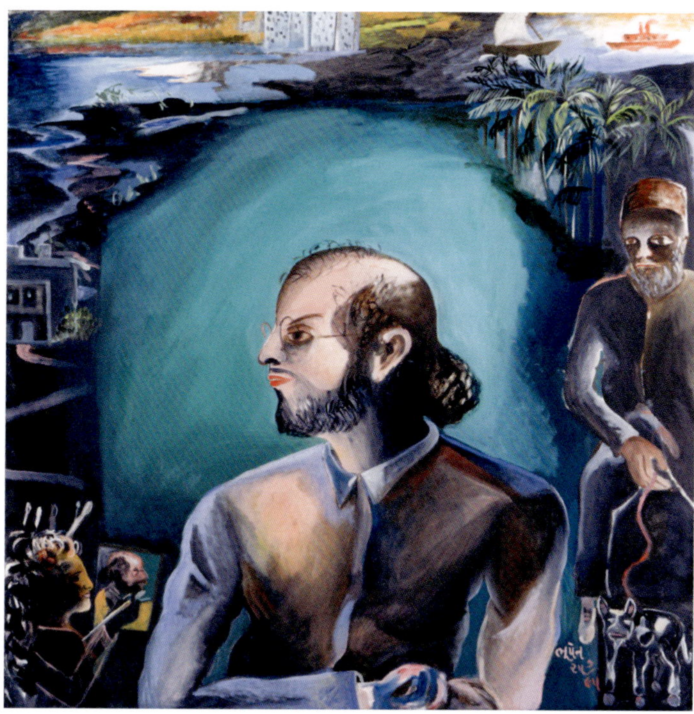

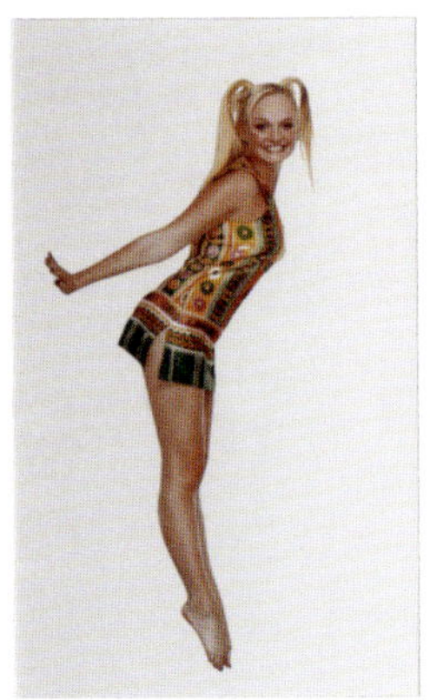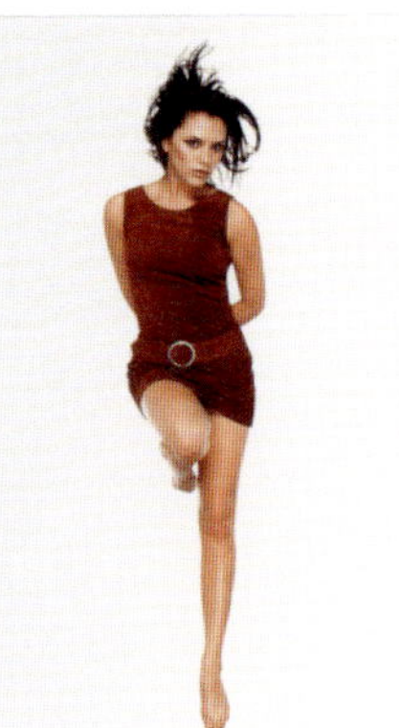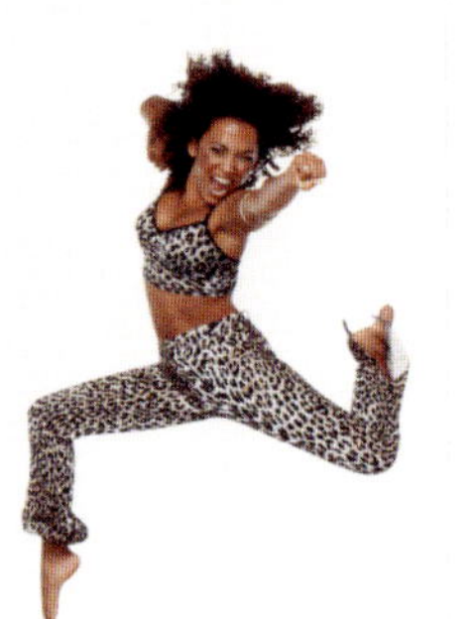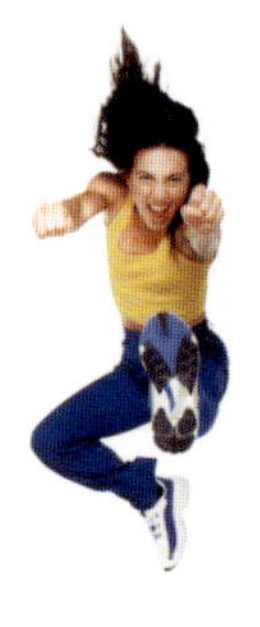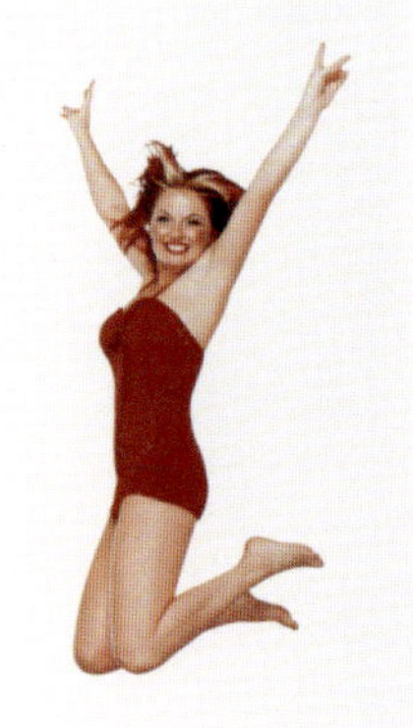

Spice Girls
Lorenzo Agius, 1997
Inkjet prints,
502 × 302mm each
NPG x88062

Promoting the triumphant slogan of 'girl power', the Spice Girls were the definitive girl group and most successful British pop act of the 1990s. Their debut single, 'Wannabe' (1996), topped the charts in 53 countries and was the first of six consecutive British number ones.

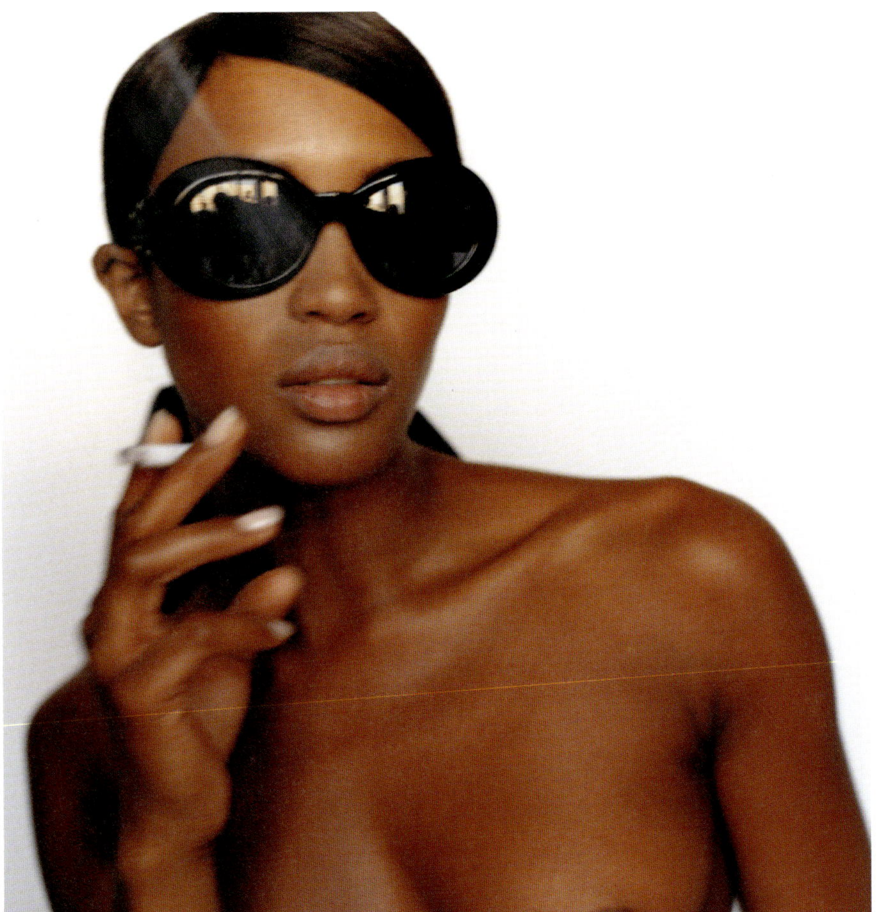

Naomi Campbell
(b.1970)
Mario Testino, 1996
Chromogenic print,
510 × 407mm
NPG P1012

Aged 17 years old, Campbell became the first black British model to feature on the cover of British *Vogue*. It was Campbell's first cover of many for the magazine, and she would go on to become one of the most iconic models in fashion.

Michael Clark
(b.1962)
Chris Garnham, 1984
Gelatin silver print,
294 × 290mm
NPG x26055

Clark is a trailblazing Scottish dancer. Aged 22,
he set up his own dance company, choreographing
scandalous punk performances to avant-garde music.
This photograph, showing Clark in various poses,
won Garnham the *Blitz* magazine Photographer
of the Year Award in 1984.

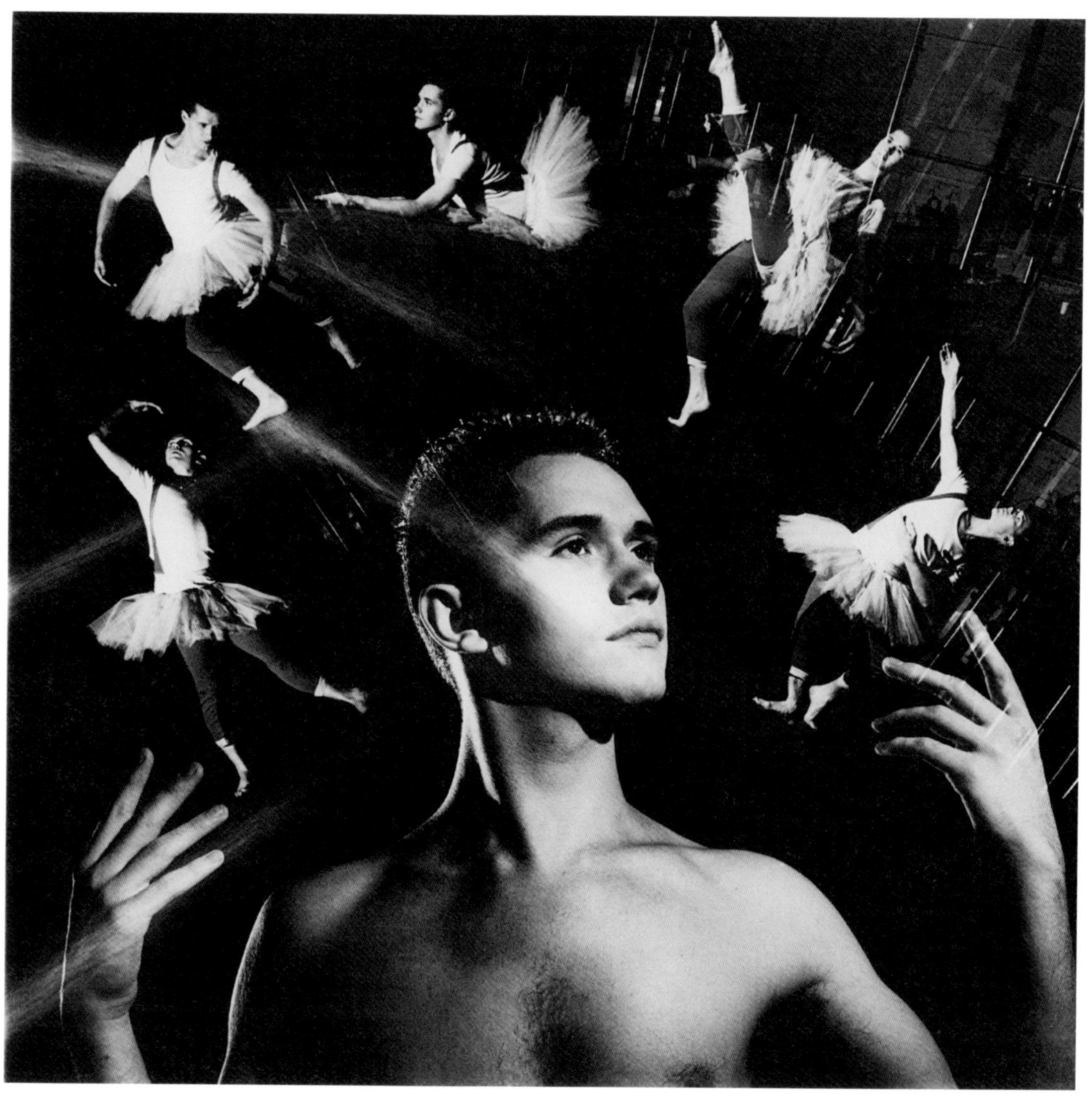

The Twenty-First Century

A rapid pace of social, technological and environmental change has characterised the twenty-first century. Today, British culture reflects the nation's complex, pluralistic and globalised society.

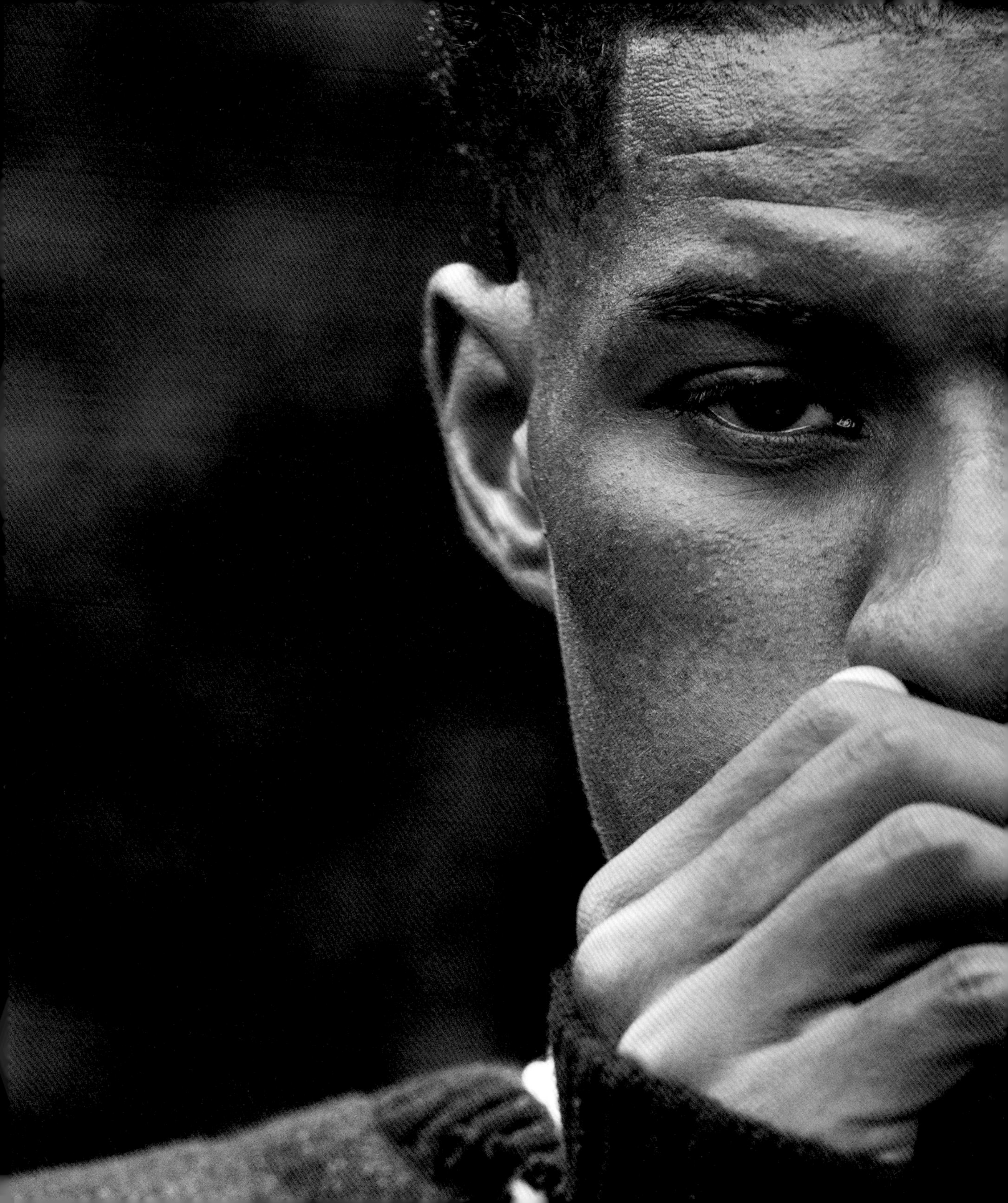

Contemporary Identities

Popular movements demanding change and legal liberalisations have been a prominent feature of the twenty-first century. Amongst the reforms carried out by the only Labour government to win three consecutive terms in office was the lowering of the age of consent for homosexual men, finally achieving legal equality between gay and heterosexual relationships. The subsequent Conservative government continued this trend by legalising same-sex marriage in 2014. Despite areas of progress, inequality and discrimination continue to be experienced by women, LGBTQIA+ and black, Asian and other minority groups.

Technology has played an ever-greater role in people's lives. During this period, the majority of the population has gained access to the internet and adopted mobile phones. Work, leisure and entertainment have increasingly taken place online. The emergence of new social and political movements have been facilitated by innovative and effective uses of social media, which have become a global phenomenon.

The process of decolonisation and the questioning of the UK's global role in the second half of the twentieth century continued into the new millennium. Britain's last major colony, Hong Kong, was handed over to China in 1997. Within the UK, some political powers were devolved to Scotland, Wales and Northern Ireland but nationalist movements continue to seek independence.

British support for the American-led invasions of Iraq and Afghanistan resulted in the deployment of hundreds of thousands of British troops. These conflicts were also a factor in terrorist attacks in the UK. Years of austerity followed the financial crisis of 2008. This contributed to a sense from some people of being 'left behind' by deindustrialisation and a globalised economy. Widespread concerns about British sovereignty led to a referendum vote to leave the European Union in 2016. Despite social differences, widely embraced moments of national unity were experienced during the 2012 London Olympic and Paralympic Games and the funeral of Elizabeth II in 2022, after 70 years on the throne.

The beginning of the 2020s was dominated by the COVID-19 pandemic. The virus has been associated with more than 200,000 deaths in the UK and resulted in national lockdowns. Beyond the pandemic, the effects of climate change, pollution and the loss of biodiversity have become increasingly urgent issues for the country to address.

Portraiture has reflected and responded to our multifaceted, ever-changing world. While structural imbalances persist, artists from diverse backgrounds, genders and ethnicities have increasingly achieved a level of recognition and success that was often denied to previous generations. Photography, digital and new media have further expanded artistic possibilities. The Gallery continues to play an important role in promoting and progressing portraiture, and commissioned many of the works in this chapter. Whether representing a household name or a less familiar face, these portraits encourage us to think about art, society and the continually evolving ways in which we define personal and national identity.

Thelma Golden and Duro Olowu (*Thelma & Duro*)
(b.1965; b.1965)
Catherine Opie, 2017
Pigment print, 1956 × 1473mm
NPG P2076

Olowu is a Nigerian-born British fashion designer and curator. His designs are celebrated for their cross-cultural aesthetic and he was named New Designer of the Year in 2005. Olowu is married to Golden, Director of the Studio Museum in Harlem, New York, who is shown here wearing his designs.

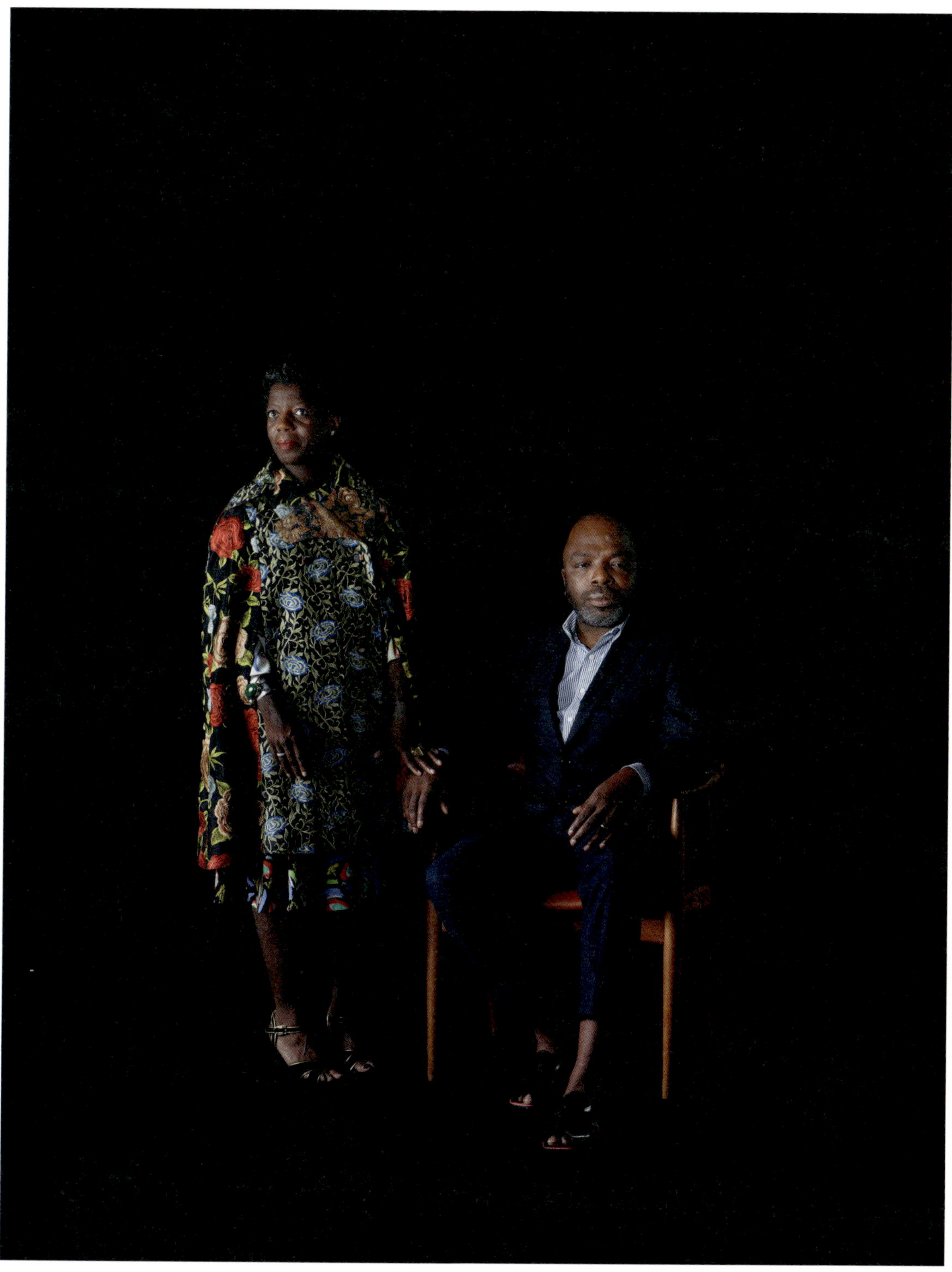

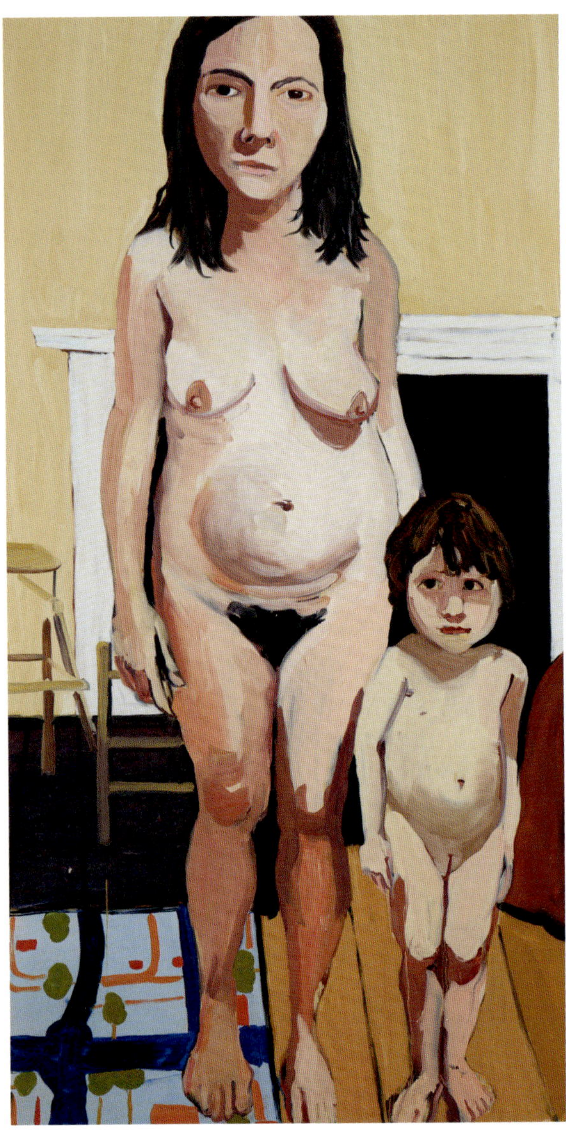

Chantal Joffe (*Self-Portrait with Esme*)
(b.1969)
Self-portrait, 2008
Oil on board, 3050 × 1530mm
NPG 7013

Joffe is a painter in the figurative tradition whose work reflects upon the contrived nature of female representation in art. Central to her practice, self-portraits present a way to consider time passing, something Joffe felt acutely while watching her daughter, Esme, grow up.

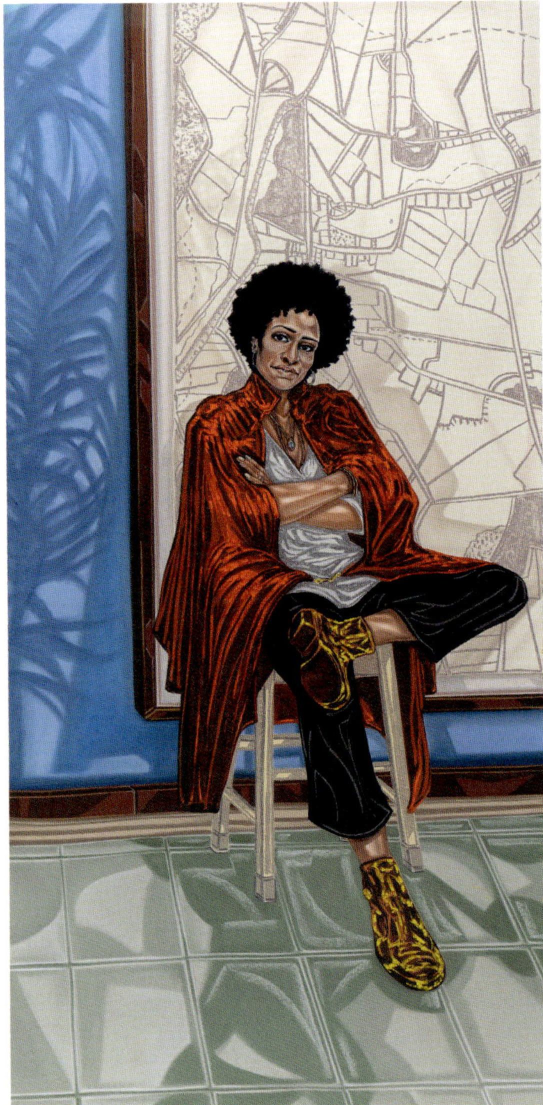

Zadie Smith (*Sadie*)
(b.1985)
Toyin Ojih Odutola, 2018–19
Pastel, charcoal and graphite on paper, 2235 × 1066mm
NPG 7105

Smith is an internationally published writer who became a prize-winning, best-selling author at the age of 25 for her first novel, *White Teeth* (2000). Smith has described Odutola as the 'central light in a thrilling new generation of black artists'.

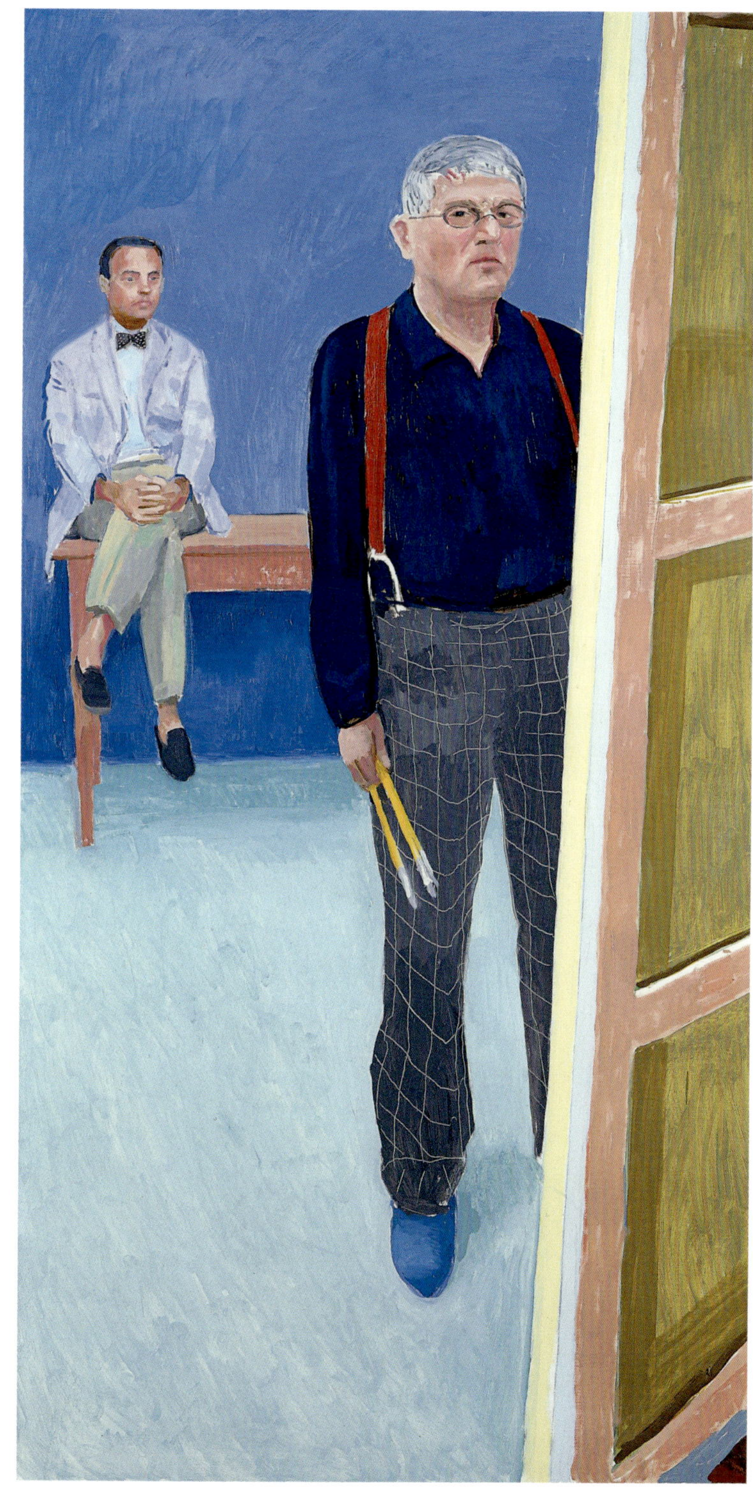

David Hockney (*Self-Portrait with Charlie*)
(b.1937)
Self-portrait, 2005
Oil on canvas, 1829 × 914mm
NPG 6819

One of Britain's most celebrated contemporary artists, Hockney is fascinated with observing and depicting relationships. He painted this large-scale portrait of himself and his close friend, the curator Charlie Scheips, in his light-filled studio in the Hollywood Hills.

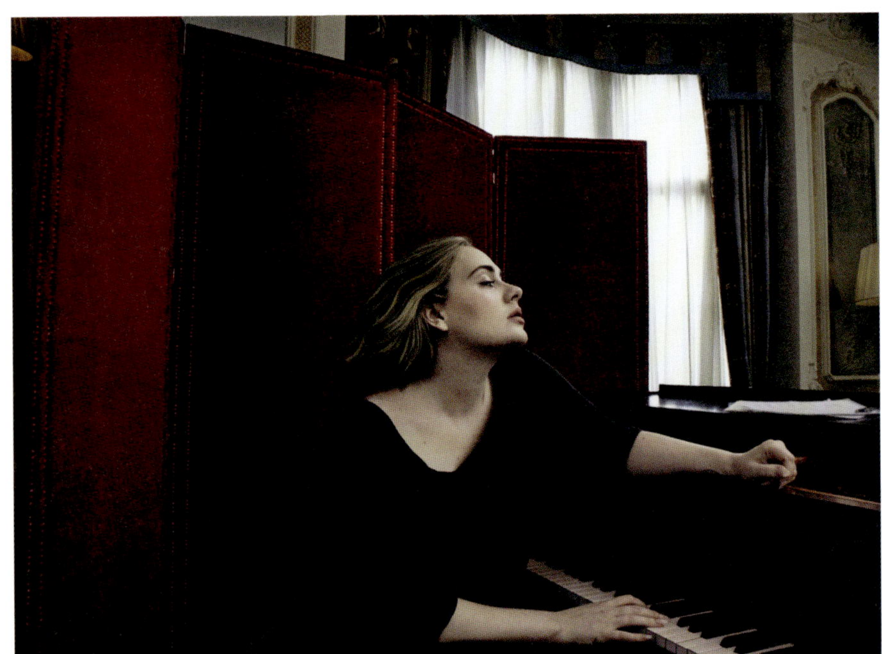

Adele
(b.1988)
Annie Leibovitz, 2015
Pigment print, 508 × 660mm
NPG P2096

Adele is one of the world's most popular music artists. She released her debut album, *19*, in 2008, which gained her critical and commercial success, and has subsequently issued further best-selling albums. This portrait was taken by Leibovitz in Claridge's hotel for *Vogue*.

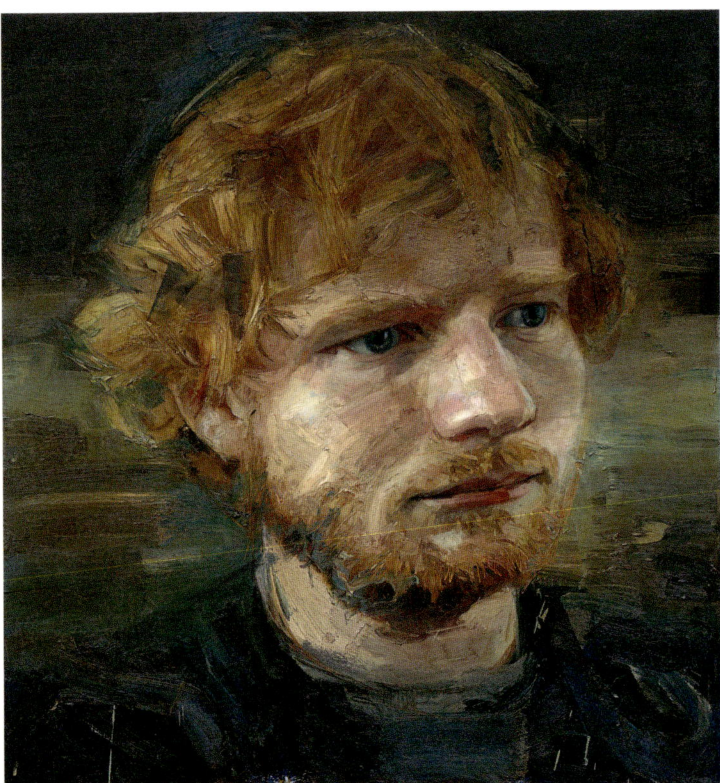

Ed Sheeran
(b.1991)
Colin Davidson, 2016
Oil on linen, 1270 × 1170mm
NPG 7035

Sheeran's musical style is an eclectic blend of acoustic, pop, folk and hip-hop. This portrait, by Northern Irish artist Davidson, shows the globally successful singer-songwriter in a quiet moment of introspection.

Michael Eavis
(b.1935)
Sir Peter Blake, 2022
Oil on canvas, 900 × 900mm
NPG 7132

Eavis is a dairy farmer and the co-creator of the Glastonbury Festival, which takes place at his farm in Somerset. In this picture, painted by Blake, he appears in front of Glastonbury's Pyramid Stage, where many famed musical performances have taken place since the festival was founded in 1970.

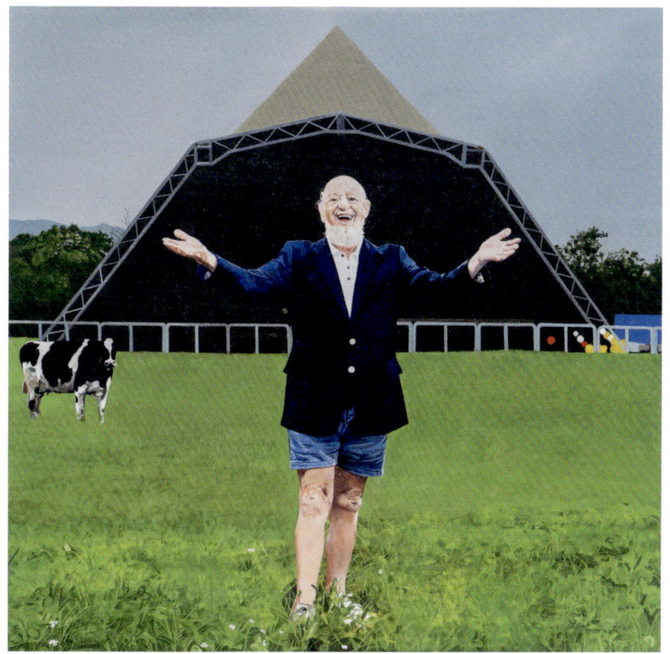

Amy Winehouse (*Amy-Blue*)
(1983–2011)
Marlene Dumas, 2011
Oil on canvas, 400 × 300mm
NPG 6948

This commemorative painting of the Grammy-winning singer and songwriter was made following her death at the age of 27. The translucent blue colours used by Dumas refer to Winehouse's troubled life and also her musical influences.

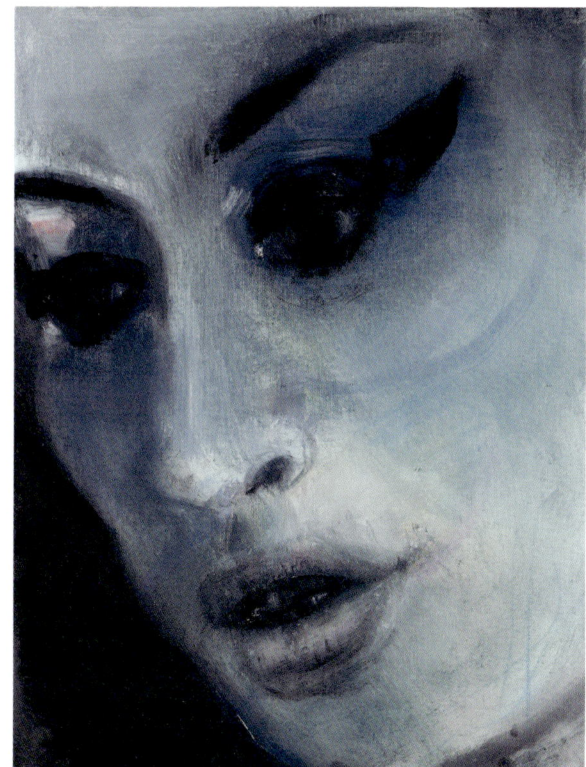

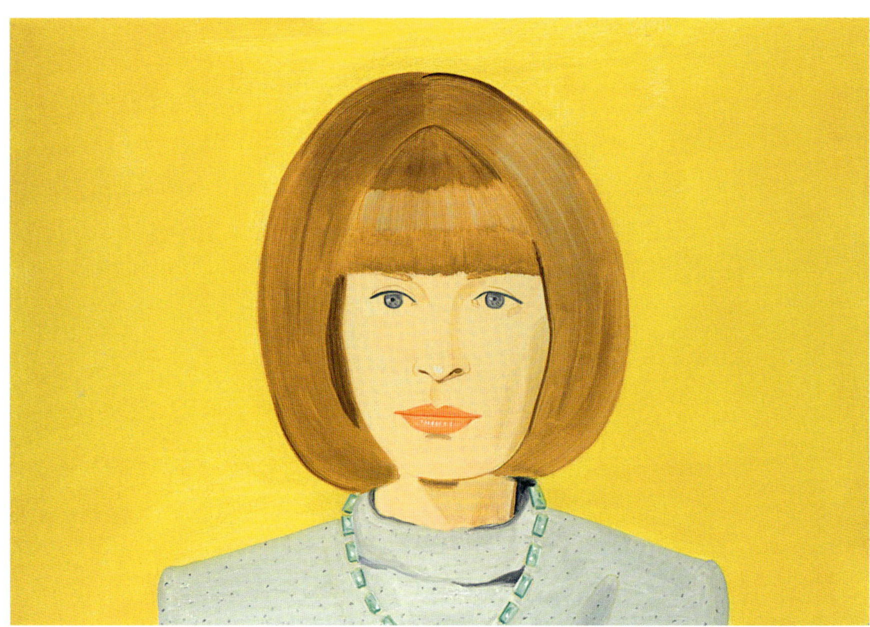

Dame Anna Wintour
(b.1949)
Alex Katz, 2009
Oil on linen, 1524 × 2134mm
NPG 6908

Appointed editor-in-chief of American *Vogue* in 1988, British-born Wintour has made a global contribution to the fashion industry. The eminent American artist Katz described painting this portrait as 'like shooting a fish in a barrel. There was no way I could miss it. She's made to order. Highly styled.'

Dame Zaha Hadid
(1950–2016)
Michael Craig-Martin, 2008
LCD screen, 1257 × 749mm
NPG 6840

Hadid was born in Iraq and studied at the Architectural Association in London. Her innovative buildings, including the London Aquatics Centre (2011), are renowned for sweeping curves, multiple perspective points and fragmented geometry. Her computer-aided design is complemented by Craig-Martin's digital portrait that is in a state of perpetual flux.

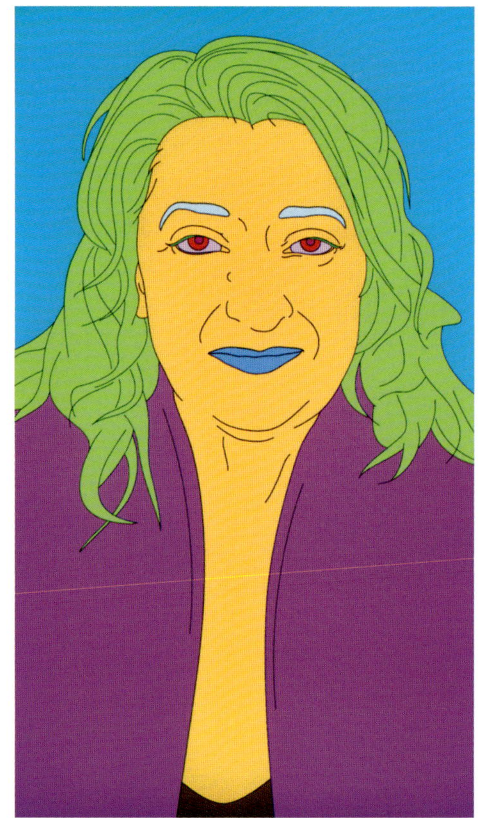

Doreen Lawrence, Baroness Lawrence of Clarendon
(b.1952)
Thomas Ganter, 2020
Oil on board, 660 × 440mm
NPG 7113

Baroness Lawrence has campaigned against racism since the murder of her son, Stephen, in a racially motivated attack in south-east London in 1993. Following a complacent police response, Lawrence campaigned for an investigation, which concluded that institutional racism in the Metropolitan Police was a factor in their failure to solve the case.

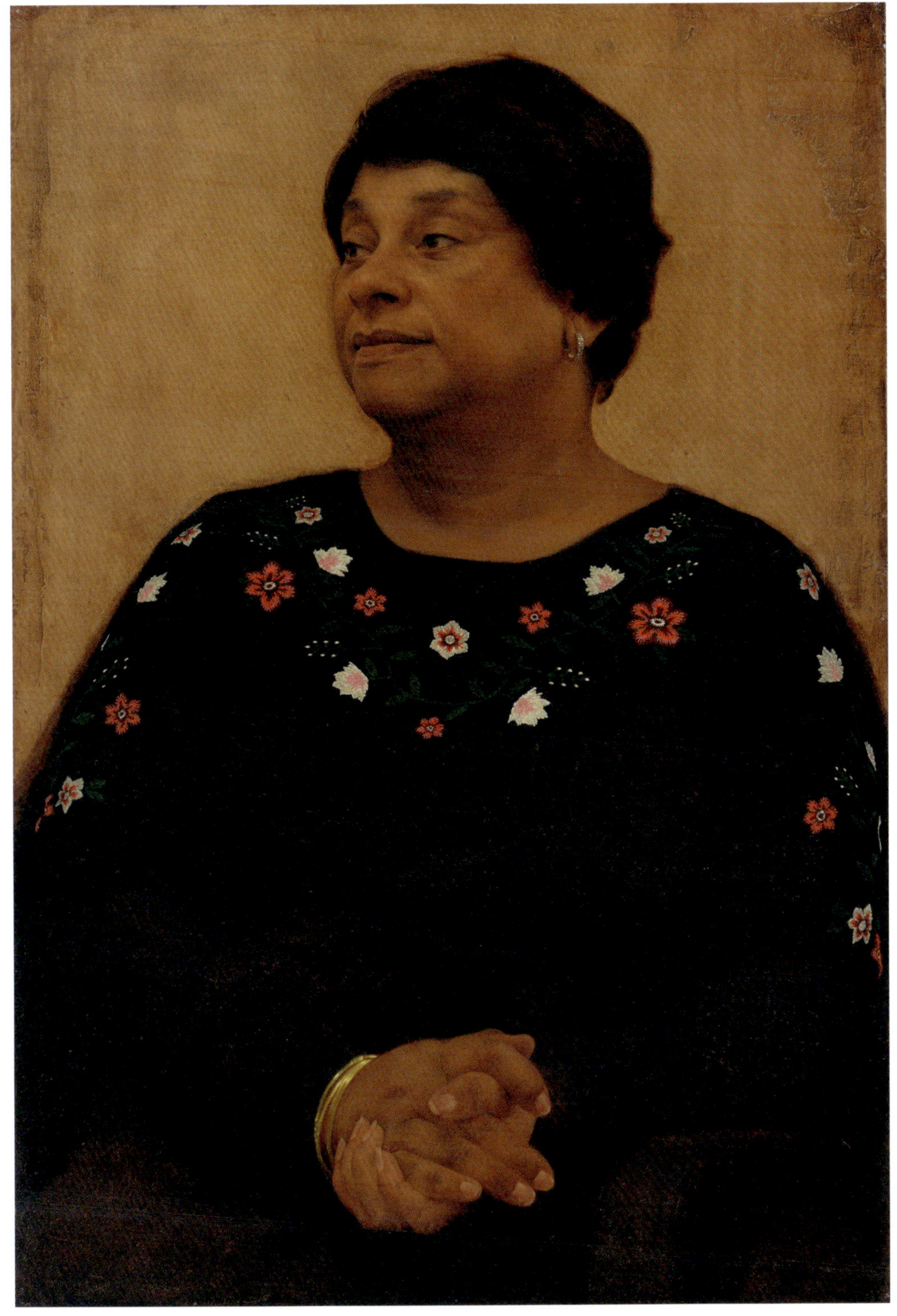

Sir David Attenborough
(b.1926)
Sam Barker, 2015
Inkjet print, 456 × 386mm
NPG x199654

Attenborough has shared the wonders of the living world
with audiences globally for more than six decades. A
naturalist, writer and broadcaster, his contribution to
broadcasting and wildlife film-making has received
international acclaim.

Attenborough's distinguished broadcasting career
began in 1952 when he joined the BBC. He launched his
first Natural History programme, *Zoo Quest*, in 1954, and
in 1957 formed the BBC's Travel and Exploration Unit. As
Controller of BBC Two (1965–9), Attenborough oversaw
the introduction of colour television and commissioned the
groundbreaking arts programme *Civilization*, presented by
Kenneth Clark in 1969. Returning to writing and presenting in
the 1970s, he set new standards for nature documentaries
with the *Life* series, beginning with *Life on Earth* (1979)
and including *The Living Planet* (1984) and *The Trials of
Life* (1990). In recent years, his documentaries *Blue Planet
II* (2017) and *Frozen Planet II* (2022) have radically raised
public awareness about pollution and climate change. He
is the recipient of numerous awards, including the Order of
Merit, and was voted Britain's greatest living icon in 2006.

This photograph, commissioned by *The Sunday Times*
to mark Attenborough's 90th year, concentrates our gaze
to the 'great mind'. Barker (b.1971), the son of the poet
George Barker and writer Elspeth Barker, has worked as a
photographer in editorial and advertising since 1997.

'Right now we are facing a
man-made disaster of global
scale, our greatest threat in
thousands of years: climate
change. If we don't take
action, the collapse of our
civilisations and the extinction
of much of the natural world
is on the horizon.'

Sir David Attenborough, 2018

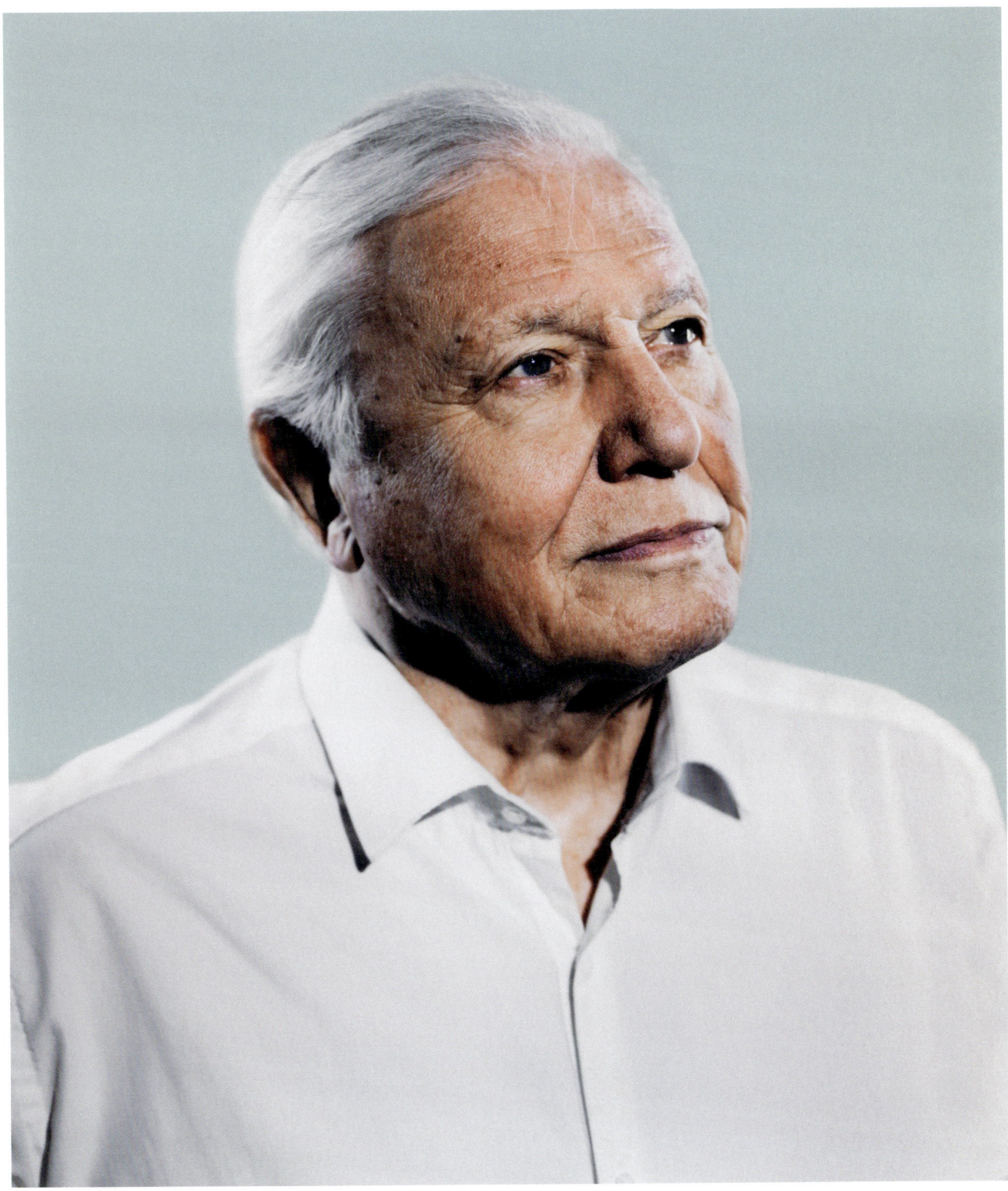

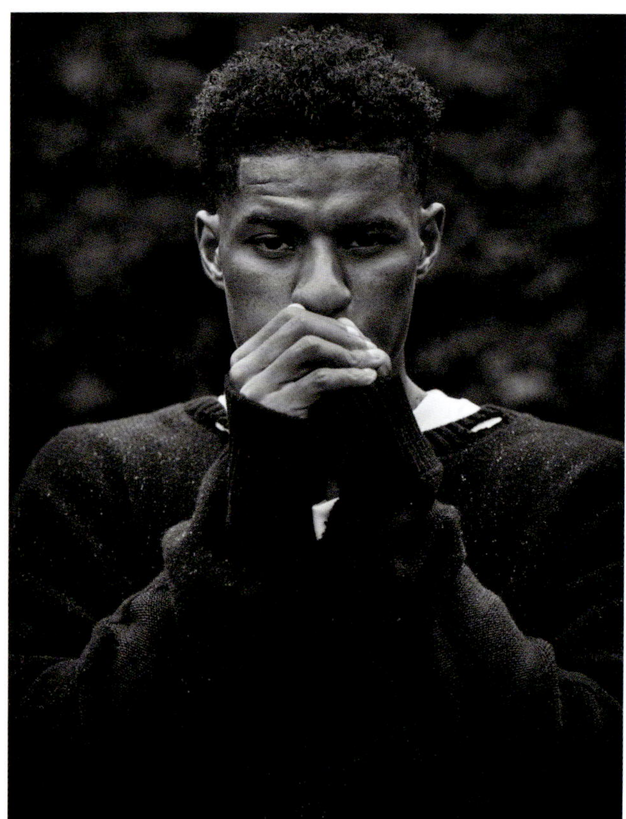

Marcus Rashford
(b.1997)
Misan Harriman, 2020
Gelatin silver print,
587 × 434mm
NPG x201380

Rashford is an English national team footballer who joined his home city club of Manchester United at the age of 7. He scored two goals on his first-team debut aged 18. As a campaigner against racism, homelessness and child hunger, he has been praised for using his platform to drive societal change.

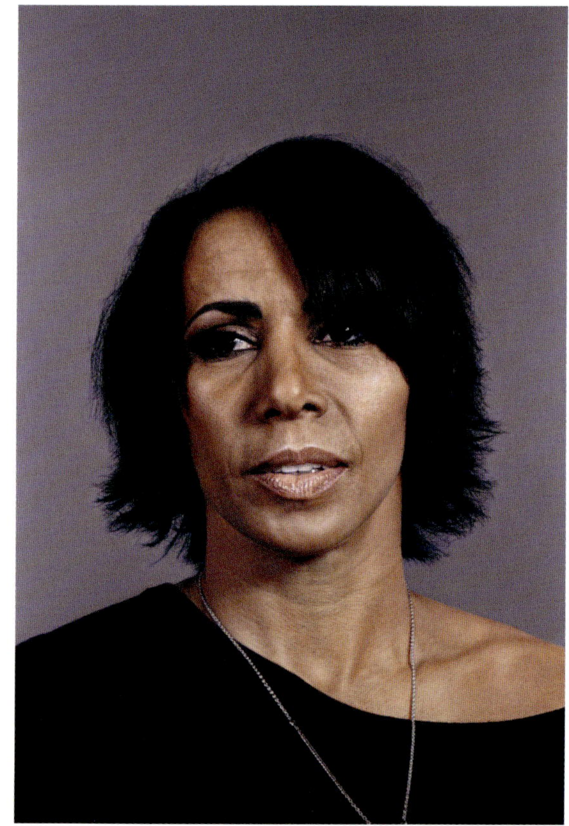

Dame Kelly Holmes
(b.1970)
Craig Wylie, 2012
Oil on canvas, 1728 × 1152mm
NPG 6944

Holmes was a sergeant in the British Army before becoming a full-time athlete in 1993. She shot to fame by winning gold in the 800m and 1,500m at the 2004 Olympic Games in Athens and was made a dame the following year. By coming out as gay in 2022, Holmes helped to challenge prejudice against gay athletes and military personnel.

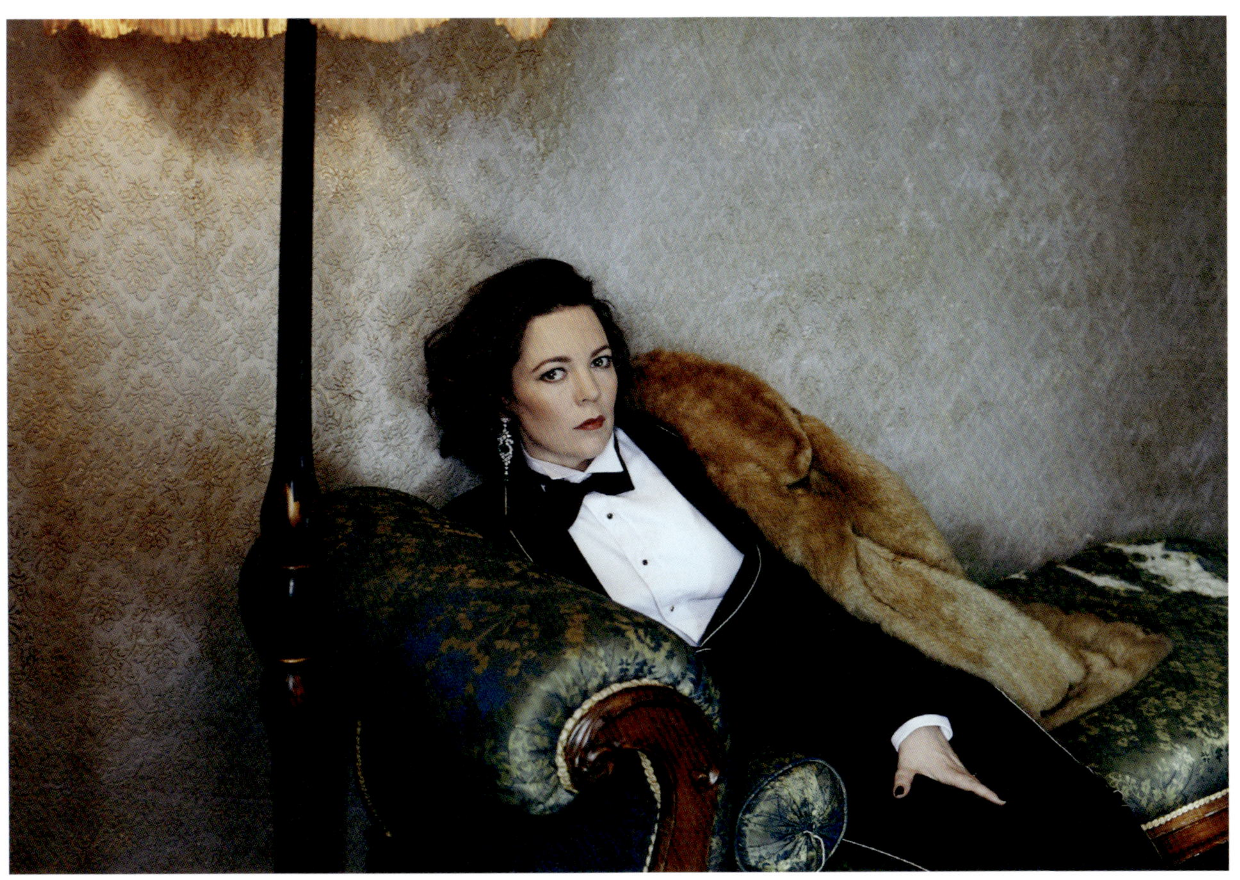

Olivia Colman
(b.1974)
Hana Knizova, 2014
Chromogenic print,
418 × 592mm
NPG x139974

Following training at Bristol Old Vic Theatre School, Colman has gone on to work extensively in film, television and theatre. She has been nominated for multiple Academy Awards, including for *The Father* (2020), and she won Best Actress for her performance as Queen Anne in *The Favourite* (2018).

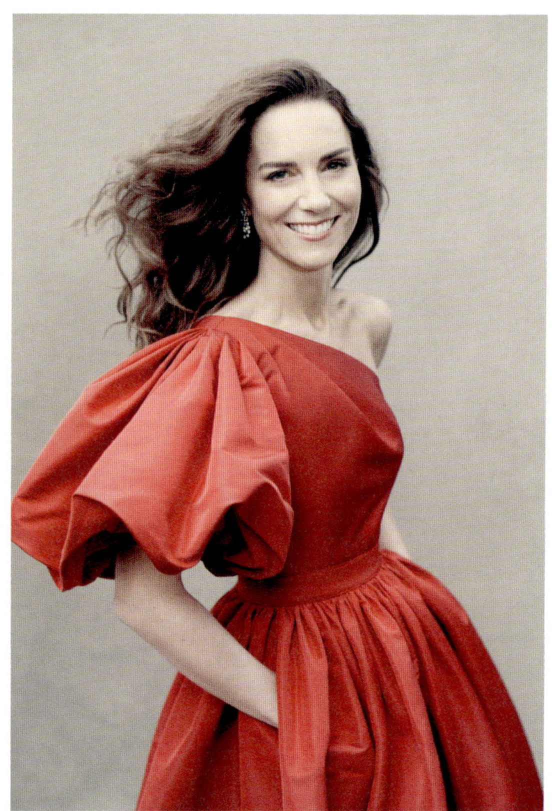

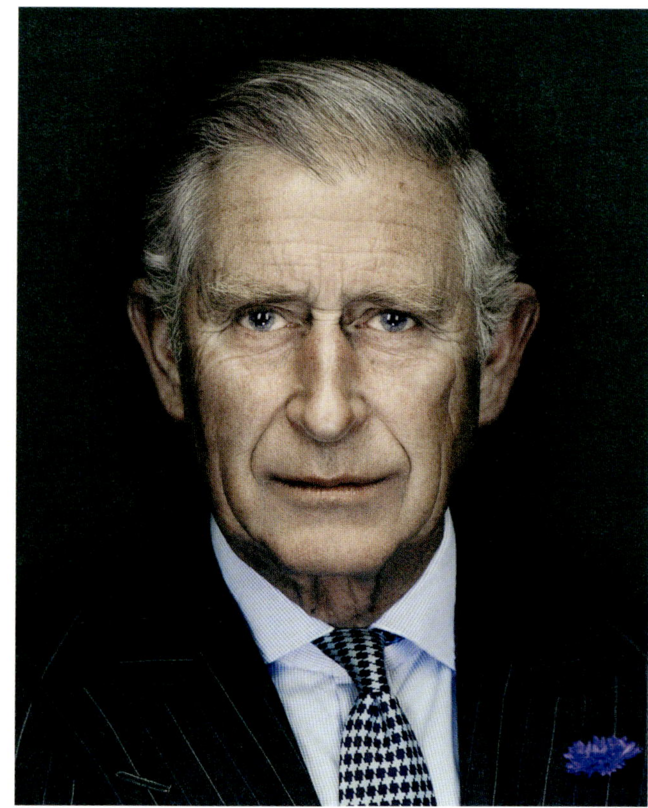

Catherine, Princess of Wales
(b.1982)
Paolo Roversi, 2021
Inkjet print, 500 × 330mm
NPG x201522

Catherine, Princess of Wales, is married to William, Prince of Wales, and is patron of several charities, including the Royal Photographic Society and the National Portrait Gallery. This is one of three portraits taken by the highly respected Italian portrait and fashion photographer Roversi to mark the princess's 40th birthday.

King Charles III
(b.1948)
Nadav Kander, 2013
Chromogenic print,
1565 × 1220mm
NPG P1989

Charles III acceded to the throne on 8 September 2022, following the death of his mother, Elizabeth II. He had been Britain's longest-serving heir apparent. Kander's close-cropped, highly charged portrait suggests both regal composure and human vulnerability. It appeared on the cover of *TIME* magazine in 2013.

**Prince Philip, Duke of
Edinburgh and
Queen Elizabeth II**
(1921–2021; 1926–2022)
Thomas Struth, 2011
Chromogenic print,
1633 × 2062mm
NPG P1665

This photograph was taken
shortly before Prince Philip's 90th
birthday and was commissioned
by the Gallery to mark Queen
Elizabeth II's Diamond Jubilee in
2012. Struth photographed the
royal couple at Windsor Castle
away from their official and
ceremonial roles.

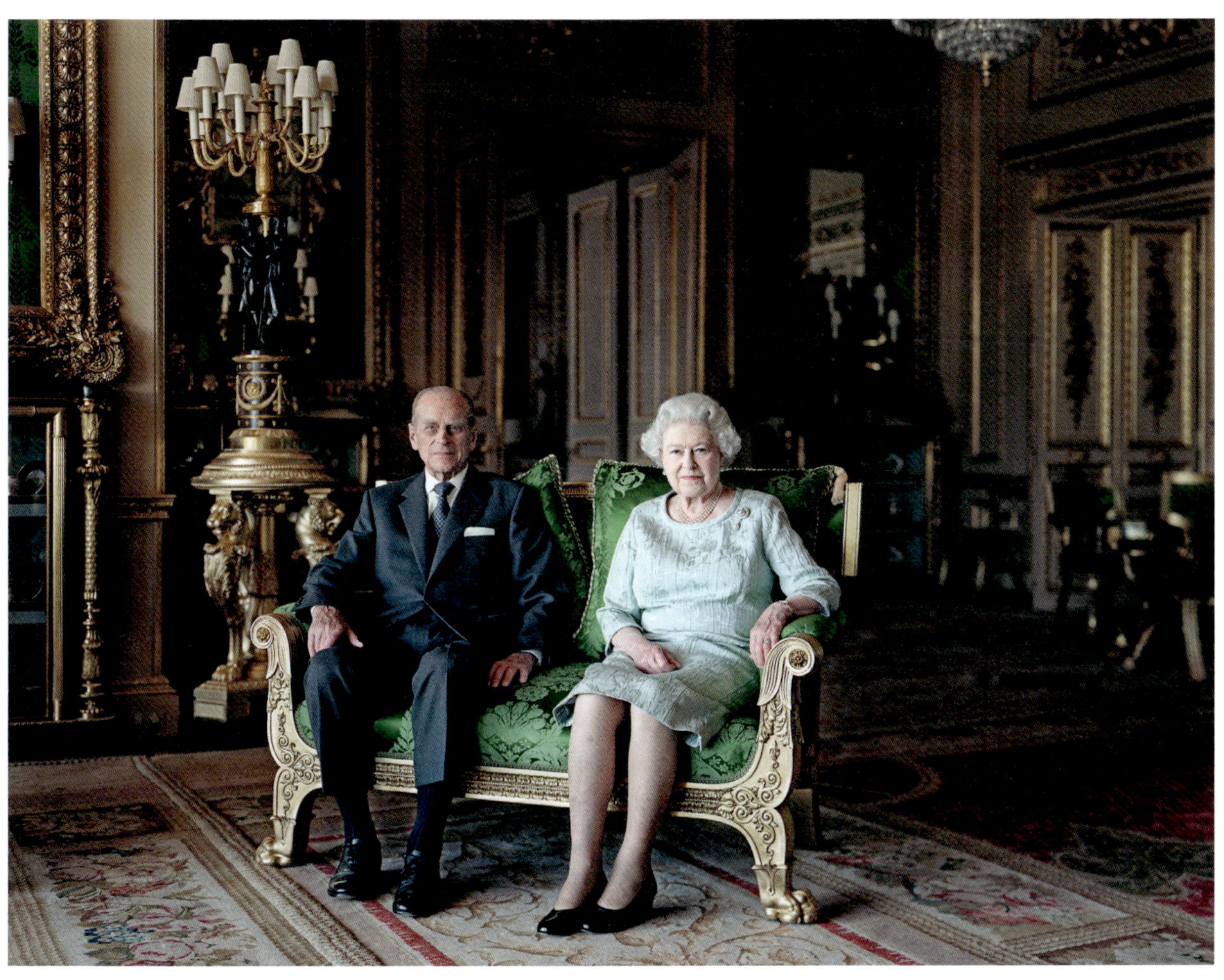

Malala Yousafzai
(b.1997)
Shirin Neshat, 2018
Archival ink on gelatin silver
print, 1524 × 1016mm
NPG 7052

Born in Mingora, Pakistan, Yousafzai is a human rights
activist for female education and the youngest recipient of
the Nobel Peace Prize. She came to prominence in 2009 by
writing for the BBC World Service about her life during the
Taliban occupation of her town in the Swat Valley and the
ban on girls' education. In October 2012, she was shot by a
Taliban gunman on her school bus. Remarkably, Yousafzai
survived the murder attempt and woke up ten days later
in a hospital in Birmingham, England, where she had been
transferred for treatment and where she chose to remain
with her family.

Yousafzai founded the Malala Fund in 2013, which is
dedicated to ensuring that all girls have the right to 12 years
of free, safe, quality education. Her work was recognised
with the Nobel Peace Prize in 2014. Yousafzai's memoir,
I Am Malala (2013), is an international bestseller and the
documentary film *He Named Me Malala* was nominated for
an Academy Award in 2015.

This portrait is an outstanding commission by the Gallery.
It is by the New York-based Iranian artist and film-maker
Neshat (b.1957), whose work often explores themes of
womanhood and the oppression of women. Here, she
has applied calligraphy directly onto a black-and-white
photograph that she took in her studio. The text comes from
the Pashto poem 'MALALA II: (Malala Yousafzai)', written by
Rahmat Shah Sayel in 2011. The poem addresses the Afghan
folk hero Malala of Maiwand and praises Yousafzai, while
making connections between the two formidable women.

'I am honoured to have my
portrait included in the
National Portrait Gallery ...
I hope it will remind visitors
that girls everywhere are
fighting for change in their
communities and countries;
their stories must also
be heard.'

Malala Yousafzai, 2018

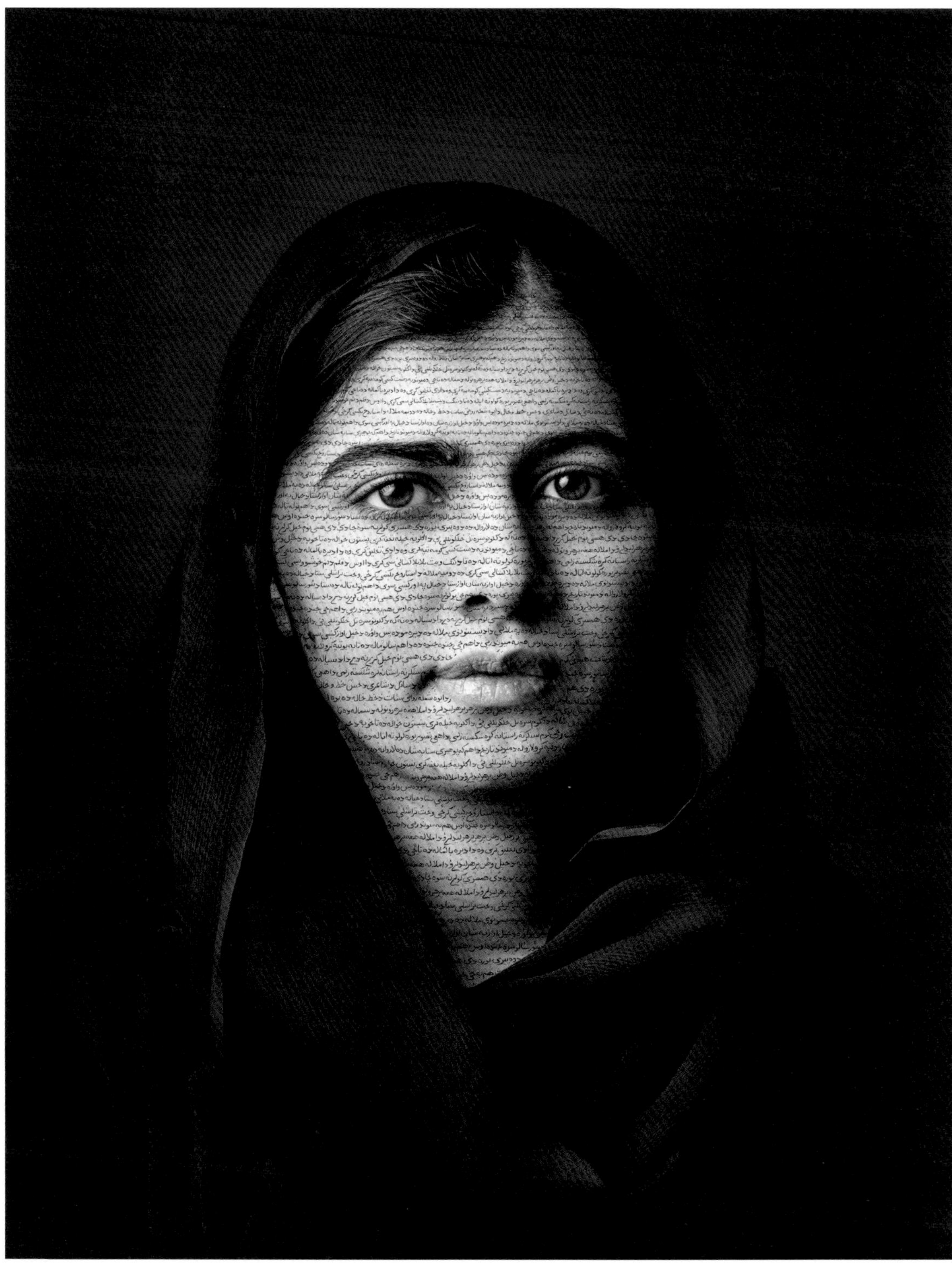

Picture Credits

Unless otherwise stated, all illustrations are © National Portrait Gallery, London. Additional commissioning and acquisition information is provided. The National Portrait Gallery would like to thank the copyright holders for granting permission to reproduce works illustrated in this book. Every effort has been made to contact the holders of copyright material, and any omissions will be corrected in future editions if the publisher is notified in writing.

p.2 Commissioned with kind support from the CHANEL Culture Fund for *Reframing Narratives: Women in Portraiture*, 2023; p.5 (left) © Courtesy the artist, Frith Street Gallery, London, and Marian Goodman Gallery, New York/Paris. Photo: Mathew Hale. Purchased jointly with the Royal Academy of Arts, London, with Art Fund support, 2018–19; (right) © Steve McQueen. Courtesy the artist, Thomas Dane Gallery and Marian Goodman Gallery. Photo: Richard Ivey. Commissioned with support from Scott Collins, in partnership with Outset Contemporary Art Fund, 2022; p.6 (left) Purchased with the Portrait Fund, 2021; (right) Given by Hassan Akkad, 2021; p.8 Bought jointly by the National Gallery and the National Portrait Gallery, with the generous support of Sir Martyn Arbib and his children, 2022; p.9 © the artist and White Cube. Given by Michael Armitage and White Cube, 2023; p.14 Given by James Thomson Gibson-Craig, 1862; p.15 (right) By permission of the Archbishop of Canterbury and the Church Commissioners; on loan to the National Portrait Gallery, London. Lent by Church Commissioners for England, 2011; p.17 (left) Purchased with help from the Gulbenkian Foundation, 1965; p.19 Given by Harold Lee-Dillon, 17th Viscount Dillon, 1925; p.20 (above) Purchased with help from the National Heritage Memorial Fund and the Art Fund, 1994; (below) Purchased with help from the Art Fund and the Pilgrim Trust, 1959; p.21 (below) Purchased with help from the Art Fund, the Pilgrim Trust, H.M. Government, Miss Elizabeth Taylor and Richard Burton, 1972; p.25, p.31 Purchased with support from the National Lottery Heritage Fund, the Art Fund in honour of David Verey CBE (Chairman of the Art Fund 2004–14), the Portrait Fund, The Monument Trust, the Garfield Weston Foundation, the Aldama Foundation, the Deborah Loeb Brice Foundation, Sir Harry Djanogly CBE, Mr and Mrs Michael Farmer. Matthew Freud, Catherine Green, Dr Bendor Grosvenor, Alexander Kahane, the Catherine Lewis Foundation, the Material World Foundation, The Sir Denis Mahon Charitable Trust, Cynthia Lovelace Sears, two major supporters who wish to remain anonymous, and many contributions from the public following a joint appeal by the National Portrait Gallery and the Art Fund, 2014; p.27 Given by Francis Egerton, 1st Earl of Ellesmere, 1856; p.29 (above) Purchased with help from the Art Fund, 1957; (below) Purchased with help from the Art Fund, the Portrait Fund, the American Friends of the National Portrait Gallery in memory of David Alexander (President 2003–10), Richard Aylmer, Sir Harry Djanogly CBE, the Golden Bottle Trust, Terry and Maria Hughes, Lady Rose Monson, Sir Charles and Lady Nunneley, Sir David Scholey CBE and Lady Scholey, and two anonymous supporters, 2013; p.32 (left) Transferred from British Museum, 1879; (right) Purchased with help from the National Heritage Memorial Fund, through the Art Fund (with a contribution from the Wolfson Foundation), Camelot Group plc, David and Catharine Alexander, David Wilson, E.A. Whitehead, Glyn Hopkin and numerous other supporters of a public appeal including members of the Chelsea Arts Club, 2005; p.35 Bequeathed by John Neale, 1931; p.37 Purchased with help from the Art Fund, 1936; p.42 (below) Bequeathed by Jane, Lady Shelley, 1899; p.43 OM.762, Lusail Museum, Doha, Qatar. Lent by Qatar Museums, Qatar Museums Authority: Doha: Qatar, 2010; p.45 (left) Purchased with help from the Art Fund, 1965;

(right) Purchased with help from the National Heritage Memorial Fund, 1985; p.48 (left) © National Portrait Gallery, London, and the Harris Museum & Art Gallery, Preston. Purchased jointly with the Harris Museum & Art Gallery, Preston, with help from the National Heritage Memorial Fund, the Art Fund, the Portrait Fund, PRISM, the Friends of the Harris, The Headley Trust, Sir Harry Djanogly, the Halecat Charitable Trust, Nicholas and Judith Goodison through the Art Fund and many other donations, 2008; (right) Purchased with help from the Handel Appeal Fund and H.M. Government, 1968; p.49 Given by Dr D.M. McDonald, 1977; p.50 (right) Purchased jointly with Gainsborough's House with support from the Drue Heinz Acquisition Fund, 2019; p.51 © National Portrait Gallery, London / National Museum Cardiff / Captain Cook Memorial Museum, Whitby. Purchased jointly with the Captain Cook Memorial Museum, Whitby, and the National Museums & Galleries of Wales, with help from a private benefactor and local trusts, the Art Fund, the Garfield Weston Foundation, Flora Fraser and Peter Soros, Sir Christopher Ondaatje, Linda L. Brownrigg, Randolph and Lara Lerner, Jon and Lillian Lovelace, the Clore Duffield Foundation, Sir Harry Djanogly, Hans and Mārit Rausing, Lawrence Banks, the Swan Trust, Amanda Sebestyen, Sir David Attenborough, Lord Plymouth and Lord Windsor and many other donations, 2003; p.53 Given by executors of Sir Robert Harry Inglis, 2nd Bt, 1857; p.55, p.67 (left) Accepted in lieu of tax by H.M. Government and allocated to the Gallery, 1975; p.57 Private Collection; on loan to the National Portrait Gallery, London. Lent by a private collection, 2012; p.59 (left) Purchased with support from the Portrait Fund, 2020; (right) Purchased with help from the Friends of the National Libraries, 1948; p.60 Given by Queen Victoria, 1900; p.61 (left) Lent by Gerald Pointon, 2017; (right) Purchased with help from the Friends of the National Libraries and the Pilgrim Trust, 1966; p.64 (right) Given by Cordelia Curle (née Fisher), 1959; p.65 Given by Mr and Mrs A. J. W. Vaughan, 1972; p.67 (left) Purchased with help from the National Lottery Heritage Fund and Gallery supporters, 2008; p.68 (left) Transferred from Tate Gallery, 2015; (right) Bequeathed by Sir Charles Wentworth Dilke, 2nd Bt, 1911; p.71 Given by the sitter's son, William Erasmus Darwin, 1896; p.72 (left) Given by William Henry Smith, 3rd Viscount Hambleden, 1945; p.73 Given by Roger Fry, 1930; p.75, p.89 Given by the sitter and artist, Gluck (Hannah Gluckstein), 1973; p.77 Reproduced with permission of The Estate of Dame Laura Knight DBE RA 2022. All Rights Reserved / Bridgeman Images; p.78 (left) On loan from a Private Collection. Lent by Mrs Jennifer Loehnis, 2013; (right) Given by the sitter's sister, Annie Wynick (née Rosenberg), 1959; p.79 Purchased with help from the Art Fund, 1987; p.81 Given by the Art Fund to mark Sir Alec Martin's 40 years service to the fund, 1965; p.83 (left) Acquired, 1940; (right) © William Hustler and Georgina Hustler / National Portrait Gallery, London. Given by the photographer's sister, Susan Morton, 1976; p.84 © Lee Miller Archives, England 2022. All rights reserved. leemiller.co.uk; p.85 (above) © Karsh. Given by the estate of Yousuf Karsh, 2010; p.86 © Estate of Augustus John / Bridgeman Images. Purchased with support from the Art Fund (with a contribution from the Wolfson Foundation), the National Heritage Memorial Fund and The Thompson Family Charitable Trust, 2018; p.87 (above) Given by Mrs Mary Behrend, 1973; (below) Given by Delmar Banner, 1948; p.88 Bequeathed by Una Elena Vincenzo (née Taylor), Lady Troubridge, 1963; p.91 © Patrick Heron Trust. All rights reserved, DACS 2022. Purchased with help from the Contemporary Art Society, 1965. Portrait adopted by the T.S. Eliot Foundation; p.93, p.105 © 2022 The Andy Warhol Foundation for the Visual Arts, Inc. / Licensed by DACS, London; p.95 © Barry Lategan. All rights reserved, DACS 2022; p.96 (left) © Estate of Sylvia Plath / Faber & Faber Ltd. Purchased with help

from Mrs T.S. Eliot, the Art Fund and Roy Davids, 2005; p.96 (right) Given by the sitter's mother, Ethel Sara Turing (née Stoney), 1956; p.97 Cecil Beaton Studio Archive © Conde Nast. Accepted in lieu of tax by H.M. Government and allocated to the Gallery, 1991; p.99 © The Lucian Freud Archive / Bridgeman Images; p.100 © Don McCullin; p.101 (above) Paul Trevor © 2021. Purchased as part of Citizen UK: Tower Hamlets, funded by The National Lottery Heritage Fund and Art Fund, 2021; (below) © Pogus Caesar/ OOM Gallery Archive. All Rights Reserved; p.103 Photo Duffy © Duffy Archive & The David Bowie Archive™; p.104 Commissioned, 1981; p.106 (above) Commissioned, 1985; (below) © Fred Cuming. Given by Stephen William Hawking, 2006; p.107 (above) Commissioned, 1995; (below) © Estate of Bhupen Khakhar; p.108 (above) © Lorenzo Agius; (below) © Mario Testino; p.109 © estate of Chris Garnham; p.111, p.122 (left) © Misan Harriman / Conde Nast 2020. Given by Misan Harriman, 2021; p.113 © Catherine Opie, courtesy of Regen Projects, Los Angeles and Thomas Dane Gallery, London. Purchased with support from Ivor Braka, 2018; p.114 (left) © Chantal Joffe. Given by Victoria Miro Gallery, 2015; (right) © Toyin Ojih Odutola. Courtesy of the artist and Jack Shainman Gallery, New York. Purchased with support from Zekiye Cingillioglu, 2020; p.115 © David Hockney, Collection National Portrait Gallery, London. Purchased with help from the proceeds of the 150th anniversary gala and Gift Aid visitor ticket donations, 2007; p.116 (above) Adele, London, 2015 © Annie Leibovitz. Given by Annie Leibovitz, 2022; (below) © Colin Davidson; p.117 (above) Commissioned, 2022; (below) © Marlene Dumas; courtesy of the artist and Frith Street Gallery, London. Purchased with help from the Art Fund, 2012; p.118 (above) © Alex Katz/VAGA at ARS, NY, and DACS, London, 2022. Purchased with help from the Art Fund, 2010; (below) Commissioned; made possible by J.P. Morgan through the Fund for New Commissions, 2008; p.119 Commissioned as part of the First Prize, 2014 BP Portrait Award, 2021; p.121 © Sam Barker; p.122 (right) Commissioned as part of the First Prize, 2008 BP Portrait Award, 2012; p.123 Commissioned as part of the 2013 John Kobal New Work Award, 2014; p.124 (left) © Paolo Roversi / The Princess of Wales released to mark the occasion of The Princess of Wales' 40th birthday in January 2022. Given by Paolo Roversi, 2022; (right) © Nadav Kander; p.125 © Thomas Struth, 2011. Commissioned, 2011; p.127 Commissioned with support from Scott Collins and Lotta Ashdown, in partnership with Outset Contemporary Art Fund, 2018.

Quotation Sources

p.4 T. Carlyle, letter to D. Laing, 2 May 1854, National Library of Scotland. Carlyle was a prominent Victorian intellectual who was, and remains, controversial due to his racial prejudice; p.18 A. Collins, *Letters and Memorials of State*, vol.1, 1746, p.386; p.22 R. Brown (ed.) *Calendar of State Papers Relating To English Affairs in the Archives of Venice*, vol.6, pt.2, 1877, p.1058; p.30 J. Richardson, *An Essay on the Theory of Painting*, 1715, p.41; p.34 R. Latham and W. Matthews (eds), *The Diary of Samuel Pepys*, vol.8, 1974, p.91; p.46 'Characters', *The Annual Register for 1781*, 1782, p.29; p.52 T.C. Hansard, *The Parliamentary History of England, from the Earliest Period to 1803*, vol.29, 1814, p.278; p.62 A. Schoen (Higgens), *The Church Missionary Gleaner*, vol.8, no.85, January 1881, p.22; p.70 F. Darwin (ed.), *The Life and Letters of Charles Darwin*, vol.3, 1887, p.223; p.80 G. John, letter to U. Tyrwhitt, 4 February 1910, National Library of Wales; p.90 P. Heron, *Guardian*, 24 September 1988, p.34; p.98 J. Russell, *Lucian Freud*, 1974, p.13; p.102 D. Bowie, *Heroes* album promotion, 1977; p.120 D. Attenborough, UN Climate Change Conference, 2018; p.126 M. Yousafzai, NPG press release, 2 October 2018.